TablE
OF CONTENTs

SongS	p. 3
SkitS	p. 43
GameS	p. 75
Scouter'S FIVE MINUTES	p. 109
RecipeS	p. 271
HintS	p. 307

www. scouts. ca

INTRODUCTION

The Canadian Leader cut-out pages have long been a popular feature of the magazine. Many readers have collected the pages over the years, starting their own library of quick ideas for weekly activities.

Games on "a handy page to place right in your leader's pocket record book" became *the Leader*'s first cut-out in June/July, 1965. Cut-out *Songs* were added as a centennial project in January, 1967. The pages proved so popular that the August/September 1974 issue expanded the subjects and introduced the numbering system still found in the magazine.

This small volume represents a selection of "the best" material that appeared in Volumes 11 to 19 (1980-1989) of *the Leader*. Some material has been altered slightly to incorporate more inclusive language and metric measurements.

We hope this first collection of material is a welcome addition to *your* Scouting library.

While most of the material is credited to its source, it is not possible to acknowledge individually the many Scouters who shared their ideas through contributions to *the Leader,* local and provincial Scouting publications or the publications of other world Scout organizations.

We thank you all and encourage you to keep sharing material for use in the magazine.

Good Scouting!

Scouts Canada National Council © 1990
ISBN 0-919062-56-3

Cat. No. 20-510

Printed in Canada

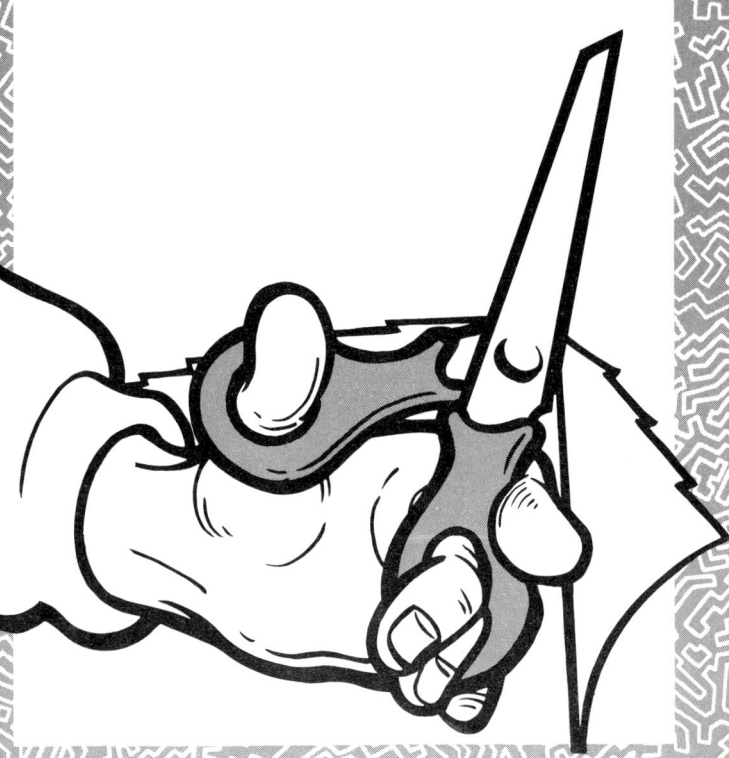

SONGS

Here for Fun
(Tune: *Auld Lang Syne*)

We're here for fun right from the start,
So drop your dignity
Just laugh and sing with all your heart,
And show your loyalty.
May all your troubles be forgot
May this day be the best
Join in the songs we sing today,
Be happy with the rest.

We Have a God Who Keeps Us
(Tune: *Battle Hymn of the Republic*)

We have a God who keeps us
on the road that we should go,
By whatever name we call Him,
He's the one that we all know.
He's Jehovah, He is Allah,
He's the mighty Manitou,
Our one and only Lord.
Chorus:
We will praise his name for ever, (3x)
Our one and only Lord.

With our brothers and our sisters,
every colour, every creed,
There is Guiding and there's Scouting
in all countries that are free.
Every Ranger, every Pathfinder
can go to Him in need,
Our one and only Lord.

SONGS

He's the God of every Beaver,
every Venturer and Cub,
And He shows the Scouts and Brownies
how to pass around his Love,
As he leads the Guides and Rovers
and all peoples everywhere,
Our one and only Lord.

He's the One who led our Founder
to that isle across the sea,
There to plant the little acorn
that became the great oak tree,
That is spreading out from Brownsea
down the years to you and me,
Our one and only Lord.

— *by Doreen Smith, Thunder Bay, Ontario*

THAT'S WHERE IT ALL BEGAN
(Tune: *Davy Crockett*)

General Baden-Powell was a Scouting man,
He rounded up some boys for he had a plan
To Brownsea Island they did go,
And that was the start,
   the start of our show.
That's where it all began!

He taught them to camp and to pioneer,
To scout in the dark and to have no fear.
The games that were played
   and the songs that were sung,
In the years between,
   round the world have rung

Songs

Brownsea, Brownsea Island,
Thats where it all began!

He gave them the law and the promise too,
And the good turn that every Scout must do
He gave them their motto "Be Prepared"
That millions of Scouts round the world
   have shared,
Brownsea, Brownsea Island, etc ...

Our Beavers as well can belong and share,
And show the world that they really care
With hearts of gold and a cheery face
Love and joy for the human race.
Brownsea, Brownsea Island, etc ...

The little brothers of the Wolf Cub pack
Down the jungle trails they all must track,
Opening their eyes until that shining day
They 'go up' to the troop in the Scouting way
Brownsea, Brownsea Island, etc ...

Venturers and Rovers across the land
Service to all and to lend a hand
Adventure and challenge and honour, too,
Future leaders, we're proud of you.
Brownsea, Brownsea Island, etc ...
          —With thanks to THE OUTLOOK

SONGS

CALL A SCOUT
(Tune: *If you're Happy and You Know It*)

When you're down and feeling blue
   CALL A SCOUT
They'll know just what to do
   CALL A SCOUT
If you're ever in a hurry
Don't take the time to worry
All you have to do is shout
   CALL A SCOUT!

If you need a helping hand
   CALL A SCOUT
They'll take your garbage out
   CALL A SCOUT
If the traffic that you meet
Has you scared to cross the street
They'll be there to help you out
   CALL A SCOUT!

Now the Scouts are always helpful
   Don't you see
They will lend a helping hand
   To you and me
For they're wise in what they do
They are kind and cheerful too
And they always help you out
   CALL A SCOUT!

—*Lyrics by Esther Handy*

SONGS

CUBS, CUBS!
(Tune: *Hail, Hail, the Gang's All Here*)

Cubs, Cubs, We're friendly Cubs,
We all work together
In fair or stormy weather
Cubs, Cubs, we're busy Cubs
Helping hands and happy hearts.
Fun, fun, we all have fun
Camping, cook-outs, races
Give us smiling faces
Fun, fun, it sure is fun
Making friends and taking part.
— *Lyrics by Linda Florence*

THERE ARE EATS
(tune: *Smiles or Tipperary*)

There are eats that make us chew,
There are eats that take away our pleasure,
Such as hash, and pork and beans, and stew.
There are eats that give us indigestion
There are eats that put us all to bed;
But the eats that make us all so happy,
Are the eats that we've just been fed.

IF YOU HAD FOLKS LIKE MINE
(tune: *Good Ol' Summertime*)

If you had a Dad (Mom) like mine
If you had a Dad (Mom) like mine
No matter what mistakes you make
He (She) always says, "That's fine."

SONGS

And even when it's dull with clouds
He (She) puts the sun in sunshine,
I know that you would have more joy
If you had a Dad (Mom) like mine

BROTHERHOOD OF SCOUTING
(tune: *When You're Smiling*)

When you're Cubbing, when you're Scouting
   You're in a world-wide brotherhood:
When you're Cubbing, when you're Scouting
   The Aim is all for good.
For when you see boys with purpose in life
They will help you in stress and in strife,
So keep on Cubbing, and keep on Scouting
   For a world-wide brotherhood!

HAPPY BIRTHDAY TO US
(tune: *On Top of Old Smokey*)

We're all at the table
   On Scouting's birthday
Our family together
   The true Scouting way.

Then somebody shouts out
   We're 75 years old
I just can't believe it,
   Though I have been told.

They bring out the cake then,
   With candles on top,
I try hard to count them,
   But they never stop.

Songs

It sets me to thinking,
   It's true what they say,
This Scouting gets older
   And better each day.

So sing out our song now,
   And make a big fuss
We're healthy and growing
HAPPY BIRTHDAY TO US!
               — *by Linda Florence*

God, We Thank You *(Jesus Loves Me)*
God, we thank You every day,
For our work and for our play,
You show us, in all You do,
Love and goodness flow from You.
   Thanks, God, we love You,
   Thanks, God, we love You,
   Thanks, God, we love You,
   We'll do our best for You.

Lucky Are We
(What Do You Do With a Drunken Sailor?)

Lucky are we for the sun and showers,
Lucky are we for the birds and flowers,
Happy are we, for the Lord He loves us,
How can we ever thank Him?
Chorus: Thank Him for all the goodness
          Thank Him for all the beauty
          Praise Him for all he gives from
          Every day's first dawning.

SONGS

Help another person, that will thank Him,
Make somebody happy, that will thank Him,
Cherish the world and that will thank Him,
Show the Lord you love Him.
(repeat chorus)

Pumpkin Wonderland *(Winter Wonderland)*
Screech owls hoot, are you list'nin?
Neath the moon, all is glist'nin,
A real scary sight, we're happy tonight,
Waitin' in a pumpkin wonderland.

In the patch we're watching for
   Great Pumpkin!
We've been waiting for this night all year,
We've tried to be nice to everybody,
And to grow a pumpkin patch
   that is sincere... (repeat first verse)

Turkey Song *(My Bonnie)*
My turkey went walking one morning,
The October weather to see,
A man with a hatchet approached her,
Oh, bring back my turkey to me.
Chorus:
   Bring back, bring back
   Oh, bring back my turkey to me, to me,
   Bring back, bring back,
   Oh, bring back my turkey to me.

I went down the sidewalks a shoppin'
The sights in shop windows to see,
And everywhere hung great fat gobblers,
Oh, bring back my turkey to me. *(Chorus)*

SONGS

I went out to dinner and ordered,
The best things they had could see,
They brought it all roasted and sizzling,
They brought back my turkey to me.

Final Chorus:
  Brought back, brought back,
  They brought back my turkey to me, to me,
  Brought back, brought back,
  They brought back my turkey to me!

Oh, B.-P. Don't You Weep
(Oh Mary Don't You Weep)
If I could, I surely would
Go to the camp where B.-P. stood;
The whole Scout movement's in good hands,
Oh, B.-P. don't you weep.

CHORUS
Oh B.-P. don't you weep, don't you mourn,
Oh B.-P. don't you weep, don't you mourn;
The whole Scout movement's in good hands,
Oh B.-P. don't you weep.

I'm going Scouting and I'm glad to say,
With B.-P.'s guidance,
I'll find the right way,
The whole Scout movement's in good hands,
Oh B.-P. don't you weep. *(chorus)*

SONGS

B.-P. went to heaven and he stood at the gate,
St. Peter took him in and said,
   "I'm glad you're not late!"
Because the whole Scout movement's
   in good hands,
Oh B.-P. don't you weep. *(chorus)*
—*from Tony Douglass, Dawson Creek, B.C.*

The Spirit Still Lives On
(Battle Hymn of the Republic)
It was 75 years ago,
When Scouting had its birth,
It has spread from dear old England
To all corners of the earth,
Baden-Powell would be so happy,
If he only knew the truth,
That the Spirit still lives on.

CHORUS: Hurrah, Hurrah for Baden-Powell,
   Hurrah, Hurrah for Baden-Powell,
   His challenge let us not forget
   So the Spirit will live on!

There are Venturers and Rovers,
Cubs and Scouts without a doubt,
And more recently the Beavers
So that no one is left out,
Each section is important,
And it serves a special need,
The Spirit must live on. *(chorus)*
The Scouting movement's purpose
Is to make men out of boys,
With programs and activities
That any boy enjoys;

SONGS

It helps to build strong character,
That we can be proud of,
The Spirit must live on. (chorus)
So, let's celebrate this special year,
It's what we all should do,
And what better way to celebrate,
Than take Wood Badge Part II;
But the message cannot stop here,
We must spread it to our boys,
And the Spirit will live on! *(chorus)*
— *by a Beaver leader: thanks to Glenn Barned, Saint John, New Brunswick*

Scouting Across Canada
(Yellow Rose of Texas)
There are Scouting groups in B.C.
We have Scouts in Alberta,
We're growing in Saskatchewan,
And in Man-i-to-ba;
Oh, we're Scouting in Ontario
In Quebec, New Brunswick, too,
In PEI and Newfoundland,
The Spirit still shines through.
Yes, you'll find us in the Yukon
And we're Nova Scotia's best,
From the Northwest Territories
To the south and east and west;
Oh, we're Scouting on in Canada,
And we do the best we can,
To make the world a better place,
Through the brotherhood of man.
— *lyrics: Linda Florence*

Songs

Swimming Jim *(Incy, Wincy Spider — Action)*
Oh Jemima, look at your Uncle Jim,
He's in the duck pond learning how to swim;
First he does the breast stroke,
Now he does the side:
Now he's under water,
Swimming against the tide.

Lucky Beavers *(Clementine)*
In a country, big and lucky.
Lived some Beavers all alone,
Found a Rusty and a Rainbow,
And a special place their own.
We are sharing, we are caring
For the world as best we can;
By our sharing and our caring,
We will help our fellow man.

Three Little Pigs *(Polly Wolly Doodle)*
A jolly old sow lived in a sty,
And three little pigs had she,
And she waddled about saying umph, umph, umph,
While the little ones said wee, wee.
"My dear little brothers," said one little pig,
"My dear little piggies," said he,
"Let's all in the future say umph, umph, umph,
It's so childish to say wee, wee.
Then these little piggies grew skinny & lean,
And lean they might well be,
For somehow they couldn't say umph, umph, umph
And they wouldn't say wee, wee.
A moral there is to this little song,

A moral that's easy to see;
Don't try when you're young
　to say umph, umph, umph,
When you only can say wee, wee.

Nothing like Cubbing *(My Bonnie)*
We're the (pack name) Cubs in the jungle,
A bright jolly crowd don't you see,
We have a good time, do you wonder;
There's nothing like Cubbing to me.
Chorus: Cubbing, oh Cubbing,
　There's nothing like Cubbing to me, to me:
　Cubbing, oh Cubbing,
　There's nothing like Cubbing to me.
Akela's the Wolf in the jungle,
The leader and head of the pack,
Bagheera will teach us good hunting,
You can't beat a panther for that. *(chorus)*
The laws of the jungle are many,
Baloo knows them all off by heart,
And Chil, the great bird of the tree-tops,
Will teach us to take our own part. *(chorus)*
We learn to be useful and happy,
Serve others instead of just ME,
And to grin when things aren't so easy,
There's nothing like Cubbing to me.
(Final chorus)

Campfire's Close *('Til We Meet Again)*
By the blazing council fire's light,
We have met in comradeship tonight,
Round about the whispering trees
Guard our golden memories;

Songs

And so, before we close our eyes in sleep,
Let us pledge each other that we'll keep,
Scouting friendship strong and deep
'Til we meet again.

Light the Fire (round)
(Row, Row, Row Your Boat)
Let's watch Akela (Skipper) start the fire
Will he get it to light?
I see a spark,
And now the flames,
It's campfire time tonight.

— *Eleanor Newsome*

Beaver Hymn *(Jesus Loves Me)*
We are Beavers, brown and blue
God gives us a job to do,
Serve Him well, and His world, too,
That's the job that we must do.

Chorus: Yes, we are Beavers
Yes, we are Beavers
Yes, we are Beavers
We have our job to do.

We will promise to obey
And work hard at fun and play,
We will spread His love around,
Make His world all safe and sound.
(chorus)

— *Cathie Slessor, Alliston, Ont.*

SONGS

Blue Springs *(Dixie)*
I wish I was in the land of Blue Springs;
Old times there are not forgotten,
Take me back, take me back,
Take me back, to Blue Springs land.
In Blue Springs land,
   where I was trained;
Knowledge, friends, I truly gained;
Take me back, take me back,
Take me back to Blue Springs land.
I wish I was in Blue Springs,
   Hooray! Hooray!
On Blue Springs land, I wish to stand;
Away, away, away in hills of Halton,
Away, away, away in hills of Halton.
                 — *Cathie Slessor*

The 12 Days of Cub Camp
On the first day of Cub camp,
Akela gave to me
A neckerchief tied up in a knot.

On the second day of Cub Camp,
Akela gave to me
Two lost Cub caps
And a neckerchief tied up in a knot.

On the third day of Cub camp,
Akela gave to me,
Three wiggly woggles... etc...

On the fourth day of Cub camp,
Akela gave to me
Four hefty Cub books... etc...

Songs

On the fifth day of Cub camp,
Akela gave to me
Five lengths of rope... etc...

On the sixth day of Cub camp,
Akela gave to me
Six bouncy balls... etc...

On the seventh day of Cub camp,
Akela gave to me
Seven badges to sew on... etc...

On the eighth day of Cub camp,
Akela gave to me
Eight knots to tie up... etc...

On the ninth day of Cub camp,
Akela gave to me
Nine knots to untie... etc...

On the tenth day of Cub camp,
Akela gave to me
Ten fires to light... etc...

On the eleventh day of Cub camp,
Akela gave to me
Eleven pails of water... etc...

On the twelfth day of Cub camp,
We gave to Akela
All our dirty laundry... etc...
— Eleanor Newsome, Ottawa, Ont.

We Are Gathered (*Kumbaya*)
We are gathered, Lord, come be here,
In Your presence, Lord, come be here,
As we worship, Lord, come be here,
O Lord, come be here.

Songs

Make us humble, Lord, come be here.
Make us loyal, Lord, come be here.
Make us courteous, Lord, come be here,
O Lord, come be here.

> — *St. Joseph's High School and Rev. Hallam Johnston, Ottawa*

Thank You, Lord *(Edelweiss)*
Thank you Lord, on this day,
For our many good blessings,
Thank you Lord, on this day,
For our many close friendships.

Glory to God, may you hear our prayers,
Guide us on forever,
Thank you Lord, on this day,
For our blessings and friendships.

Lord we ask, as we go
Into all of life's pathways,
That each day, we may know
You are calling us onward.

Glory to God, may you hear our prayers.
Lead us on forever,
So each day, we may know
You are leading us onward.

Grant us Lord, on this day,
Deeper insights and challenge,
That each day, we may grow
In faith and knowledge and wisdom.

Glory to God, may you hear our prayers,
Guide us on forever,
Grant us Lord, on this day,
Deeper insights and challenge.

Songs

Taps (variation)
Great spirit come; beat the drum,
Journey now, with each one, through the dark,
Take our hands; lead us all
Safely home.

Beaver Pride *(Mickey Mouse)*
B-E-A-V-E-R P-R-I-D-E!
Beaver pride, Beaver pride
Forever let us wear our tails up high;
Green and blue and red and white
We'll all be here tonight
B-E-A-V-E-R P-R-I-D-E!
— *Rusty Bill Rivers, 1st Devon, Alta.*

I'm A Little Leprechaun *(for Mar. 17)*
I'm a little leprechaun, short & green,
Here is my shamrock but I can't be seen,
When you pull my feather, hear me scream
   (everyone scream)
I'm a little leprechaun, short & green.
— *The leaders of 1st St. Pat's Beavers,
Carbonear, Nfld.*

Christmas Time *(Jingle Bells)*
School is out, we won't pout.
All Cubs shout, "Hurray!"
Something special's coming soon,
It is Christmas Day;

Wrap the gifts, trim the tree,
Fill your hearts with cheer,
Soon we'll hear the bells ring out,
Christmas will be here.

SONGS

In the Good Old Wintertime
In the good old winter time,
In the good old winter time,
I love the snow, the sleet, the ice,
Blizzards sure are fine;
I'm frozen in, I'm frozen out,
Just watchin' the snowdrifts climb,
We'll all be diggin' tunnels soon,
In the good old winter time.

Pollution Song *(My Bonnie)*
The litter blows over the highway.
The litter blows over the park:
Unless we do something to stop it.
The world will be litterly dark!
Pick up, pick up, oh pick up the litter you see, you see
Pick up, pick up, oh pick up the litter you see.

The cars that drive over the highway,
Are spewing exhaust in the air.
We're leading our world to extinction
And yet just don't seem to care.
Bring back, bring back, bring back a clean world to me, to me
Bring back, bring back, please bring back a clean world to me.

God gave us clean air for our breathing.
But we just don't keep it that way;
Instead we pollute it from smokestacks
And breathe in the garbage each day!
Bring back, bring back, bring back a clean world to me, to me
Bring back, bring back, please bring back a clean world to me.

Songs

God's Good Earth *(Jesus Loves Me)*
Let's take care of God's good earth.
Water, forests, air and soil
Don't toss out that used tin foil
Ride your bike and don't burn oil.
Chorus
Love one another
Share with each other
Save God's good earth
And learn to do with less.
Only buy the things you need
Enjoy the simple things in life
Do a hobby, play some games.
Eat at home, invite some friends.

> — Thanks to Scouter Doug Brown, Chatham, Ont., for sending these two pollution awareness songs.

Ha, Ha, This Way *(Have You Ever Seen a Lassie?)*
When I am a Beaver
A Beaver, a Beaver,
When I am a Beaver,
I slap my tail.
Chorus
Ha, ha, this away
Ha, ha, that away
Ha, ha, this away
Then, oh then...
(Carry on with: I chop the wood: I swim all day: I build a dam: etc., and appropriate movements.)

> —*from the Trenton District Beaver Songbook*

SONGS

Jungle Song *(A Bear Went Over the Mountain)*
Baloo went into the forest (3x)
It took him two days to get out.
It took him two days to get out (2x)
Baloo went into the forest (3x)
It took him two days to get out.
Akela is a lone wolf (3x)
The wisest in the pack.
Kaa ate up the Banderlog (3x)
Now there's none of them left.
Rama ran over Shere Khan (3x)
And trampled him to death.
Bagheera killed an old bull (3x)
That brought Mowgli to the pack.
Chil helped Mowgli (3x)
And carried the message home.

> *— composed by the Cubs of the 1st Twillingate Pack, Nfld., while on a hike. Thanks to Akela David Wair*

SONGS FOR SCOUT WEEK GATHERINGS

Boom, Boom
Chorus:
Boom, Boom, but it's great to be crazy.
Boom, Boom, but it's great to be crazy.
Giddy and foolish all day long.
Boom, Boom, but it's great to be crazy.
Akela, Akela, he sells socks,
Ten cents a pair, and a dollar a box,
The longer he wears them, the stronger they get.

Songs

He puts them in the water and they don't get wet.
Our Kim and a Beaver and three Brownies nice,
Sat on a curbstone shooting dice,
Kim fell off and landed on the three,
And together they all shouted, "There's a Kim on me!"

Way down south where bananas grow,
A Beaver stepped on an elephant's toe,
The elephant said, with tears in his eyes,
"Pick on someone your own dam size!"

Way up north where there's ice and snow,
There lived a Wolf Cub, his name was Joe,
He got so tired of everything white,
He wore pink pants to the dance last night.

A Scout he promises to be prepared,
He never shows that he is scared,
So why at camp do they always flee,
When a leader says, "Who'll help me?"

Venturers, Venturers, they go forth,
If one points south, another points north,
How they get there, we surely don't know,
But when someone yells "Pathfinders", they're never slow.

— *by Scouter Judy Fearon, 66th Clareview Cubs, Edmonton, Alta.*

A Salute to Leaders
(*Battle Hymn of the Republic.*)
We thank you all our leaders,
But we know we bring you joy,
For each and every week we send
To you our quiet boys:

Songs

Alone they're very silent
But together quite a noise,
And the troops go marching on.
Chorus:
Thank you all for being leaders.
Thank you all for being leaders,
Thank you all for being leaders.
Of our Beavers, Cubs and Scouts!
The boys arrive here right on time.
In proper uniform;
Their hair is always combed real fine,
Like when they just left home;
They all sit down and quietly wait,
Until the fall-in call,
And the troops go marching on!

*— by Ruth Johnson, 1st Dundas Ladies'
Auxiliary, Ont.*

Benediction *(Eidelweiss)*

May the Lord, mighty God, bless and keep you
  forever,
Grant you peace, perfect peace, courage in every
  endeavour;
Lift up your eyes and see His face, know His
  grace forever,
May the Lord, mighty God, bless and keep you
  forever.

— Thanks to Jean Layman Georgetown Ont.

SONGS

Sing a Song

O Lord, It's Great to be Wolf Cubs
(O Lord, It's Hard to be Humble)
O Lord, it's great to be Wolf Cubs,
Our pack's getting better each day,
Earning our stars and our badges,
With the Old Wolves to show us the way;
You may think that we are just bragging,
But we'll be the best Scouts some day,
O Lord, it's great to be Wolf Cubs,
Doing our best every day.

O Lord, it's great to be Wolf Cubs,
Doing good turns every day
Keeping the Law and the Promise,
As we work and we sing and we play;
There's snow fun and outings and camping,
And friends who we meet on the way,
O Lord, it's great to be Wolf Cubs,
Doing our best every day.

So let's give a cheer for the Wolf Cubs,
Let's hear it, hip, hip, hooray!
O Lord, its great to be Wolf Cubs,
Doing our best every day.
(shout) What are we doing?
We're doing our best every day!
— *by Flo Hayden, 2nd North Sydney, N.S.*

I'm a Little Beaver
I'm a little Beaver, short and brown,
Rather be in the water than on the ground:
When you hear my tail slap (hit floor)
That's my sound,
I'm a little Beaver, short and brown.
— *August Baker, 5th Deer Lake, Nfld.*

SONGS

Big Brown Beaver Swims
Taking an idea from the Travelers, Scouter Anne Barbour, 1st McGregor Beavers, Essex, Ont. developed a song that's "lots of fun, especially when parents are around". Use the tune of the *Skater's Waltz* or *The Loveliest Night of the Year* and simply sing:

Big Brown Beaver swims
(lines 1,3,5,7)
Bi-ig Brown Beaver Brown Beaver swims (lines 2,4,6,8)

Sing the whole song together a few times, then arrange the Beavers in four groups (lodges work well) with at least one adult in each. This time, assign each group only one of the words to sing.

When the groups manage to put the song together smoothly this way, ask each group to stand up whenever it's time to sing their word, and sit down when they're done.

Campfire Reflections *(If You're Happy)*
We are gathered by the campfire's light,
At the close of a very busy day,
We've had fun and we've made friends,
The Scouting spirit has prevailed,
We are gathered by the campfire's light.

We will hike along the nature trails,
Finding everything we can from A to Z,
We'll be working, we'll be playing,
And we'll learn some new things too,
That will help us grow as we go on.

SONGS

We will help our friends along the way,
To make the most of each and every day,
We'll be sharing, we'll be caring
And we'll try to do our best,
To make this the greatest camp we've ever had.
— *Monika Perrault, St. Albert, Ont.*

Cub Vesper *(O Christmas Tree)*
Softly falls the light of day,
As our red flower fades away,
Silently each Cub should ask.
Have I done my daily task?
Have I kept my Cub Law too,
Taught to me by old Baloo,
Always tried to do my best?
God grant me, a quiet rest.

Celebrate Scouting
From the Bull Patrol at a Feb.'86 troop Wood Badge course in Ontario, here's a fine song for Scout/Guide Week. The tune is *This Land is Your Land*.

I am a leader with Scouting Canada,
I was a Beaver, a Cub, a Boy Scout,
And after Venturers, I was a Rover,
This is what Scouting's all about.
By sharing, sharing, we do our best
To be prepared to meet the challenge,
Of serving others throughout our world,
This is the message Scouting sends.
From Beaverees to Rover Moots,

Songs

We gather often to share our fun,
And all across our great land,
Scouting is for everyone.

Get ready for spring with these offerings from the
New Zealand Scout News.

Litter Droppers *(Drunken Sailor)*
What shall we do with the litter droppers?
What shall we do with the litter droppers?
What shall we do with the litter droppers?
Early in the morning.

Chorus: Put them in the bin and let the garbage
truck take them (3x)
Early in the morning.

What shall we do with the bottle smashers? (etc.)
What shall we do with the tin can tossers? (etc.)
What'll we do if they take no notice? (etc.)
So pitch right in and put your litter in the litter bin
(etc.)

O Dear, What Can the Matter Be?
Chorus: Oh dear, what can the matter be,
This poor old world, it ain't what it used to be,
Oh dear, what can the matter be,
What have they done to our land?
Our rivers are full of detergent and dung,
The fish are all dying, the streams hardly run.
The sea is so pongy that swimming's no fun.
Oh what have they done with our world?
Our people are needing more pills than they
should be,

SONGS

Their faith in their God is not what it could be,
Abuse and pollution, it seems such a tragedy.
What have they done to our world?
Final Chorus: Oh dear, what can the matter be,
The poor old world, it ain't what it used to be.
The job, it seems, is just up to you and me.
Let's make a much cleaner land.

Wouldn't It Be Loverly?

All I want is a world somewhere,
Far away from polluted air,
With lots of love and care,
Oh, wouldn't it be loverly?
Lots of places where streams run clear,
Lots of children who have no fear,
Pure seas, pure land, pure air,
Oh wouldn't it be loverly?
Oh so loverly it would be without the smells and smoke,
We would see they cleaned up all their horrors before we choke;
(Repeat first verse)

A Song for Closing

After adding a verse for each of their sections while on a canoeing trip in Algonquin Park, the 3rd Aurora Borealis Venturers and Nomad Rovers shared this all-section closing song "heard around many campfires" in their South Lake Simcoe District, Ont. The tune is *O Christmas Tree*.

SONGS

Softly falls the light of day, as our campfire fades away,
Silently each Beaver asks, have I done my daily tasks?
Did I give the world my care, remembering to smile and share?
Beavers turn to God in prayer, knowing He will always care.

Softly falls the light of day ... etc.
Silently each Cub shall ask ... etc.
Have I kept my Cub laws too, taught to me by Old Baloo?
Have I tried to do my best? God grant me a quiet rest.

Softly falls the light of day... etc.
Silently each Scout shall ask... etc.
Have I kept my honour bright? Can I guiltless sleep tonight?
Have I done and have I dared, everything to be prepared?

Softly falls the light of day ... etc.
Silently each Venturer asks ... etc.
Have I kept my challenge true? Side by side, we'll see it through,
Have I turned to God today? Let Him help show us the way.

Softly falls the light of day... etc.
Silently each Rover asks ... etc.
Have I served my fellow man, guided by our Founder's hand?
Rovers try to do their best; God will help them with the rest.

Songs

Leaders, Goodnight *(Goodnight Irene)*
Last Saturday night I joined Wolf Cubs,
Me and my pack settled down,
Now me and my pack are learning,
To do our best all around.
Chorus:
Akela, goodnight; Raksha, goodnight;
Goodnight Baloo, Goodnight Bagheera.
I'll see you here next week.

Sometimes we go to the country,
Sometimes we stay in the town,
Sometimes we take a great notion,
To just fool around like clowns. *(chorus)*

Whatever it is that we're doing,
We always have fun in our pack;
Earn a star, earn a badge, or just do a craft.
We can't wait for next week to come back.
— *by Carole Richardson, 1st Wetaskiwin Cubs, Alta.*

Pumpkin Bells
Dashing through the streets,
In costumes bright and gay,
To each house we go, laughing all the way.
Hallowe'en is here, making spirits bright,
What fun it is to trick or treat,
Singing pumpkin songs tonight.

Pumpkin bells, pumpkin bells,
Ringing loud and clear,
Oh what fun Great Pumpkin brings,
When Hallowe'en is here!
— from *The Beaver's Bark*, Northern B.C.

Songs

Lament for Akela
(Tune: Clementine)
Chorus: Oh Akela, Oh Akela
Oh Akela, friend of mine.
You are lost and gone forever,
Dreadful sorry, friend of mine.

Once there was a pack of Wolf Cubs
Went out for a winter hike.
But Akela couldn't keep up.
So she went home for her hike. *(Chorus)*

She went over to the river.
Right up to the water's brim.
But she fell in and we lost her.
For Akela couldn't swim. *(Chorus)*

We just stood there, sad and helpless
Feeling anything but brave.
Saw Akela floating by us,
Carried on a great big wave. *(Chorus)*

Down she swept right to the ocean.
Oh how sorry was our lot,
But we went home for our supper.
And Akela, we forgot. *(Chorus)*
— *Elizabeth Watson, 2nd Windsor Cubs, NS*

Snowman, Snowman
(Twinkle, Twinkle, Little Star)
Snowman, snowman where did you go?
I built you yesterday out of snow,
I built you high and I built you fat,
I put on eyes and nose and a hat;
And now you're gone, all melted away.
But its sunny outside, so I'll go and play.
— *Sandra Hards, 1st North Bay Beavers, Ont.*

Songs

It's a Long Way to Our Campsite *(Tipperary)*
It's a long way to our campsite,
It's a long way to go,
Its a long way to our campsite,
To the best in life we know;
Goodbye television,
Farewell old armchair,
It's a long, long way to our campsite,
But we'll soon be there.
—from Scouting (UK) magazine

Why Am I in Scouting? *(Wasn't It a Party)*
Must have been my big mouth,
Must have been their grin,
Must have been that "One night a week" commitment,
Boy, how they sucked me in;
My calendar's so booked up,
I often sit and cry,
Tell me, me oh me oh my.
Why am I in Scouting?

Wasn't for the prestige,
Wasn't for the pay,
Wasn't for the uniform,
I can't stand green or grey;
My family only sees me,
To wave a quick good-bye,
Tell me, me oh me oh my
Why am I in Scouting?

Has to be the fellowship,
Has to be the fun,
Has to be the trainers,

They've all been number one,
The boys all love the movement.
No need to question why,
Tell ya, me oh me oh my
I'm proud that I'm in Scouting!

> *— thanks to Sandy Bard, Northern Alberta Region, and participants of a 1983 "Campfire Magic" weekend.*

Come Down to CJ
(Frosty the Snowman)
Chorus
The Scouting spirit is alive
And fine in P.E.I.;
Come show you care
And meet us there,
Just drive, or sail, or fly.

Come down to CJ,
Come down to our jamboree.
Won't you all come down
To Charlottetown,
Lots of fun for you and me;
Come down to CJ,
Come and have a merry time,
There is loads to do
And we sure want you,
Down at CJ'89! *(chorus)*

Yes, come down to CJ,
Come and join our happy crew,
Come and work and play
In the Scouting way,
We'll have good times, me and you:
Come down to CJ,

Songs

Now's the time to plan to go,
And I promise you,
I swear its true,
We'll put on a real good show. *(chorus)*

Sure, come down to CJ
Where the Scouting spirit's strong,
And if you're not there,
It just won't seem fair,
Come and join our cheerful throng:
Come down to CJ,
Cement friendships old and new,
We'll have a real good time,
At CJ'89,
Where our Scouting dreams come true.

— *by Frank Townson, National Capital Region, Ont.*

O Lord, We Stand Before You
Major Gwenyth Redhead, Vancouver, B.C., wrote new words to the hymn tune *Aurelia (The Church's One Foundation)* for The Salvation Army B.C. South Division, who used it at their united Divine Service Parade in 1987 and their annual Fourfold Fellowship Banquet in 1988.

O Lord, we stand before you,
Our loyalty declare,
To You, our Great Creator
And to our country fair.

Please help us to be faithful
To promises we've made,
To reach out hands to others,
And help someone each day.

Songs

We thank you, Lord, for Guiding,
And Scouting groups for boys.
For chances to discover
The secrets of real joy,
The challenges of learning,
Developing new skills
That help to make us ready
Your purpose to fulfil.

Winter Snow *(Edelweiss)*
Winter snow, winter snow,
Each day I look for you;
Fresh and white, clean and bright,
Full of wonder, I greet you.
Snowbank of snow may you grow and grow,
Grow and grow all winter;
Winter snow, winter snow,
Stay in my yard forever.
— *by Becky Lindstedt*

Song for Swim Up
(Tune: *Frère Jacques*)
Lucky Beaver, lucky Beaver,
Growing up, growing up,
Remember all our good times,

Remember all our good times,
Wish you luck, wish you luck.

Fun and sharing, fun and sharing,
That's the track, that's the track,
Now you'll do your best, (2x)
In the pack, in the pack.

Songs

Leaving Beavers, leaving Beavers,
Don't be sad, don't be sad,
Swimming up to Wolf Cubs (2x)
Aren't you glad, aren't you glad?

Regina 59 Troop Song
(Tune: *Toronto Blue Jay's theme song*)

We've got nine and ten,
A pack... and a tent,
And that's not all
We've got a map and a compass
From fall 'til fall
What d'ya say...
Let's go hike
OK! OK!
Fifty-nine, fifty-nine
Let's go hike.OK! OK!
Fifty-nine, fifty-nine
Let's go hike!

—from Kendall Kerr, Regina, Sask.

When the Cubs Come Marching In
(*x marks a hand clap*. Tune: *The Saints*)
Oh when the Cubs, x x
Come marching in x x
Oh when the Cubs come marching in, x x
Akela, we'll x be in that number, x x
When the Cubs come marching in, x x
Oh when the Grand x x
Howl is begun, x x
Oh when the Grand Howl is begun, x x
Akela, we'll x be in that number,
When the Grand Howl is begun. x x

Songs

Oh when Ake-x x
La ties a knot, x x
Oh when Akela ties a knot x x
Akela (etc.)

Oh when the pack, x x
Goes on a trip, x x
Oh when the pack goes on a trip, x x
Akela, (etc.)

That's all there is x x
To this small song, x x
That's all there is to this small song, x x
Akela, please x write us more verses x x
And we'll all sing along. x x
                — *Thanks to Eleanor Newsome*

It's an Insect Covered World
(Tune: *It's a Small World*)
It's a world of centipedes,
A world of moths,
It's a world of katydids,
A world of wasps,
There's so much that we share
That it's time we're aware,
It's an insect covered world.

Chorus: It's an insect covered world (4x)

It's a world of beetles,
It's a world of fleas,
A world of caterpillars,
And a world of bees,
In this world that we know,
There's so much we can show,
It's an insect covered world.

SKITS

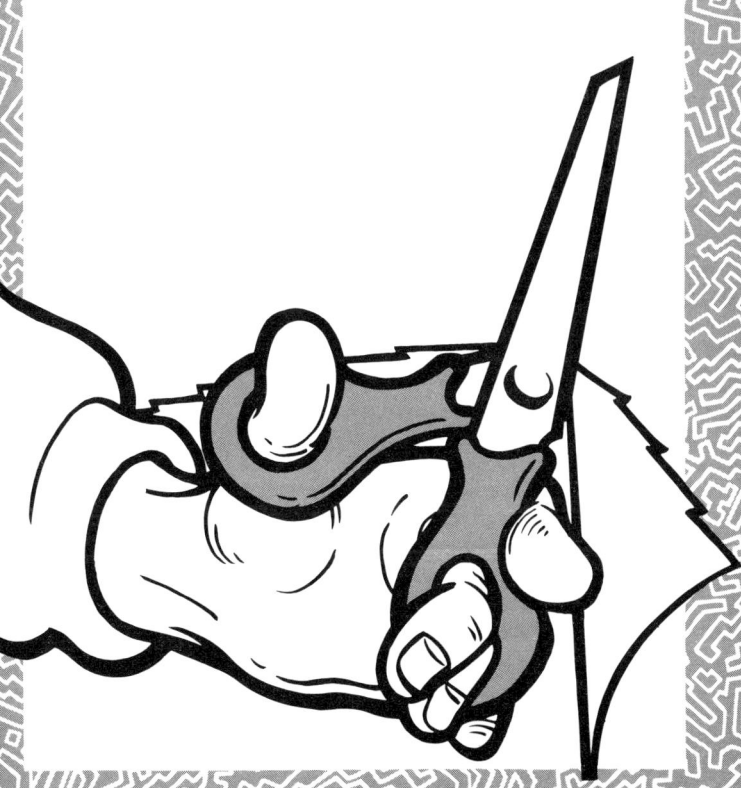

SKITS

THE CONTEST

Cast: 6 Cubs
Five Cubs sit in their clubhouse (indicated by appropriate signs) playing a game.

Cub 1: (runs in, very excited) Hey, you guys! Did you hear about the big contest?
Cub 2: What contest? What's it about?
Cub 1: The 'Keep Canada Beautiful' contest, that's what!
Cub 3: Are there prizes? A contest is no good without prizes.
Cub 1: Sure, lots of prizes. Neat ones like bicycles and radios, and lots of good stuff!
Cub 4: (gloomily) I bet it's hard. Contests with neat prizes are always hard.
Cub 1: Nope! It's easy. Even the rules say it's SIMPLE — in big letters. The winner is the one who picks the easiest way.
Cub 5: The easiest way to do what?
Cub 1: The easiest way to keep Canada beautiful. That's what I've been talking about!
Cub 6: (with a swagger) Ha! Then I'm a cinch to win!
Cub 1: Why is it so cinchy for you? What's your great way to keep Canada beautiful?
Cub 6: (takes out a comb and combs his hair) See! That's the easiest way *I* know to keep Canada beautiful.
(The others look at him, then at each other. Quickly they surround him, carry or drag him to a large box marked TRASH, and dump him in).
Cub 1: Like he said, fellas, we're a cinch to win! That's the easiest way *I* know to keep Canada beautiful! (They exit, laughing while Cub 1 stands up in the trash box with a disgusted look on his face).

SKITS

WITCHES BREW

Scene: The Macabre Restaurant (two tables appropriately set up). Sign reading: *Soup of the Night — Alphablood (or Ghoul Gruel, or anything repulsive and gruesome)*. Three or four ghosts, witches, etc., sit at one table and pantomime eating and talking. Enter a cackling witch, who takes the other table.

Waiter (a Dracula type): What will it be, madame?

Witch: I'll try your Soup of the Night.

Waiter: Coming up, madame. (glides away and returns with suitably macabre-looking bowl of soup). Voilà, madame.

Witch (tasting soup): Screech! Waiter — I can't eat this soup! Bring me the cook!

Waiter: Of course, madame, Right away, madame! (flaps off, returns with cook, another witch).

Cook: What seems to be the trouble?

Witch: This soup is flat! It needs some eye of-bat!

Cook: Yes, madame. I'll get some eye-of-bat right away madame (scoots off, returns and puts something into the bowl with appropriate cackles, stirrings and witchly mumblings). That should be fine now, madame. Try it.

Witch (taking another taste): No, still not enough spice. It needs some crushed beetle and extract of spider.

Cook: Of course, madame. Coming up. (hobbles off, returns and adds something to the soup, again cackling, stirring, etc. Customer witch joins the cackles and mumbles). There madame, I think that should be just right!

Witch (tasting once more): You fool! It's missing toad-tails! (Repeat routine of fetching, adding ingredient, cackles and stirs, but have cook witch sneak away while customer witch continues the mumbo-jumbo over the bowl).

Witch (comes out of trance, looks around, tastes soup and slams down spoon): Screech! Waiter! WAITER!

Waiter (swooping over): Yes madame?

SKITS

Witch: I can't eat this soup!
Waiter (exasperated): Why ever not, madame?
Witch: Screech! Because it's cold, you fool!

• • • • • • • • • • • • • • • • • • •

PEANUT BUTTER
Scene: Noon on a work project. Several workmen with lunch kits, one who is "star". Announce each act in words or by sign.

Act I
Star: (Takes out lunch, looks through lunchbox carefully, picks out a sandwich, unwraps it, examines and scowls) Peanut butter! (Throws sandwich away while others look on).

Act II
Star: (Smiles in anticipation, takes out lunchbox, looks through it carefully, picks out sandwich, unwraps it, lifts bread to examine filling, scowls and yells) Peanut butter! (Hurls sandwich away while others look on, shake their heads).

Act III (Star repeats action of Act II, another workman speaks.)
Workman: Excuse me for butting in buddy, but I've noticed that every day you look at your sandwich and throw it away. Why don't you tell your wife you don't like peanut butter?
Star: You leave my wife out of this. I make my own sandwiches!
—*Thanks to Helen Singh, Little Fort, B.C.*

• • • • • • • • • • • • • • • • • • • •

Jungle drums
Cast: Mowgli, who drums out messages on a tom-tom; several Cubs in full uniform; Akela. As Mowgli beats out messages, Cubs take turns translating for Akela. (Mowgli drums)
Akela: What's he saying?

SKITS

Cub 1: Mowgli says there will be a special meeting next week. (Akela nods. Mowgli drums again and Akela looks puzzled)
Cub 2: Mowgli says that it will be a very exciting meeting. (Nod, drumming and puzzled Scouter routines repeat)
Cub 3: He says that many Cubs will receive special awards at the meeting. (Repeat nod, drum, head-scratching)
Cub 4: Mowgli says there will be singing and games, and many visitors from the families of Akela's pack. (Akela nods again and Mowgli beats out another message. All the Cubs shake heads, shrug. Mowgli drums again. Cubs still indicate they don't understand. Mowgli determinedly beats out the message one more time as Akela and Cubs listen intently. Akela smiles, nods.)
Cub 5: I don't get it! What did he say?
Akela: I got it! Mowgli says to telephone him if there's anything special we want him to bring to the meeting.
Cubs: (in great disgust) Telephone! Oh, Good Grief! (exit all)

Is the Train Comin?

Members of a six or patrol stand in a straight line facing the audience. Pa stands at one end, next to Ma and an assortment of sons, daughters, cousins, etc. All speak in slow, southern drawls.

Pa turns head toward Ma and drawls, "Hey Ma, is the train comin' from Calahoo?" Ma turns to next in line and drawls, "Hey Baby Joe, is the train comin' from Calahoo?" Baby Joe passes on the message, and it continues down the line until it reaches the last boy. He steps forward, peers intently to the right, steps back into line and says, "Nope" to the person next to him, who passes it on to the next person, and so on up the line until it reaches Pa again.

In a leisurely drawl, Pa says, "Hey Ma, is the train comin' from Keremeos?" Ma dutifully starts the question down the line until it reaches the last person, who steps forward, peers intently to the left, steps back and says, "Nope." His answer returns slowly up the line until it finally reaches Pa once more.

SKITS

Pa scratches his chin, spits, then drawls, "Well, then, I guess I kin cross the track now." The whole tribe moves forward, turns right, and exits.

• • • • • • • • • • • • • • • • • • • •

Peanuts
Cast: policeman; three boys; police chief. (Policeman hustles scuffed-looking boys up to boy sitting at table marked CHIEF.)
Policeman: Here's a bunch of trouble-makers for you, sir.
Chief: Okay, constable. I'll deal with this. (dismisses officer, turns sternly to Boy 1) Well, now. Why are you here?
Boy 1: (embarrassed) I threw peanuts into the lake. (Chief looks puzzled)
Chief: (sternly to Boy 2) And why, then, were you brought in?
Boy 2: (defensively) I threw peanuts into the lake. (Chief scowls angrily)
Chief: (bellows at Boy 3) And you! What have you got to say for yourself?
Boy 3: I'm Peanuts, sir! (exit all)

• • • • • • • • • • • • • • • • • • • •

THE ROCKIES
Scene: a painted backdrop of high mountains. A Scout, with World Jamboree insignia prominently displayed, stands near railing (a line of chairs) looking at the view. The first of a series of people enters to join him in view gazing.
Scout: Hi! What do you think of these mountains, eh? 1st Man: High.
Scout (a little louder): Hi! What do you think of these mountains, eh?
1st Man: High, I said.
Scout: Hi to you, too. But what do you think of these mountains?
1st Man: High! High! I said they were high, didn't I? (walks away in disgust)

SKITS

Second man, carrying shopping bag, enters.
Scout: Hi! Say, what's it like living in these mountains, anyway?
2nd Man: Well, I guess you could say it's sort of like an umbrella.
Scout (amazed): An umbrella?
2nd Man: Yep — sometimes up; sometimes down! (walks away chortling)
Third man enters. The two stand quietly for a minute and Scout fidgets, wondering if he should try again.
Scout: Say, aren't these mountains something?
3rd Man: You bet! Just like music.
Scout: Well, I never thought of it that way. Music?
3rd Man: Yup — all HARD ROCK! (slaps his thigh, guffaws, exits)
Fourth man enters.
4th Man: Say, you're one of them Scouts, aren't you? Up from the Kananaskis Valley, eh? Tell me, what do you think of these mountains?
Scout: To tell you the truth, I'm a bit puzzled. I haven't seen a squirrel all day, and I figure this is a perfect place for squirrels.
4th Man: Yeah? How's that?
Scout: Well, from everything I've heard since I got here, these mountains are definitely full of nuts!
(Exit all)

THE FARMER & THE OX
Cast: farmer, three merchants, hired hand
Farmer (enters and falls on knees): Oh, woe is me! It's time to plough and I have no oxen (raises arms to sky). Oh, whatever fates there are, please, please send me an ox so that I can plough my fields and plant my crops!
(Enter merchant)
1st Merchant: Whatever are you doing, man?

SKITS

Farmer: I'm begging the fates to send me an ox so that I can plough my fields and plant my crops. Without an ox, my children will starve. Oh, woe is me!

1st **Merchant:** Oh you poor, poor man. I would stay to help, but must get to town without delay (turns to audience). Will no one out there help this poor man? Often the fates ignore one voice, but will listen to two. *(The merchant coaxes a volunteer from the audience, arranges him on his knees with the farmer and instructs him to lift his arms to the sky and repeat over and over, "Please, please send an ox!" The merchant leaves and a second merchant enters, repeats the routine and brings up a second volunteer. A third merchant does the same. When all three volunteers are kneeling and wailing with the farmer, the hired hand enters, looks amazed and shouts...)*

Hired Hand: Boss! Boss! Truly it's a miracle we see. You prayed for one ox, and the fates have sent you three jackasses!

• • • • • • • • • • • • • • • • •

Quick and Foolish

Boy and Matches
A boy enters with a large box of matches. He removes a match and strikes it, but it doesn't light, so he throws it away and takes another match out of the box, He repeats the performance several times. Finally, he strikes a match which lights. He blows it out quickly, puts it back into the box, looks at the audience, smiles and says, "That's a good one. I'd better keep it!"
   Exit

The Traveller
A cast of two; the traveller and a hotel clerk who sits behind a table. Traveller approaches hotel desk.
Traveller: I'd like a room for the night, please.

Clerk: With tub or shower?
Traveller: What's the difference!
Clerk: Well — you sit down in a tub!
       Exit

Reindeer Game

Announcer (bursting with enthusiasm):

Good evening ladies and gentlemen, and welcome to our program. Tonight, some lucky member of our audience will win $10,000 — if he correctly answers our skill testing question!
(Scans audience and picks out his planted helper). You, sir, would you like a chance at this great prize?

Helper:
Oh yes, sir! (Leaves audience and joins announcer on stage)

Announcer:
Tonight, our question is: "Name two of Santa's reindeer!" You have 10 seconds to think about it. No help from the audience, please. (Buzzer sounds) Time's up! Now, give me one of the two reindeer names.

Helper:
Would one be Rudolph?

Announcer (jumping with joy):
Yes! That's absolutely correct! You are half way to $10,000! Now, can you give me one more name?

Helper (thinks, scratches his head):
Well, how about Olive?

Announcer (groans):
Olive! Whoever heard of a reindeer named Olive?

SKITS

Helper:
Well, they sing about her in the song about Rudolph. You know! We've all heard them. They sing, "Olive the other reindeer!".
— *Jo Brygider, Maple Ridge, B.C.*

The Bouquet

Cast: six Cubs on an outing.

1st Cub (glumly):
I don't think Akela is having such a great time.

2nd Cub (looking at 3rd Cub):
Well, you didn't help much — giving her that garter snake!

3rd Cub:
I was just trying to help her collect stuff for our nature display.

4th Cub:
And, you heard what she said. "Nothing, ever again, that moves by itself!"

3rd Cub:
So, now I know better.

5th Cub:
Don't worry about a thing, guys. I'm going to fix everything!

6th Cub:
Yeah? How?

5th Cub:
Well, you know how she likes flowers! So, I picked her this neat bunch of flowers (holds up bouquet trailing ivy) — see!

6th Cub:
Oh, no! Now we'll never get to go on another hike!

5th Cub:
How come?

6th Cub:
Because, silly — that's poison ivy!

SKITS

(The other five Cubs make disgusted, horrified noises and run off stage. The 5th Cub, left standing, drops the bouquet, starts to scratch and exits)

• • • • • • • • • • • • • • • • • • •

Pure Corn with Joe & Moe

At the Pet Store

Moe stands behind the counter. Joe enters.

Joe: May I have 25¢ worth of birdseed, please
Moe: How many birds do you have?
Joe: None yet, but I'm gonna grow some!

The Fortune Teller

A turbaned Moe sits at a table on which there is a crystal ball. Joe enters.
Joe: Do you tell fortunes?
Moe: Yes, I do. Moe the Marvellous knows all, sees all, tells all — for a price.
Joe: How much do you charge?
Moe: Well, today's a slow day — bargain rates: $20 for two questions.
Joe: Wow! Isn't that a bit much for just two questions?
Moe: Yes. Now, what's your second question?

Billy the Bully
Moe stands at a table making a sandwich. Battered, bruised and bandaged, Joe limps in.
Moe: What on earth happened to you?
Joe: I had a run-in with Billy the Bully on the way home from school.
Moe: What happened?

SKITS

Joe: Well, he said he had half a mind to beat me up.
Moe: And you agreed to let him beat you up?
Joe: Not exactly, I agreed he had half a mind!

The Trackers
Carrying all the gear needed to make plaster casts, Joe and Moe are out in the wilderness looking for tracks.
Joe: Some tracks! A raccoon passed here.
Moe: Those are bear tracks!
Joe: No they aren't, they're raccoon tracks.
Moe: Bear tracks!
Joe: Raccoon tracks!
(The argument continues, getting louder and louder. Quietly start a tape of an approaching train. Gradually increase the volume and end with a train whistle, pounding wheels, Joe and Moe yelling "Aaargh!" and lights out.)

The Western
Joe and Moe are watching a cowboy movie on television (make a mock screen from a cardboard box). You can tape sound effects for a chase (whoops, hollers hoofbeats, gunshots) ahead of time, or post "live" noisemakers in the wings.
Moe: I betcha that cowboy hits his head on a tree branch and falls off his horse.
Joe: You're on! I betcha he doesn't.
(The chase sounds get wilder until the sound effects indicate the cowboy indeed runs into the tree branch.)
Joe: Oh, no!
Moe: See, I told you he would! But then, I've seen this movie before.
Joe: So what. I've seen it before, too.
Moe: What? Well, if you've seen the movie before, why on earth did you bet the cowboy wouldn't hit a branch and fall off his horse?
Joe: Well, I didn't think he'd be so stupid the second time around!

SKITS

At the Movies
Director, cameraman, clapper board man, a couple of lighting men (with flashlights) and mother are on stage as action begins. Son, doctor and undertaker wait in wings.

Director: Lights, Camera, Action!

Clapper Board Man: Scene One, Take One!
(The actors play the scene without the least sign of emotion as lighting people follow and cameraman films. Mother is flipping pancakes at the stove when son walks in.)

Son: Mom, I don't feel too well. (He collapses.)
Mom: (Goes over, looks at son.) Oh, I'd better call the doctor. (Moves to phone, dials making click, click sounds.) Doctor, come quick. My son's collapsed.
Doctor: (Enters, checks pulse and breathing.) He's dead. I'd better call the undertaker. (Goes to phone, dials making dialing sounds like Mom did.) Undertaker, you'd better come. I have a dead body here.
Undertaker: (Enters and begins to measure the body.)
Director: (Jumps up) Cut! Cut! That was terrible. You had no emotion at ALL. Let's do it again. This time, give me more emotion!
Cast: (Exiting) Right. More emotion.
Director: Lights, Camera, Action!
Clapper Board Man: Scene One, Take Two!

(The actors re-do the scene, using exactly the same words, but with great hammy histrionics. Mother weeps uncontrollably throughout, son dies very dramatically, etc. At the same point as in Take One, the director yells, "Cut! Cut!")
Director: That was better, but too fast. Let's try again. This time, slow it down. Lights, Camera, Action!

Clapper Board Man: Scene One, Take Three!

SKITS

(The actors re-do the scene in slow motion — talking slowly, moving slowly. For example. when the telephone is dialled, it goes "click... click.. click", and after the doctor checks the son's pulse, the son's hand falls slowly back to the floor, etc The director yells, "Cut!" in the usual place.)

Director: That was far too slow. One more time. Let's speed it up!

(This time, the actors do the scene so quickly that the son throws himself to the ground, the doctor is there before Mom can hang up, and so on.)

Director (at the same place): Cut! That was absolutely terrible! Actors? Do you call yourself actors!!??

Cast: Actors? Who said anything about actors?
We're the cleaners! (All pick up brooms and exit.)
— Thanks to *Scout* magazine, Australia

Flora the Flea
(The performer is putting his trained flea Flora through all her tricks. His eyes follow every flip, jump, etc. as she performs and lands back in his hand. Then he asks her to jump to the ceiling. His eyes lose her and she doesn't return. He looks high and low, and finally looks in someone's hair.)
Performer (delighted): Flora, there you are! I'm so glad to have you back. (Looks more closely. But... say, this isn't Flora!

SKITS

Sound Effects for Skits

Sound effect people working at hidden microphones can add a whole lot of realistic fun to your skits. Try these ideas.

Hoofbeats: Beat coconut shell halves on a pillow (distant), or a wooden board.

Breezes: Wave narrow streamers of newspaper.

Burbling water: Several people blow through straws into glasses of water.

Rain: Slowly drop sand on tightly drawn cellophane.

Hail: Pour grains of rice onto an overturned baking tin or a piece of wood.

Wind: Cut a narrow slit in a sheet of paper. Hold the paper about 12 mm from lips and blow.

Airplane: Hold heavy paper so that it strikes the blades of an electric fan.

Fire: Crumple cellophane into a ball and release for crackling sound.

Thunder: Shake a 30 cm x 90 cm piece of tin suspended from a bar or frame.

Breaking glass: Put an old piece of window glass in a sack; drop on the floor.

Crashes: Fill a wooden box with broken glass and some stones, then nail down top. Tip box or drop, depending on the type of crash you want.

SKITS

Train: Put small nails or BB shot inside a flat tin and shake back and forth. Or try sandpaper or wire on metal.

Shot: Slap a yardstick on a hard, flat surface. Screeching brakes: Slide the open end of a drinking glass over a pane of glass.

• • • • • • • • • • • • • • • • • • • •

THE EMPTY BOXES

You need a manager, guard, three workmen, and a few large cardboard boxes. Setting: a factory gate.

Manager (to new guard): I'm giving you the very responsible position of gate guard at this factory. Because of the lack of vigilance by your predecessors, the workers have stolen so many finished articles that the firm is heading for bankruptcy. Your duty is to ensure this is brought to an end. Do you understand?

Guard: Yes sir. I am to stop stealing.

Manager: That's right. You can search people if necessary. Now it's up to you, and let's see some results.

Guard: Very good, sir. *(Manager leaves; guard takes post; first workman enters carrying a clothdraped box.)*

Guard: Just a moment. What have you got in that box?

Workman 1: What do you mean? Guard: What have you got in that box? It's my duty to see that no one takes stuff out of the factory.

Workman 1: Why didn't you say? There's nothing in the box. Look! *(He shows everyone the box is empty).*

Skits

Guard: Oh, well, that's all right then. *(Workman 1 leaves and second workman enters, box draped as before. Guard and workman go through routine of looking in box. Repeat with the third workman. After the third man has left, manager races in enraged).*

Manager: You idiot. I hired you to stop this pilfering. You've only been here half an hour and already we're losing things!

Guard: But the only people who went out were three men with boxes. I stopped them all and they had nothing in them.

Manager: You fool! We make boxes!

• • • • • • • • • • • • • • • • • • • •

Mounted Scouts
Cast: Scouter; Scouts Tom, Dick and Harry; other Scouts.

(Camp scene with tent, backpacks. etc. Troop is gathered around Scouter.)

Scouter: Okay, guys, rest day. You're on your own to go fishing, exploring, whatever. But I'm sick and tired of you guys being late all the time and coming up with wild excuses, so I'm making just one rule. Everybody — and that means every Tom, Dick and Harry of you — must be back in camp by
5 p.m. Got it?

Scouts: Right, Scouter... Gotcha, Scouter, etc.

(Scouts scatter and move off-stage. When they're gone, Scouter looks around, props a backpack against a chair "tree", stretches out and pulls down his cap over his eyes to have a snooze. Noise of returning Scouts off-stage. Scouter jerks awake, looks at watch. First pair of Scouts comes in.)

Skits

Scouter: Good work, men. Only 4:55. *(Scouts go to fire circle, start messing with pots and pans, etc. Other Scouts come in, and Scouter greets them, checking the time against his watch — 4:56; 4:58; etc.)*

Scouter: Time's up! 5 o'clock! *(Silently counts gathered Scouts)* Where's Tom? Where's Dick? And Harry?

(Scouts shrug, move off to do different things. Scouter paces, looking at watch. Finally, Tom staggers onstage, all tattered and torn.)

Scouter: You're late! What happened?

Tom: (gasping) I went canoeing. The boat sank. I swam to shore, found a horse, and rode it a couple of miles. But it collapsed! I hiked the last 20 miles! *(Tom collapses. Dick staggers in, tattered and torn.)*

Scouter: What on earth happened to you?

Dick: I went canoeing. The boat sank. I swam to shore, found a horse, and rode it a couple of miles. Then it collapsed. I had to hike the last 20 miles! *(Dick collapses. Harry crawls into camp, tattered and torn.)*

Scouter: No, don't tell me. I know, I know. You went canoeing; your boat sank; you found a horse and rode it until it collapsed

Harry: No, no, no! You've got it all wrong! My horse couldn't get through! There were two collapsed horses blocking the trail!

Ghost Story
Boys lined up in file tiptoe onto the stage and suddenly stop. The message is passed in a mock whisper from the head of the line to the foot and vice versa.

SKITS

Head: (points) That's where I saw the ghost!
Foot: Where?!
Head: About six metres away!
Foot: How big was he?
Head: About three metres tall!
Foot: How long ago?
Head: About two weeks ago!
Foot: Then why are we whispering?
Head: 'Cause I've got a cold!

Another Ghost Story

Scout stands alone on dimmed stage whistling and darting glances here and there. Second Scout enters.

Scout 2: What are you doing?
Scout 1: Whistling.
Scout 2: Why?
Scout 1: To keep the ghosts away
Scout 2: But there aren't any ghosts around here.
Scout 1: See! It's working!

Canned Skits

A good way to stimulate skit-making skills is to provide the actors some starting points. When young people have not had much experience at creating original skits, it helps if they can start with a setting, situation, and character.

Prepare three cans or paper bags filled with cards or slips of paper. One can will offer different settings, the second a variety of situations, and the third a selection of characters. Skit teams draw one

SKITS

card each from the first two cans and enough cards from the third can to give each player a character.

Once your bunch are more experienced at creating skits, try some of these other ideas.

• Fill a bag with punchlines (e.g. They told me there'd be days like this . . . I knew I should have minded my own business. . . But it seemed like a nice little pussy cat . . . etc.). Challenge teams to create a skit leading up to the punchline they draw.

• Fill a bag with fairy tale or nursery rhyme titles. Challenge teams to create skits that give the story a surprise ending.

• Challenge teams to act out a situation using only nonsense words (gobbledygook) or only numbers. How about a skit using sounds only?

• Fill a bag with situations: e.g. shopping at the supermarket; rearranging the furniture in a room; giving the dog a bath; etc. Challenge teams to act out the situations with no props (i.e. using people as doors, typewriters, lamps, etc.).

• Give each team one item; e.g. a hat, scarf, pair of shoes. Challenge them to create a skit using that item.

• Fill a bag with a list of song titles. Challenge teams to mime the song (tell its story in movement only— no words).

Quick Skit

Announcer: Ladies and Gentlemen: Professor X will now give his address.

Professor: Ladies and Gentlemen. My address is 498 Maple Street. *(Professor bows: announcer and professor exit)*

SKITS

Measurement problem

(Two Scouts come on stage carrying a long pole. They prop it up, then stand back and look at it.)

Scout 1: Now, there are several ways we can figure out the height of this pole. How do you want to start?

(The Scouts unsuccessfully try various methods of estimation to calculate the height of the pole. The conversation goes something like...)

Scout 1: According to my calculations, that pole is about 2 m high.

Scout 2: There's no way. It has got to be shorter than that. Just look at it.

(This kind of exchange repeats several times as the Scouts obviously become more and more exasperated. A Cub strolls onto the stage.)

Cub: Hi! *(he watches a bit)* What are you guys trying to do?

Scout 2: We're trying to measure the exact height of this pole.

Scout 1: We haven't had too much luck, yet, but we'll get it.

Cub: Why don't you just lay the pole on the ground and measure its length?

Scout 1: (scornfully) Cubs!

Scout 2: I'll say. *(To the Cub)* Didn't you hear right? We want to know how tall the pole is — not how *long* it is!

SKITS

Two for Christmas
by Greybeard

Trimming the Tree
Characters: Mother, Father, Child

Props: Scout staff with sprig of evergreen lashed to the top. Some materials to make snipping and sawing sounds (you can pre-record these on cassette tape).

Mother is on stage, father and child out of sight.

Father tells child to go ask mother how the tree looks.

Child runs onstage and asks.

Mother peers through imaginary kitchen window, hints and says it needs more off this side.

Child runs off stage and repeats her directions. Sounds of sawing, snipping, etc.

Repeat several times, with mother pointing in different directions each time, father perhaps becoming impatient, and child becoming more and more tired.

Finally many sounds of sawing and snipping. Father marches on stage with staff, shows it to mother and audience.
"Now is it right?!"

SKITS

• •

The New Computer
Characters: Computer, Child
Props: instruction book (or simply use mime)

This is a monologue with the opening words left to the imagination of your boys.
Computer is onstage, crouched on hands and knees with arms covering head. Child runs on, announces that Santa has been here and left him a new computer.
Child opens up computer and sets it up *(computer faces audience, bends over, puts hands on knees).*

Child says something like, "Hmmm, here's the instruction book. Uh ... lessee... (reads) "To start your computer, insert a disk."

(Pantomime inserting disk, continue reading) "Then type the word 'Run' and press the 'Return' key

(Puts down book, makes a big show of typing) "R-U-N"
When he presses the return button, the computer runs off stage.

The child's look of surprise *(face the audience!)* adds to the ending.

• •

Dinner Special
Characters: two customers, waiter. Let actors develop actions and dialogue from the situation.
Props: table with tablecloth, candles, menus, etc. Most important — a storybook.

Two customers enter a fancy seafood restaurant, study menus, etc. Waiter arrives to take orders. One customer orders shrimp. The second says, "I'd like a lobster tail, please."

SKITS

Waiter says appropriate things, goes away, returns with storybook, sits down near customer two but facing audience, and begins reading: "Once upon a time, there was a little lobster . . . ."

• • • • • • • • • • • • • • • • • •

Quick & Corny
Scout 1: Whatcha doing?
Scout 2: Writing a letter to my little brother.
Scout 2: Why are you writing so slowly?
Scout 1: Because my little brother can't read very fast!

• • • • • • • • • • • • • • • • • •

Campfire Skits

We thank Linda Kish, Lethbridge, Alta., for sharing her collection of favourites.

Campfire Conference
Six or eight weary-looking campers enter the campfire circle, silently circle the campfire once, and sit in a ring around the fire. After a pause, the first camper sighs and says "What a day!" There's another pause for deliberation before the second camper sighs and says, "What a day!", and yet another before the third repeats, and so on around the circle until they reach the last camper. He sighs and says, "Yes sirree!" (or "You betcha", or something similar).

After a long silence, the first camper says in disgust, "If you can't stick to the subject, I'm getting out of here!" Then he rises and leaves the campfire, followed by all the others.

SKITS

Good Soup!
A number of players are tasting and admiring a bowl of soup. Ad lib comments about how wonderful and delicious it is. Camp cook runs out waving floor mop and yelling, "Get out of my mop water!"

Bad Breath
One blanket-covered player is the terrible dragon with the terrible breath. Plant three or four "volunteers" in the audience who come up, one by one, to say hello to the dragon. Each time the dragon replies, "Hello!", the "volunteer" falls over dead (lots of scope for hams, here). Then, ask for a real volunteer to say hello to the dragon. When he says, "Hello, Dragon", the dragon falls over dead.

The Bike Shop
You need a bike shop owner, four "bikes" who line up in a row on hands and knees, and a customer. The shop owner sets the scene, points out the virtues of each bike, etc. Customer enters, says he wants to buy a bike, and sits on each in turn to try it out. The first bike falls down, the second is too big, the third is too small, and the fourth is the wrong colour. He says he really likes the first bike, but every time he picks it up and tries to sit on it, it falls down.

The shop owner assures the customer he can fix the bike in the time it will take him to walk around the block. The customer leaves and the shop owner asks a volunteer from the audience to help hold up the bike. When the volunteer is in place, the customer returns and sits on the bike. This time, it stays up.

"It was a simple problem," the shop owner explains. "All I needed was the right nut to hold it together."

Hot News
Setting: a newspaper office. The city editor is talking to a brand new reporter. Editor tells reporter he will get ahead by developing a "nose for news". "Learn to spot it almost before it happens," he says. Reporter ad libs okay sure loss, I'll try, etc. Editor sends reporter out to get some "hot news".

SKITS

Reporter leaves, returns with "hot news" that a train wreck happened last week. Editor says it's no good and sends him out again. Reporter returns with "hot news" that a boat sank yesterday and four people drowned. Editor is furious. Old news is no news, etc., etc., if you don't get some hot news this time you're fired, etc., etc. Reporter leaves, rushes back in...

Reporter: Boss, boss! Really hot news this time. Building across the street just blew up!

Editor (skeptical): Yeah? *(Follow immediately with sound of explosion from off-stage)*

• • • • • • • • • • • • • • • • • • •

The Lost Lollipop
Cast: little boy, two passers-by

A little boy sits on a chair crying. A passer-by stops. The suggested dialogue is only a guide. Let the actors use lines that come naturally to them.

Passer-by 1: What's wrong, little boy'? Why are you crying?

Boy: I lost my lollipop!

Passer-by asks boy if he has looked for it. Boy tearfully replies he has looked everywhere under his bed, in his sock drawer (use the imagination) even in the pocket of (name someone in the audience). "I can't find it anywhere!" He cries even louder.

Passer-by 1: Have you tried chanting?

Boy: What?

SKITS

Passer-by 1: Chanting. I've heard that it often works. Think very hard about the lollipop until you can see it in your mind and chant its name softly over and over again.

Boy: Like this? (Boy closes eyes tight, chants "Big red lollipop, big red yummy lollipop, big red lollipop". Passer-by nods approval and leaves. Boy chants for awhile then starts to cry again.)

A second passer-by stops to ask what is wrong. Boy repeats his story, describes the "big red yummy lollipop". Passer-by asks what he's done to find it. Boy repeats places he's looked and adds, "I've even tried chanting."

Passer-by 2: What?

Boy: Chanting. Someone told me that it often works, but nothing happened. Say, maybe it will work if you help me. (Boy explains how. He and passer-by close eyes and chant, "Big red lollipop, big red yummy lollipop, big red lollipop, etc." Nothing happens. Boy begins to cry again.)

Passer-by 2: Please don't cry. Maybe we just need more help.

Boy: You think so?

He turns to audience: "I need all of you ... my only chance to get my lollipop back ... please help" and asks them to close eyes, think hard about the big red lollipop and softly chant, "Big red lollipop, big red yummy lollipop, big red lollipop, etc." When he and the second passer-by successfully get the audience going, the first passer-by returns. Boy tells audience to keep chanting softly.

Passer-by 1: Hi, little boy You look more cheerful. Did you find your lollipop?

Boy: No, I didn't. But I certainly found a whole lot of suckers!

SKITS

The Check-Up

You need a doctor, patient, two chairs, and a table. Patient is on chair and doctor peers down throat, listens to heart, tests reflexes, etc., making appropriate noises ("Ahh!" "Hmmm!", "Ah-ha!") as he goes. Patient begins to look worried. Doctor completes examination, sits behind table and scribbles out three prescriptions.

Doctor: This should do it. (Gives patient first paper) These are blue pills. Take one every morning with a glass of water. (Hands patient second paper) These are yellow pills. Take one every noon with a glass of water. (Hands him third paper) These are red pills. Take one every night before bed with a glass of water.

Patient: Holy cow, Doc, give it to me straight! What's wrong with me?

Doctor: You're not drinking enough water!

Those Wonderful Machines

For the first two skits, decorate cardboard boxes as futuristic machines with lots of dials, cranks, buttons and, if you're really ambitious, flashing lights. Include sound effects people, too, to "turn on" the machines on cue.

The Growing Machine: The cardboard box needs to be large enough to hold one of the players and various props. "Load" it and push it on stage, where a narrator explains that this marvellous machine has been invented by tonight's guest, Professor ... who will demonstrate its tremendous powers. He introduces the professor, who enters carrying a bag of his props.

The professor explains he has invented a wonderful machine that makes things grow. He proceeds to demonstrate. He pulls a small

SKITS

piece of paper from his sack, pushes buttons, etc., and throws in the piece of paper (sound effects, flashing lights). The player inside throws out a paperback book. The demonstration continues with small ball in, large ball out; piece of string in, hunk of rope out; etc. Finally, the professor throws in a baby doll. The player inside jumps out in baby clothes, cries "Daddy!", and chases him off stage.

The Hair Cut Machine: The cardboard box needs to be large enough for a player to poke in his head. Face the opening away from the audience. Set up a striped pole and use a few other barbershop props. The "customer" wears a tightfitting light-coloured bathing cap to hide his hair and, over the cap, a long scraggly wig loose-fitting enough that he can shake it off when he needs to but well enough anchored that it won't fly off too early.

Barber is on stage. Customer enters and asks for a hair cut. Barber checks him out, announces he thinks this is a job for his brand new haircut machine, and convinces the customer to try it. Customer sticks his head into the back of the box and barber turns it on (sound effects). Customer yells, flails, flops and goes through incredible contortions, shaking off the wig in the process. Barber, unperturbed, turns off the machine. Customer pulls out "bald" head and races screaming off stage.

Is it Time Yet? Six to 10 players sit in a line facing the audience, legs stretched out in front of them, left leg crossed over right at the ankle. The player at one end of the line asks the one beside him, "Is it time yet?" The question passes from person to person down the line. The last player looks at his watch and tells the person beside him, "No, not yet" — The reply passes from player to player back up the line to the first person. Players send question and answer up and down the line three or four times, each time becoming more impatient and fidgety. Finally, the end player replies, "Yes, its time now." The news passes from one to another up the line to the first player who says, "Oh, thank goodness!". At this point, all the players uncross their legs and re-cross them right over left.

SKITS

A Quiet Day: One player stands with his ear to a fence (an old painted sheet will work) as if listening intently. Several others enter to watch. One of them asks, "What do you hear?"

"Listen!" he says dramatically. They all listen, look puzzled. Another says, "I don't hear anything."

"Listen!" first player says again. The routine repeats once or twice more. Finally one player says with great disgust, "I don't hear anything !"

"Funny," says the first player, "it's been like that all day!" Players exit.

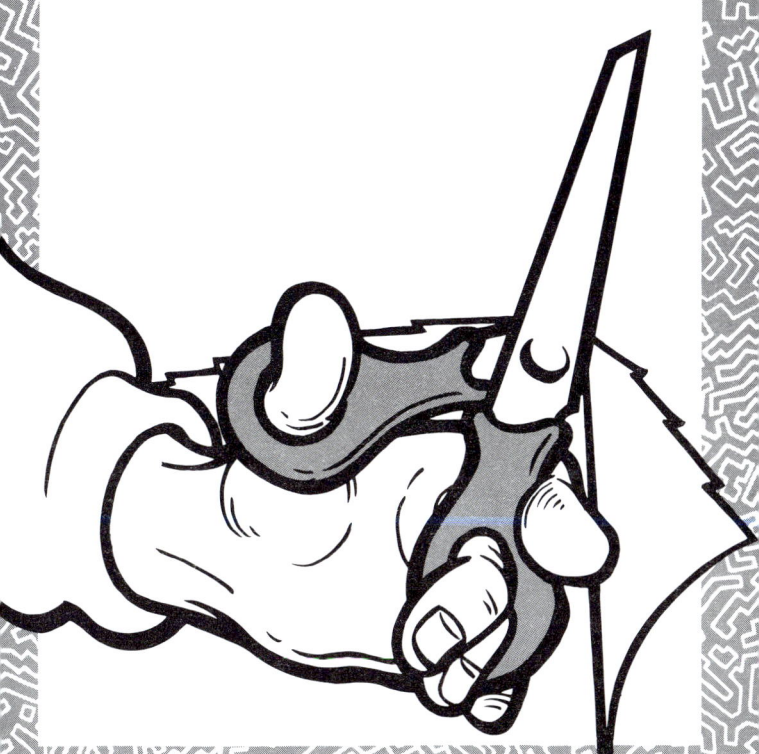

GAMES

That's Christmas!

Are you planning a Christmas get-together this month? Here's a presentation you might find good to use. Adapted from the 1979 Circle Ten Pow Wow Book, BSA, it is suitable for almost any size Cub pack. Given a small group of a dozen boys, you can assign each a couplet to recite. With larger numbers, assign groups of two or three boys to recite each pair of lines.

The boys enter carrying parcels, decorations or whatever symbols are appropriate to their words in the presentation. They arrange themselves in a line or semi-circle and proceed to speak the parts in turn.

1: Secrets, secrets, in the air,
   Merry greetings everywhere!
        That's Christmas!

2: Cedar boughs in every nook,
   Holly everywhere you look!
        That's Christmas!

3: Christmas trees with baubles bright,
   Flashing in the candlelight!
        That's Christmas!

4: Hearth fires leaping high to show
   Faces in the firelight's glow!
        That's Christmas!

5: Spicy smells of things to eat
   Promising a welcome treat!
        That's Christmas!

6: Bundles big and bundles small,
   Peeking's not allowed at all!
        That's Christmas!

GAMES

7: Little whispers all about
   But we can't find one thing out.
       That's Christmas!

8: Such a lot of things to do,
   Shopping trips and wrapping, too.
       That's Christmas!

9: Time for fun and song and play
   Just the year's most happy day!
       That's Christmas!

10: Manger, star and shepherds' joy
    Greet the holy infant boy.
        That's Christmas!

11: Bells sing out the Christ child's birth.
    Hope and peace for all the earth.
        That's Christmas!

12: Joy in all we have and do,
    Wishing joy to others, too!
        That's Christmas!

All: So we gladly join to say,
   Have a happy Christmas day!
       Merry Christmas everyone!

Quick and Foolish

Boy and Matches

A boy enters with a large box of matches. He removes a match and strikes it, but it doesn't light, so he throws it away and takes another match out of the box. He repeats the performance several times. Finally, he strikes a match which lights. He blows it out quickly, puts it back into the box, looks at the audience, smiles and says, "That's a good one. I'd better keep it!" Exit

GAMES

HALLOWEEN FUN FOR BEAVERS

Witch and the Cat
One boy is chosen to be the witch and another is chosen to be the cat. The remainder of the boys form a circle by holding hands. The witch stays in the circle all the time and the cat darts in and out or across the circle as he wishes. The witch tries to catch the cat any time he enters the circle. A new contestant can be chosen by the old one after the witch has succeeded in catching the cat.

Goblins and Fairies
Goblins form a line along one side of the room and fairies form a line on the opposite wall. Goblins face the wall. On a signal from the leader, the fairies creep up behind the goblins. When they have come about half way, the leaders call: "The fairies are coming". The fairies turn about and head for home and the goblins give chase. If they catch any, the boys go to the other side. (With 5-year-olds, it is a good idea not to let those creeping up get too close to those facing the wall. The children love this game if they never catch anyone.) Fairies take a turn facing the wall.

GAMES

Pick a Pumpkin
Cut a five-inch pumpkin from orange construction paper for each group of five or six children. Each boy is given five pumpkin seeds (toothpicks will do). The pumpkin is put in the centre of the group. Each boy takes a turn until all five of their seeds are used up. They throw it and try to get the seed to land on the pumpkin.

The Witch has Lost her Cat
Beavers form a circle. The old witch covers her eyes as she sits in the centre of the circle. The cat (bean bag) is passed from hand to hand outside the circle. When the witch calls "STOP" whoever has the cat keeps it hidden behind his back. The witch has three chances to find it; if she does not succeed, the one holding the cat trades places with her. If she finds it in the three chances she gets another turn. (Also known elsewhere as "The Beaver has Lost his Brother".)

Special Halloween Treat
Wrap a special treat to be given out to the Beavers, in a box with layers and layers of paper. The Beavers form a dam. When the leader blows a whistle the package is passed around the circle. When the whistle is blown again, whoever is holding the package starts to unwrap it until the whistle is blown again, and the package continues to be passed around. This continues until the final wrapping has been removed and whoever has it must share with all the other Beavers.

Halloween Toss
Cut a good sized hole in an old sheet and drape it over a chair or table. The Beavers could draw a face on it similar to a jack o'lantern. The hole becomes the mouth and each boy takes a turn throwing a sponge through the hole. Let them have a trial throw first to get used to the light weight of the sponge.
—*from "The Loop" South Saskatchewan Region Scout newsletter.*

GAMES

For Beavers

• *Hit the Deck* — One Beaver is captain of the sailing ship, the others are the crew. A definition of terms is necessary to set this ship afloat. The captain calls, "All hands to: starboard, port, bow or stern", and the sailors race in the appropriate direction. When the captain calls, "Boom coming over!", sailors 'hit the deck' by throwing themselves down on their bellies. Rotate captains either randomly or by choosing the first or last sailor to 'hit the deck'.

• *Corral that Horse* — Best outdoors. All Beavers, except one who is the horse, form a line, they build the corral by holding the boy in front around the waist. On signal, the corral tries to surround and pen the horse, without failing apart. Let energetic Beavers play the game several times with different horses.

For Cubs

• *Night Trail* — In the dark, Cubs follow a string onto which different objects have been tied at intervals. Their job is to identify the objects by touch, and to remember all of them when they report in at the end of the trail. It can be an individual effort, or a collective challenge for sixes.

• *Sharp-eyed Scavenging* — Leaders prepare an outdoor trail by placing man-made objects along it. Some of the items should be obvious (a coloured balloon tied to a branch; a lightbulb among the daisies), and others should be less easily spotted (a piece of black rubber hose in a damp area of tangled sticks; a red bead under a fruit-heavy berry bush; a scrap of brown cloth in the crook of a tree).

Send the Cubs along the path with directions to note what 'litter' they see without disturbing any of it and without pointing it out to their buddies. At the trail's end the boys quietly report to a leader the number of objects they spotted. Unless they've made a perfect score

GAMES

on the first pass, the leader tells them there's still more, and sends them back for another go. When all (or nearly all) have been spied, retrieve the object and talk about why some were easy to see and others were not.

It's a good 'observing' game and a novel introduction to camouflage. A number of spin-off activities are possible, including an outdoor session on looking at ways that natural things camouflage themselves.

For Scouts

• *Wet Egg Toss* — Fill small balloons generously with water for an inexpensive version of an egg-toss. Scouts in pairs toss the fragile missile back and forth between them, increasing the distance tossed with each successful catch. A great game for a hot day!

• *Rollercoaster* — For this one, may we suggest a piece of ground with a little 'give'. Scouts lie as closely-packed as possible side by side on their stomachs. The Scout at the starting end rolls over onto his neighbour, and continues rolling all down the line until he's back on his stomach at the end. At this point the next Scout gets rolling. Once things are in motion, the rollercoaster starts moving along at quite a clip. Put two or more rollercoasters in motion and have a race.

BEAVER GAMES

Wicked Troll — Beavers must cross a bridge (bench or gym mat) guarded by a wicked Troll (a leader, or a succession of Beavers). The Troll makes sure that each Beaver crosses the bridge in a different manner (running, hopping, rolling, etc.)

— *from* Beaver Tales, *Greater Winnipeg Region*

GAMES

Who Are You? — A game to follow discussion or learning about the inter-relationships of animals; predators (meat-eaters) and prey (plant-eaters). For the game, predators are "enemies", prey animals are "friends" and the hunter is a special enemy.

Beavers sit in circle formation. A leader calls out the names of different animals. If the animal named is a "friend", Beavers give a big grin; if an enemy, they scowl and bare their teeth. If "hunter" is named, Beavers yell, "Bang! Bang!". When played quickly, the game becomes hilarious and soon has Beavers rolling in the aisles.

Name Him — Beavers stand in circle formation. One boy is blindfolded and stands in the middle holding a stick. Players move around the circle while the blindfolded Beaver taps the ground three times with his stick. On the third tap. Beavers in the circle freeze. Middle Beaver points his stick at someone in the circle and says, "Cow!" or "Dog!" or the name of some other animal. The Beaver indicated makes the noise of that animal and the blindfolded Beaver tries to guess the boy's name. If he's successful, the two change places. If not, he has two more tries before a leader chooses another Beaver to take the centre.

KIM'S GAME VARIATIONS — CUBS/SCOUTS

Travelling Salesman — A stranger comes to the meeting with a suitcase full of goods he wants Scouter to buy. Boys listen, then after the salesman has been turfed out on his ear, they are asked to:
• make a list of articles offered, including the price the salesman asked for each:
• give the sales pitch used by the man to try to convince Scouter to buy each article.

Kidnap — Make sure room is cleared of obstacles before turning off lights. Boys run around in the dark. Scouter throws a blanket over a boy and yells, "Kidnap!" The boy huddles to the floor under the blanket so that no one can see him, and an assistant turns on the lights again. The first boy to identify who has been kidnapped wins a point for his six or patrol.

SPACE INVADERS — CUBS/SCOUTS
Bring a popular electronic game alive with this idea from *Scouting* (U.K.). Make chalk marks across the hall, about three feet apart. Divide boys into two teams: the Invaders, who form a line along the wall at one side of the room. and the Defenders, who have tennis balls and line up along the opposite wall. The Invaders side-step across the hall in their line. When they reach the far wall, they step forward a pace to the next chalk-line, and side-step across to the other side of the hall. The Invaders' advance continues in this manner while Defenders fire at them by rolling their balls across the floor. Wh en an Invader is hit, he falls out, and the round is over when all invaders are dead, or when Invaders reach the Defenders' line. Add to the fun by having invaders mimic the sounds and movements of the machine version of the game.

CAMP COOLERS

• **Diamond Hunt:** Teams in relay formation, each facing a tub of muddy water in which you've placed marbles. In turn, players run up to the tub, jump in, muck about until they find a marble, then run back to tag oft the next in line. Follow up with a good swim.

• **Obstacle Race:** Teams in relay formation, a bucket full of water directly in front of the first boy in each team, and an empty bucket at the end of the course opposite each team. Lay a number of obstacles between the buckets. In turn, boys fill a cup from the full bucket and transport it over and under the obstacles. At the end of the course, they pour whatever water remains in their cups into the empty bucket,

GAMES

then race back to tag off the next boy by handing him the cup. The bucket containing the most water after all boys have run belongs to the winning team.

• **Fill the Bucket:** Each team has a waterfilled bucket and an empty bucket, the empty one placed at some distance from the full one. Without moving either bucket, and without using any equipment, teams must transfer the water from the full to the empty bucket in the quickest possible time.

• **Up a Tree:** Let Scouts hold a race to see which team is quickest to move all of its members and two buckets full of water at least two metres up a tree.

• **Barber:** Another good one for Scouts. Boys in two teams. Members of one team hold water-filled balloons on their heads while the others, equipped with razors and cans of shaving soap, try to lather up and shave the balloons without getting their customers wet.

• **Gotcha:** Two teams line up on opposite sides of the playing area, facing each other. A small pail of water sits centred between the two lines. Team members number off, and when a leader calls a number, the appropriate members of each team race to the water. First to reach it sloshes the other guy with it.

• **Water Wall:** This one is for all ages. Two teams line up in waist-high water, facing each other over a good splashing distance. On signal, the lines furiously splash each other, until one side retreats. Can be played many times on a hot afternoon.

WILD ANIMALS
• **Snake in the Grass:** Again a game for any section. Mark out a 30 square metre snake pit, and name a snake who can move only by slithering and wriggling around on his belly. The other players move

GAMES

freely within the snake pit until a leader calls, "Snake in the grass!" The players then must freeze while the snake wriggles around to tag as many of them as he can before a whistle sets them all in motion again. Tagged players become snakes and join the first snake in the belly-down position. Continue the game until the snake pit is full of wriggling snakes.

• **Turtle Tag:** Good for Beavers or Cubs. One or two boys are "it" and try to tag the others. Players can save themselves by "turning turtle"; i.e., by lying on their backs with arms and legs in the air. When players "turn turtle it counts to 10, at which time turtles must jump up and take at least 10 steps before turning turtle again. A tagged turtle exchanges places with "it" and the game continues.

HAT DUEL — Have Beavers or Cubs make and decorate tall "birthday hats" for themselves. Give each boy a long balloon, and tell the boys to arrange themselves in pairs. Blindfold the duellists, give each a triple spin, and send them out with balloons swinging to knock off their opponents' hats.

CUT THE CAKE — Make several flour cakes by filling a cake tin to the brim with flour, placing a plate over the top, turning over the tin and gently tapping out the "cake". Very carefully set a piece of chocolate in the centre of the cake. Players sit around a circle with the cake in the middle, and a leader starts some music. As the music plays, pass a blunt kitchen knife around the circle. The one who holds the knife when the music stops must cut a slice from the cake before returning to his place. If his cut collapses the cake, he must kneel, put his hands behind his back and, with his teeth, try to retrieve the piece of chocolate from the mess. A hilarious game which is why you'll want to have more than one cake!

— from *Scouting (UK)*, Dec. '81

TOOTHPICK KIM'S GAME — In relay formation. Each player has a supply of toothpicks, and a toothpick design has been set out at

GAMES

the end of the course opposite each team. On signal, the first one in each team runs to the design, examines it, then races back to the next player for whom he tries to duplicate the arrangement. Meanwhile, record and remove the original design. The second player memorizes the duplicate design and races to the opposite end to make his own copy, and so on. When everyone has run, compare the final toothpick design with the original and award points for any signs of similarity.

JUNGLE RESCUE — Write the names of jungle animals on slips of paper and hide the papers throughout the room. Tell Cubs that the animals have lost both their memories and themselves and give the Cubs five minutes to find as many as they can. When they gather again at the signal, each Cub describes the animals he's found. In order to rescue the animals, the others must guess who they are from the descriptions. Beavers will enjoy the game if you hide animal pictures.

CRAZY BEETLES (A Knotty Game) — Give each patrol or six a *Crazy Beetle* kit: giant cardboard beetle head and body with holes for legs and tail; seven 80 cm ropes, hanked (legs and tail); two antennae made from 25 cm lengths of wire in which you've bent a small loop; two eyes; one long rope; sticky tape. Give each team a pair of dice as well.

On signal, each boy in turn throws the dice. To get the beetle body and start the assembly process, someone must roll a 6. When they have the body, they must roll a 5 to get the head, which they attach to body with a sheet bend. They continue to roll for other parts of the bug, but the assembly order no longer matters. Four gets a leg, which they attach with a round turn and two half hitches; 3 gets the tail, attached with a reef knot; 2 gets an antenna, attached with tape; 1 gets an eye, also attached with tape.

When the critter is complete, the team ties the long rope around its neck with a bowline and tows it across the room to Scouter, who checks to see that it is properly knotted. First successful team wins. Other knots may also be used.

— from *Scouting (UK)*, Dec. '80

Games for Harvest & Hallowe'en

Body Builders: Place empty food containers or pictures of food at one end of the playing area. Make most of them nutritious foods, but scatter some junk-food items like potato chip bags, candy wrappers and pop tins among them. Arrange teams in relay formation and have boys in each team number off. Then, call out a number and the starting letter of a food: e.g. "Three C!" The number three boy in every team runs to choose a carton or picture representing a food that starts with "c" (cheese, cookies) and races back to his line. Give the boy who has chosen the most nutritious food a peanut to hold in his hand, then call out another number and letter. When everyone has run, boys divvy up their peanuts and eat them.

Crazy Pea Games: A jar full of dried peas is an inexpensive and versatile element of pack equipment. You can devise any number of relay games involving drinking straws and peas: blow peas across table or floor; transfer peas from container to container, and so on. Or, you can use peas in *Red Light Green Light* variations.

For the basic game, line up boys at one end of the hall and place a leader, with back turned, at the other. Scatter the pea jar's contents all over the playing area. On signal, boys start to pick up peas as fast as possible. When leader turns to face them, they freeze. A boy caught moving must drop all of his peas and return to the starting point.

In variation one, post the leader at a light switch and play the game in the dark. Boys freeze whenever the light flashes on.

Variation two is also played in the dark but the leader uses a strong-beamed flashlight.

GAMES

Whoever is caught in motion by the searchlight, drops his peas and returns to the starting line.

Use imagination to add Hallowe'en spookiness to the variations played in the dark.

— *Thanks to **Action Stations** in **Scouting (U.K.)** for these ideas.*

The Witch's Throne: Arrange as many chairs as there are players in an inward facing circle. Mark a chair for the leader in a special way as the "witch's throne". Players sit in the other chairs and number off 1, 2, 3, 1, 2, 3 around the circle. Then, the leader calls, "Twos change places like bats" and all players with that number move to change places, giving bat impersonations as they go. After some single calls, try something like, "Ones like ghosts and threes like goblins!" Or call all three groups to move in monstrous ways at the same time.

What about the witch's throne? Once everyone has the idea, the leader includes his or her number in the call. Whoever ends up sitting on the throne after that round becomes the new leader.

Ghost Drop: Teams in relay formation facing a book (ideally of ghost stories) placed on the floor some distance away from each. Give all players a single ply facial tissue which they hold pinched between thumb and pointer by the centre. On signal, the first one in each team runs to his book and, from eye level, drops the tissue ghost onto the book. Award 10 points if the ghost swallows the book (covers it completely), 5 points if it gulps down half or more, and 2 points if it takes a bite (touches a corner). Players run back to tag off next in line. Tally up total points when all have run.

Balloon Race

Give each six or patrol a different coloured balloon of irregular shape and each boy a large drinking straw. Line up teams at one end of the hall. Working together, each team tries to blow their balloon to the opposite end of the hall in the fastest possible time. Straws must not touch balloons.

GAMES

Space Challenge for Cubs or Beavers
Which six (or lodge) can be the first to organize itself so that it takes up 5 feet of space — 4 feet — 3 feet? For Beavers, draw different sized circles or squares on the floor with chalk.

Night Challenges
• With lights out, players walk a prescribed number of steps in one direction, turn around and walk back to their exact starting places.
• Arrange players in a straight line facing away from a number of articles you've placed about 4.5 metres (15') from them. Turn out lights and tell them to turn around, then flick on lights for a few minutes as they observe the objects. When you douse the lights again, each walks out, picks up an object and carries it back to the starting line.

Night-time Crossing
Divide pack or troop into two teams — attackers and defenders — and arrange them at opposite ends of the hall. Instruct each team to choose a secret "password". Place empty plastic margarine tubs around the floor as mines and a piece of chalk somewhere along the defender's wall. In complete darkness and silence, the attackers try to obtain the chalk, carry it to their side of the hall and make a mark on the wall. The defenders, of course, try to prevent this.

If someone touches a mine (you'll hear the plastic tub being moved), he yells "boom" and falls down on the spot to become an extra hazard. If two meet, one asks the other the password. If it's the password from the opposite team, the challenger must shout "aargh!" and fall to the floor to become yet another hazard.

Indoor Snowball Fight
You need a good supply of newspaper and two paper grocery bags. Divide group into two teams and have each players make two crumpled-paper "snowballs". Station teams in lines facing each other from a distance of about 4 metres. Two players from each team stand behind their opponents, sharing a paper bag between them. Their job

GAMES

is to pick up all the snowballs thrown over the heads of the opposing side by their team-mates and put them into the bag. On signal, everyone in the lines begin tossing their snowballs at each other. They may catch as many of the ones coming their way as they can to hurl back at the other side. The game is over when all snowballs have been bagged, or when time is called.

Cars & People — Especially for Beavers
Stand Beavers behind a line marked at one end of the hall. At a signal, they pretend to be cars and drive around the hall. When a leader calls, "People!", they all run to stand behind the line, look both ways, and cross the street. Then they change back into cars again. A good energy burner.

Games for Fun

Musical Chain
Arrange players in a long line and give the first in line something that will clatter when dropped (e.g. a pebble-filled tin). With Beavers, have Keeo or a leader start at the head of the line. The leader begins to sing a song (perhaps something Christmassy?) and marches around the room while the others sing along and march behind. He suddenly drops the rattle, a signal for everyone to sit down and stop singing. The last one down takes the rattle and leads the next round.

Freeze Game
Fun for both Beavers and Cubs. Choose two "refrigeration units" who can freeze other players solid by tagging them. Tagged players are immediately thawed when two yet unfrozen players join hands around them. Who can work faster — the freezers or the thawers?

GAMES

Blind Men
All sections will get a giggle from this one. For Beavers, use a paper bag as a blindfold. Stand one Beaver a short distance away from the others and blindfold him. The others can shuffle around a bit and change places, then the blindfolded boy walks slowly toward his mates. When he bumps into one of them, he tries identify him by touch alone. Particularly fun if you have a ticklish crowd.

Shepherd, Sheep and Wolf
Play in sixes or patrols. One player from each team is the shepherd, one is the wolf and the rest are the sheep. Sheep stand at the opposite end of the room from the shepherd and wolf and form a line, each holding the belt of the person in front. Blindfold the sheep and the wolf.

On signal, the blindfolded wolf begins to wander. Standing in one spot and using voice only, the shepherd tries to guide his sheep past the prowling wolf and safely to his side. How many sheep make it?

Gift-Wrapping
In this relay, sixers or patrol leaders stand facing their teams from a short distance away. Give the first player in each team a roll of toilet tissue. On signal, he runs to his leader and begins wrapping her from the feet up. When the whistle blows, he races back and the next in line runs up to continue the wrapping job. Players must cover all gaps and repair rips and tears in the wrapping along the way. Tie winning team will be the one that can keep its sixer or PL from bursting all his seams as he collapses in laughter.

Alphabetical Script
A zany game for fast-thinking hams. Teams can be of any size. Give each team a situation to act out and a letter of the alphabet to start their dialogue. Tie first speaker begins the script with the given letter and each successive player must start his bit with the following letter as they try to get as far through the alphabet as possible. Deduct

GAMES

points for "uumms" and other stalls. For example, a script for *Mountain Climbing*, letter *C* might go: (1) ***C****an you see the top yet?* (2) ***D****on't think so.* (3) ***E****asy does it — loose rock here.* (4) ***F****red, look out!* (5) ***G****ood grief!* (6) ***HELP!!*** Fun, eh?

Rainy Day Games

Sittin' in the Rain
Arrange two teams in relay formation. Give the lead player in each team a folding chair, a bucket with a whistle in it and an umbrella. On signal, the first two race to the end of the room, unfold their chairs and sit on them, put up their umbrellas, remove whistles from the bucket and blow them, put back the whistles, close the umbrellas, fold the chairs and race back to pass the equipment to the next in line. First team finished wins.

Sticky Tape Fun
Arrange sixes in relay formation and tip a 2 cm strip of sticky tape onto the nose of each Cub. In turn, Cubs race to the end of the room and, without using hands, try to transfer the tape from their noses to a piece of cardboard mounted on the wall. First team finished wins. Remove the competitive aspect for Beavers by providing a piece of cardboard to each lodge. When everyone has transferred the tape from nose to cardboard, reward the colony with a treat. Perhaps they'll come up with ways to help each other accomplish the trick.

Beavers and Cubs will enjoy another sticky tape game. Line up facing the wall and ask them to close their eyes. A leader walks along the line with a strip of sticky tape, running a finger down the back of each player so that everyone believes he's been "taped". During the process, the leader sticks the tape to one of the backs. When he calls, "Go!", the players run around the room trying to spot the tape while

GAMES

keeping their backs hidden from the others. When a person sees the tape, he sits quietly on the floor. The game ends when all but the one wearing the tape are sitting.

Grow a Tree

A super indoors Trees for Canada relay. Arrange Cubs in sixes. Provide each six a sign reading "Sapling", a bag containing 20 or 30 construction paper leaves, birds, blossoms, butterflies and birds' nests, some small branches and a roll of tape.

Tape a sapling sign and a paper bag full of stuff to each sixer and stand him in the centre of a circle made by his six. On signal, the Cubs begin to make their sapling grow by handing him the branches to hold and taping the contents of the bag to various parts of the branches or the sapling. The first team to "grow" its tree wins.

This can also be fun for Beavers in lodges. They start by making things they'd find on a growing tree and choose a sapling. After each helps its sapling "grow", the whole colony judges the best-looking or bushiest tree or whatever other categories you're inspired to ask about in view of the boys' handiwork.

Ummmm

Players sit on chairs in a circle. Put one in the centre and blindfold. On signal, he makes his way to the circle, finds a chair and sits on the lap of the person occupying it. Then he says. "Ummmmmm" in as silly a way as he can. The player he's sitting on replies in the same way, trying to keep his identity a secret. If the blindfolded player guesses his identity the two change places.

Christmas Games

Loading Santa's Sleigh

Sixes line up in relay formation. A distance away from each team, place a pile of presents (enough cardboard boxes of different shapes

GAMES

and sizes for every runner in the team). Beside each team place Santa's sleigh (a chair). The Sixer in each team is Santa. On signal the first Cub in each team runs to the pile, picks up a present, runs back and loads it into Santa's arms before tagging off the next in line, who runs for a present to give Santa, and so on. Santa must hold all the presents in his arms until the last one is delivered, when he may load up the sleigh (pile them on the chair). First finished is the winner.

From Santa's Sack
Beavers will enjoy this game. Fill a big bag with all sorts of dress-up clothes, including wigs and funny hats. Players form a large circle around "Santa's sack". Put on some music and have them start passing a balloon around the circle. When the music stops, the one with the balloon runs to the sack, grabs something quickly and puts it on before returning to his place. Continue until the sack is empty then hold a fashion show and judge the most colourful fashion, the funniest fashion, etc. Give everyone a prize.

Autograph Bingo
This quieter game is particularly good as a party mixer. Prepare papers with 20 or so squares on them (some number lower than the number of people at the party). As people arrive, ask them to print their names on a small card which you put into a box. Then give them a squared paper and a pencil and tell them to go around to collect one autograph in each square on the paper. When everyone is ready, play *Bingo* with the caller picking name cards from the box. The first person to complete their card yells, "Merry Christmas".

Sorting the Mail
This mixer uses old Christmas cards. For older players, cut each card into six pieces. Keeping one piece of each card for the leader who will run the game (the Postmaster), jumble up all the other pieces. The Postmaster randomly hands a piece of card to everyone and spreads the remaining pieces (including the one from each card he had) around the playing area.

GAMES

In a given time, players try to "sort the mail" by searching out the missing pieces of their cards, some held by other players, others simply scattered in the area. They'll have to work together to complete the designs as quickly as possible so they can get them into the mail before Christmas is over. When they are successful, they post the mail by reporting to the Postmaster. You can also play this game with Beavers, but cut each card into only three or four pieces.

If You Go to the North Pole With Me...
For this fun party game, form groups of at least 10, each with a leader. The leader chants: "If you go to the North Pole with me, what are the wonders you will see?"

Players call out what they might see happening at the North Pole at the moment. If an excited Beaver simply shouts, "Santa Claus", the leader asks him what he thinks Santa is doing. As a boy comes up with an idea (e.g. Santa checking over his list; the elves making toys or packing Santa's sack), ask volunteers to act out the scene. Then chant the question again and get an idea for another scene. The game is over when everyone is involved in a living tableau of the pre-Christmas scene at the North Pole.

Birds & Worms
Camouflage Game
Play in lodges or tail groups (six to nine players is best). First, prepare a box of round toothpicks by colouring 50 blue, 50 red and 50 green. Leave 50 or more their natural colour. Find a grass and weed covered spot and, with a string, mark off an area about 1 metre by 3 metres. Scatter the toothpick "worms" in this area. Ask the Beavers to pretend they area flock of birds following their flock leader on a search for some lunch. Fly around until you reach the prepared area and stop for a meal. On signal, the boys try to catch as many worms as they can

Games

within 15 seconds. When time is up, have them put the worms they've caught into colour-piles and count the number of each colour. Ask them what colour they would like to be if they were worms!
—thanks to *The Beaver's Bark,* Prince George, B.C.

Giant Leapfrog
Practise playing leapfrog in lodges (or sixes), then get the whole colony (or pack) together for a giant game of leapfrog. What's the longest distance the group can cover?

Frog Gang
Let Beavers try to hop together in lodges for as long as they can before breaking apart. Cubs play as a relay. In sixes, the Cubs squat behind their sixer. The sixer folds his arms at chest level and each Cub places his hands on the hips of the person in front. On signal, the six frog-jumps as a group from start to finish line.

Ker-Plunk
The 1st North Bay Beavers enjoy playing this action game on the nice, soft grass.

• • • • • • • • • • • • • • • • • • • •

The bunny rabbit goes hop, hop, hop;
Around and around spins the big red top;
The elephant swings her big, long trunk;
But I just fall down and go ker-plunk!
Leap, leap, leap, goes the kangaroo;
"Grrrr!" says the lion in his cage at the zoo;
The airplane flies with a zoom, zoom, zoom;
But I just fall down and go ker-BOOM!

GAMES

Flashlight Tag
Cubs will enjoy this after dark at camp. Define the playing area carefully and give IT a flashlight. As players move in the area, IT flashes the light around. A Cub caught by the light becomes IT.

Elephant Line
See how Cubs or Scouts do with this one. Players get down on hands and knees side by side and close together in a long line, alternate players facing in opposite directions. Very gently, they begin to sway back and forth. The person at one end of the line gets up and tries to crawl along the backs of the line of elephants. If he falls off, he has one more go before joining the elephant line. If he makes it to the end, he joins the line and the next in line starts.

All Around the Circle
All players but one form a circle and hold hands. IT stands outside the circle, calls out the name of a person in the circle and tries to touch them on the shoulder. To avoid being touched, the named player pulls everyone in the circle around with him. He can change directions as he likes, and everyone in the circle tries to help him. When IT touches him, the two change places.
— from Greenwood Area Beavers, Ottawa

Games from Other Lands
The first three games are more suitable for Beavers and Cubs, but Scouts will enjoy the circle game from Yugoslavia.

Doorkeeper — Afghanistan: Any number can play this after school street game with a small soft ball. All players but one are Doorkeepers who stand in a circle, legs astride and feet touching those of the players on either side. The person chosen IT stands in the centre of the circle and tries to roll the ball through the legs of one of the Doorkeepers. The player who sees it coming tries to stop it by

GAMES

quickly putting his legs together. If the ball goes through his legs, he drops out and the game continues until all players are eliminated then begins again with a new IT. But you needn't play it as an elimination game. When a Doorkeeper fails to stop a ball, he can simply change places with IT.

Fire on the Mountain — Tanzania: Play with any number of players and a leader. Players lie on their backs and choose a key word that is their signal to jump quickly to their feet. The leader begins by calling, "Fire on the mountain!" and all the players shout, "Fire!" but remain on their backs. The leader continues to call, "Fire on the ...", changing the location with each call, and the players shout back "Fire!". At any time and in any part of the sentence, the leader can call the key word and everyone jumps up. As children in Tanzania play it, the last person up is eliminated and the game continues until one winner is left, but you can simply have the last person up each time replace the leader.

Help! — Peru: Play this chasing game with four to 10 players. To choose IT, one player holds out their hand, palm up, and the others place their index fingers into his open palm. When he closes his hand without warning, the one who is caught becomes the chaser. The chaser runs after the others to try to tag them. When a runner is in danger of being caught, he shouts, "Help!" Other runners can race to his rescue and try to hold his hand before he is tagged. Both runners are safe while they are holding hands. If the chaser tags a player before he is rescued, the two change places. Play until everyone is tired.

Kolo — Yugoslavia: In this energetic game for Scouts, players form a circle and hold hands. One person is chosen Zimbo (IT). He is blindfolded and placed in the centre of the circle. To start the game, Zimbo stamps on the ground three times calling, "Kim, Kim, Kolo!" Hands still clasped, the players in the circle begin to tiptoe around, making odd noises and whispering. Zimbo suddenly darts at the circle and tries to touch one of them. When he's successful, players drop hands and scatter while Zimbo whips off his blindfold and tries to tag one of them. When he's successful, he yells, "Kolo!" and the handholding circle forms again with the tagged boy and Zimbo standing in the centre. The circle moves around the two until a leader gives a signal, then breaks again and Zimbo and the tagged player try to tag others. This repeats until all the players have been caught. Then Zimbo takes the hand of one player, and the others join up behind to form a chain that moves faster and faster behind Zimbo as in crack the whip. Zimbo stops short and the first person to let go is Zimbo for the next round.

Water Games

Balloon Burst: Again, play in a shallow area and use a time limit. Each swimmer ties a balloon to their arm. On signal, the swimmers try to pop other swimmers' balloons while defending their own.

Buddy Race: Players float on their backs and link elbows of one arm, then race as a single, flutter kicking and doing the backstroke with their free arms.

Canoe Tug-o-War: Tie two canoes together with a 20 m rope attached at the stems. Mark the centre of the role and line it up with a floating marker buoy (you can make one with a plastic bleach bottle). Canoe crews attempt to out-paddle each other to pull their opponents canoe over the centre line.

PFD Switch: Teams arrange themselves with half their players facing the other half at opposite ends of the pool or swim area. The first racer wears a PFD. On signal, he and his mate from the other end of the pool race towards each other to meet in the middle where the "dressed" swimmer removes the PFD and his teammate puts it on

GAMES

to swim back to his own side of the pool. There he passes it to the next swimmer on the team, and so on. Judge both speed and properly fastened PFDs.

Ping Pong Race: Each player swims a course (12 m maximum) while blowing a ping pong ball ahead of him. No hands.

Shark's Teeth: Teams consist of four players each. Put five corks per player into the water. Players must retrieve their corks by mouth (no hands), take them to their team's collection area and return for more. Set a time limit. The team who collects the largest number of corks in the time allowed is the winner.

Snake Race: Teams form a floating snake with each Scout holding one foot of the person in front. On signal, the snakes race a course, the lead swimmer using both arms and the rest using only free arms and legs to prowl them through the water. Watch out for disintegrating snakes.

Sponge Fishing: Partly fill balloons with water so that they are suspended at different levels in the pool, or swimming area. Use two teams of "divers" who must retrieve the balloons and put them into a pan on shore. The team with the most sponges wins.

Sweatshirt Relay: Arrange teams in relay formation in shallow water and give each team an oversized sweatshirt. On signal, the first "swimmers" don the shirt and race the course with hands on the bottom and feet kicking. At the end of the lap, they remove shirts and hand them to the next swimmers, who put them on, and so forth.

Waiter Race: Swimmers race while balancing a plastic plate and cup of water in the air on the palm of the hand. You'll need the sidestroke for this one.

Water Soccer: Players lie on air mattresses and manoeuvre by paddling with the hands. They may put the ball in the opposing team's goal by kicking, hitting, or pushing it. They may not pick up the ball or throw it.

Let's Cooperate

Beavers always play cooperative and collective games, but Cubs, Scouts, and Venturers can have great fun playing cooperatively, too. There's something for all sections here.

Ball Pass: Arrange two teams, each with an end zone. The object is for one team to get a ball into the other team's end zone by passing it from teammate to teammate. The player holding the ball may not move, although his teammates have to scramble to set themselves up for the passes.

Jumping Bean: You need an old sheet or blanket with a hole cut in the middle. Players grasp the edges of the sheet and a leader tosses a number of balls onto it. The object is for players to get the balls jumping up and dawn like jumping beans and then to manoeuvre them so that they jump out through the circle in the middle.

Lap Ball: Players sit shoulder to shoulder in a circle. The object of the game is to pass a ball around the circle from lap to lap without using hands.

Orbit Ball: Arrange players in two groups. One forms a large standing circle. The players in the other group lie on their backs with heads pointing towards the centre of the circle feet propped into a bicycling position. Players work together to keep a beachball in play while moving it around the circle. The ball alternates between inside players, who kick it with their feet, and outside players, who push it

GAMES

back with their hands. The object is to get the ball around the circle without letting it touch the ground. Count aloud the number of times the ball is exchanged between the inside and outside circles.

Pass the Mask: Players sit in a circle and a person chosen IT begins by turning to the player next to them, looking directly into his eyes, and making a funny face. The second player passes on the face to the third player, and so on. Meanwhile, IT immediately turns to the player on his other side and starts a different funny face going in the other direction. The round ends when both "masks" return to IT. Choose another IT and play again. A guaranteed howler.

Round & Round: Players form two equal circles placed fairly close together. One player in each circle begins passing a ball around the circle while all the others sing or chant: "The ball goes round and round/ It stops at every town/ And when it stops/ It stops at YOU!" The player holding the ball at the end of the verse joins the other circle and the game continues.

Rubber Band: Players form a circle and hold hands. Ask them to pretend the circle is a rubber band and try to stretch it as far as it can go without breaking. Then, have the rubber band move inward. When players all meet in the centre, they again stretch the rubber band.

Statues: Players stand in a circle facing inwards with eyes closed. Choose IT and keep their identity secret from the others by walking quietly around the circle and tapping a player on the back. Ask players to open eyes and move randomly around the hall in some interesting way (racing cars, snakes, airplanes, etc.). When you call "Statues", IT races to tag and "freeze into statues" as many players as possible in a count of 10. Players then form the circle again, and IT walks around to tap the back of the next person to be IT. Players need to observant because they don't know who IT is until he tags his first victim.

GAMES

Ghost Story Game

Try this idea from *Scouting (U.K.)* magazine for Hallowe'en with Cubs, Scouts, or even Venturers. Put an item per player (flashlight, box of matches, tooth, hat, shoe, etc.) plus a few extras into a bag or box, place it in the centre of the story circle, and start telling a ghost story. Stop after a few lines and, at random, choose a player to dip into the bag, pull out something, and continue the story, working the object into the tale. When he or she stops, another player goes up to pull out an object and continue the story.

Spaghetti Drop

For a hilarious relay with older sections at a Hallowe'en party, try this one. Teams line up in relay formation. Each chooses one member to go to the opposite end of the playing area, take off his shirt, and lie on his back with an empty pop bottle on his stomach. He may hold the bottle in place. Beside the first person in each team, place a pot of cooked, cooled and drained (but still slightly soggy) spaghetti noodles, and a pair of disposable plastic gloves. After the signal, each player in turn puts on the gloves, picks up 10 wet noodles, runs to the other end of the room, and drops the noodles into the pop bottle before racing back to take off the gloves and hand them to the next player. Declare the first team finished the winner. Declare each team's bottle-holder a hero!

Beaver on a Chair

This is a good game for Beavers early in the year. Make up a simple tune for these words.
Here sits a Beaver on a chair, chair, chair,
He's sad because he thinks no one will care,
So rise up on your feet and greet the one you meet,
The happiest Beaver you know.
Ask the Beavers to stand in a circle, place a chair in the centre, and choose one boy IT. When everyone sings the song, IT follows the words by going to sit on the chair. At the appropriate time in the song,

he gets up and shakes hands with a Beaver in the circle, who then becomes IT. Give IT different directions each time: e.g. Here sits a Beaver under a chair..., behind a chair...; Here stands a Beaver on a chair..., etc.; Here sits a Beaver with a finger in his ear..., one leg up in the air..., and so on. Some silly fun that helps Beavers relax and get to know each other.

Nature Kim's Game
Here's a variation on the familiar Cub observation game from *Canadian Guider* magazine. Define a playing area outdoors, preferably a field or park with a variety of trees and vegetation. Arrange the area with out-of-place items such as an evergreen cone on an oak tree, an acorn on a pine tree, a dandelion flower on a lilac bush, and the like. Give Cubs a certain time to explore the area and note all the "nature mistakes" they find.

Chickadee and Fly
This one from *Canadian Guider* sounds like noisy fun outdoors for Beavers. Define a playing area in a field and choose one Beaver the Chickadee while the others are Flies. Chickadee says "chickadee" and Flies buzz as Chickadee chases flies. When Chickadee tags a Fly, he becomes a Chickadee, too, and helps catch more Flies. Play until all Flies become Chickadees.

Scout Dragnet
For this test of strength and teamwork, you need a neckerchief for each patrol and a heavy rope large enough to encircle the entire troop. Place a neckerchief in each patrol corner. The Scouts, arranged in their patrols, stand inside the rope circle placed in the centre of the hall. On signal, they lift the rope to waist level. They must stay inside the rope and keep it at waist level as they try to retrieve their patrol's necker from its corner.

GAMES

Ice Hockey Squares: You need some preparation for this troop game. To make the puck, put 25 mm water in a margarine tub, freeze, and remove "puck" at game time. Have each Scout make a hockey stick from securely taped rolled newspaper. With chalk or masking tape, divide the meeting hall into quarters and put an equal sized team in each square. Place a leader with a whistle in a sideroom or outside in the hallway where he can't see the game. Place the puck in the centre of the room for a face off between a member of each of the four teams. The object of the game is to keep the puck *out* of your team's square. Players must stay in their own squares and may touch the puck only with their sticks. If the puck is in a team's square when the "blind" leader blows the whistle, the team loses a point. Start each round with a face off. End when the puck disappears.

Creepy Crawlies: Arrange Cubs in two teams, have members of one team scatter randomly in the hall and stand still with legs apart, then blindfold them. The other team are the "creepy crawlies" who must try to crawl around the room and through the legs of their opponents without being detected. If a blind Cub hears or feels anything, he bends forward to try to touch the creepy crawly who, when touched, dons a blindfold, too. Play until only one creepy crawly remains, then switch sides.

Chain Relay: Sixes line up in relay formation at one end of the room. The sixer runs to the far end and back, number two in line grasps him at the waist and the two run down and back to collect number three, and so on. Great aerobic exercise. especially for the sixer! First six to complete the job and sit quietly in line wins.

For Beavers
Round Up: Mark out a large circle in the centre of the room and organize the colony in two teams cowboys and broncos. Ask the broncos to take off their hats or scarves so that everyone knows who's who. On signal, the cowboys chase the broncos and, when they tag one, lead him to the corral (the circle). He must stay there unless one

GAMES

of the free broncos can sneak into the corral to release him. Play until all the broncos are corralled or for a set time, then change sides.

Billy Beaver's Travels: Beavers will enjoy this story game. Sit them in a circle and begin a tale about Billy Beaver's long journey, during which he must travel by plane, train, car, bus, truck, horse, camel — whatever your fertile imagination can devise. Whenever Billy boards a new mode of transport, the Beavers leap up and run once around the Pond pretending they are his transport (plane, train, camel, etc.) before returning to their places to sit again for the next part of the story. Great, noisy fun.

Thanks to *Scouting (U K.)* magazine for all these games.

SCOUTER'S
5

SCOUTER'S FIVE MINUTES

A POTTED STORY
(To read aloud and embellish as you go along.)

One Good Turn ...
Scout has been to local town looking for part-time job to help out at home as his father has been laid off from work. Returns home to country area, changes into uniform and sets off for Scouts. Meets gang of young people at bus stop who make fun of his uniform. Bus comes and one girl who was giggling at him discovers she has lost purse and must find it. Others all climb aboard bus laughing and calling out that she'll just have to catch next bus. Scout says he knows area and will help her look for it. They find it on back road. Blizzard descends and all further buses cancelled. He misses Scout meeting and girl very upset as her parents are away from home so she can't telephone them and is stranded with nowhere to stay. Scout offers to take her to his house nearby. Although his parents are poor they show her kindness and hospitality. Boy tells her something of Scouting principles and next morning puts her safely on bus. Later her father visits Scout's family, thanks them for their kindness, says should be proud of Scout son and what his uniform stands for. Offers father job at his plant in nearby town.

An Observation
Pity the poor female Cub leader —
She has to:
Look like a girl,
Play like a boy,
Act like a lady,
Think like a man,
And work like a horse!
— Alice Beals

SCOUTER'S FIVE MINUTES

A Beaver Prayer
Dear God,
I stand before You, a Beaver
All dressed in brown and blue,
I've promised to take care of the world,
A promise I'll keep for You.
Although I'm not very big or strong,
I'll do the best I can
And pray that You will help me
To help my fellow man.
— *Ruth Barlow, 2nd Scarborough East Beavers*

B.-P. SAID...
When is a Scout Not a Scout?
Some fellows are always asking themselves riddles so I am trying it myself, as that is the first question that occurs to my mind. I don't know what the correct answer is but it seems to me to be this.

A Scout is not a Scout when he thinks that Scouting is all drill and a grand array of badges, flags and brass bands.

My idea is to get into the woods and fields — especially in the spring and summer time, either in camp or on tramping hikes, and to watch and stalk and learn all that one possibly can about animal life, bird life, insect life, plant life — any kind of nature study.

Not only is it fascinating to every true boy but it is also study of God's work, and you can't do better than that.
— *1917*

There is an instinct towards noise, and to rebellion against quiet, in lively youth, in health.
— *John Masefield*

Pack Scouter's Survival Checklist
1. When the Pack won't pay attention and you feel like blowing your top, count to ten, then blow your top!

SCOUTER'S FIVE MINUTES

2. So you tied the flag on upside down. Smile knowingly, give five points to the Cub who spotted it and a lecture to the others on being unobservant.

3. Accept the boy for what he is. If that's impossible just be thankful he isn't *your* son!

4. Learn to laugh at yourself. The Cubs probably think you're hilarious anyway.

5. Too many Cubs and not enough leaders? What a compliment. It must be *you* they like!

6. When everything goes wrong remember Job. At least you don't have boils.

7. If maintaining your dignity concerns you ... quit!

8. So you feel like a failure next to the hot shot running the pack next door? Relax ... he's probably got ulcers.

9. Your spouse has threatened you with divorce if you don't slow down? Slow down... fast!

10. Forgot the Cub Promise while investing a new chum did you? Blame your diet.

11. Remember you *are* human, no matter what the boys might tell you.

12. So what if you lost your cool on parents' night? At least nobody thinks you're dull!

SCOUTER'S FIVE MINUTES

13. Running a meeting is a breeze? You're in trouble. Go take a training course.

14. You had to cancel summer camp and nobody loves you? Sure they do. Just ask who's coming back to Cubs next year'.
— *Our thanks to Judy Evans.*

A SCOUT'S PRAYER

We have hiked along life's pathways,
Our packs upon our backs,
We have pitched our tents and rested
Here and there along the tracks.
We have used our compass wisely
To guide us on our way
And hope to reach the campsite
Of our Great Chief Scout some day.

We have tried to be trustworthy —
Kept our honour high and clean,
We have been as loyal as any
To our Country and our Queen.
We have done our best at all times —
Kept our Promise — been prepared.
And hope our good deeds please Him
When at last our souls are bared.

We have lightened others' burdens,
With our smiles along the way,
We have kept our hand in God's hand,
Walked beside Him day by day.
And when our span of life runs out,

Scouter's Five Minutes

We'll make this gentle plea —
May we sit around His Campfire
At the Final Jamboree.
—*from: "Scouting in New South Wales"*

Everybody Does It

When Johnny was six years old, he was with his father when they were caught speeding. His father handed the officer a $5 bill with his driver's licence. "It's okay son," his father said as they drove off. "Everybody does it."

When he was nine, his mother took him to his first theatre production. The box office man couldn't find any seats until his mother discovered an extra $2 in her purse. "It's okay son," she said. "Everybody does it."

When he was fifteen, he made right guard on the high school football team. His coach showed him how to block and at the same time grab the opposing end by the shirt so the official couldn't see it. "It's okay kid," the coach said. "Everybody does it."

When he was sixteen, he took his first summer job at the big market. His assignment was to put the over-ripe tomatoes in the bottom of the boxes and the good ones on top where they would show. "It's okay kid," the manager said. "Everybody does it."

When he was eighteen, Johnny and a neighbour applied for a college scholarship. Johnny was a marginal student. His neighbour was in the upper three percent of his class, but he couldn't play right guard. Johnny got the assignment. "It's okay," they told him. "Everybody does it."

When he was nineteen, he was approached by an upper classman who offered the test answers for $3. "Its okay kid," he said "Everybody does it." Johnny was caught and sent home in disgrace.

SCOUTER'S FIVE MINUTES

"How could you do this to your mother and me?" his father said. You never learned anything like this at home." His aunt and uncle were also shocked.

If there's one thing the adult world can't stand, it's a kid who cheats.
— *Anon*

Quality of Leadership
Boys of promise are brought into contact with men of high purpose through Scouting experiences. When second-rate, mediocre men are in contact with boys of promise, the unfortunate result is often that the boys simply follow in their footsteps and become no better than themselves. Boys grow to be like the men with whom they live.
— *Walter MacPeek*

A New Leader's Prayer
Dear Father,
As I assume the leadership of this group, make me sensitive to the needs and capabilities of others. Help me to draw out the shy, finding in each a special ability. Help me to find useful channels for those who hunger for recognition. Help me to guide with delicate suggestion those who are experienced in taking responsibility. Help me to accept criticism, thoughtfully searching it for truth. Help me to welcome suggestions and to give credit to others with sincerity and warmth. May our objectives be clear and recognized as more important than personalities. May we work together in harmony and with an enthusiasm that will attract others to our quest. I thank Thee for this opportunity and pray that the results will find favour in Thine eyes. Amen.
— *from Josephine Robinson*

SCOUTER'S FIVE MINUTES

Points to Ponder
• Your thoughts are your own, until you express them.

• The actions of men are like the index of a book: they point out what is most extraordinary.

• You cannot be angry or emotionally upset as long as you control your voice.

• Sometimes the most difficult feat of muscular endurance is just holding your own tongue.

• Some men can talk more good in five minutes than they can do in a year.

• If you are not as close to God and His Blessed Mother as you once were, you can be sure as to which one of you has moved.
— *from Jack Dalton, Montreal*

Standing on your own two feet — a story
(Adapted from 'The Scouter's 5 Minutes')

A young religious student who was diligent at his books and wanted to be wise, was forced to stop studying one night because his lamp ran out of oil and the light went out. Troubled, he cradled his head on his folded arms and fell asleep at his studying place. Thus sleeping he had a vision in which the god of learning appeared to him. The god offered to convey all knowledge and learning to the student by breathing into his ears and mouth.

"No, thank you very much," said the student. "But, if it please you, sir, I shall be very glad to have a supply of oil so that I can pursue my studies until midnight."

SCOUTER'S FIVE MINUTES

Ten Common Fallacies About the Scouting Movement
(With thanks to Judy Evans, who sends some laughs to brighten up your winter.)

1. All Scouters are a little unhinged. *Not true.* I met one a couple of years ago who was as sound as a bell!

2. The modern Scout is not able to light a fire by rubbing two sticks together. *Yes he is,* as long as the two sticks are matches!

3. Beaver Leaders all are 5'2", cute and shaped like Miss America. I asked a 6' male Tic Tac about this, and he just grinned and said, "Not all ... but enough!"

4. Venturer Advisors just sit and listen while the boys think up all the program ideas. *Only partly true.* Venturer Advisors sit and listen and grow ulcers while the boys think up all the program ideas.

5. Cub camp is where the boy sets out with his socks and comes home with someone elses. *Not true.* Cub camp is where the boy sets out with his socks and comes home with nothing!

6. Female Scouters all have loud voices. *Untrue.* Come June, female Scouters have *no* voices.

7. No-one ever washes at Scout camp. Only true if it doesn't rain.

8. Rover Crews never run out of steam. *Yes they do.* It just seems that way because of all the hot air around!

9. Scouts don't do good turns any more. *Yes they do.* They can be depended upon to help pick strawberries, retrieve a brick from the bottom of a swimming pool on a hot summer day, or assist in any way at Girl Guide Camp.

10. All Scouters who wear short pants have knobby knees. This *has* to be a fallacy but I'm still looking!

SCOUTER'S FIVE MINUTES

Thoughts on Camping
(Adapted from the *Scouter's Five Minutes*, and from *B.-P.'s Outlook*.)

Have you ever thought how a camp helps your boys to practise living the Scout law?

For example, trustworthiness. There's hardly any place where things are as open and available as a camp, if a fellow wanted to steal. But somehow the camp atmosphere helps a Scout to be trustworthy.

A Scout demonstrates loyalty every time the flag is lowered at camp. And where else offers as many opportunities for him to be helpful? Other Scouts need help on achievements; new campers need encouragement; some boys need a lift here and there.

How about friendliness? Well, every once in a while a fellow in camp needs a friend — the kind of friend his fellow Scouts can be to him.

A Scout finds chances to be courteous any time, anywhere. At camp there are chances to be kind to animals. And courtesy is involved in treating the outdoors and the campsite with respect.

Obedience is important in many camp activities; swimming, boating, canoeing.

Finally, there's no place like camp to bring out the cheerful spirits of boys.

B.-P. summarized the values of camping when he said, "It is in camp that the Scoutmaster has his opportunity for inculcating under pleasant means the four main points of training; character, service for others, skill and bodily health. But beside all, it is his golden chance to bring the boy to God through the direct appeal of Nature and her store of wonders."

From the mouths of babes

Thanks to *Scouting in New South Wales*, Oct. 1980, we have this delightful piece written by the nine-year-old daughter of a Cub leader in response to her teacher's request to prepare a composition answering the question. "What did you do last weekend?"

SCOUTER'S FIVE MINUTES

"Nothing! My mum went away for the weekend with Mr. Haylen *(her mother's group leader)*. Daddy didn't mind because he knows him. Mum also went away with thirty other men and says that if she doesn't do these two weekends, all her others will be a waste of time.

"We are packing our bags and going to grandma's place next weekend. If mum passes her tests after her weekends, she will be able to wear a bootlace and two bits of wood around her neck."

One can only hope that the teacher who received this effort is also involved in Scouting!

A Leader's Prayer

Please God grant me —
- The spark to imagine
- The daring to innovate
- The discipline to plan
- The skill to do
- The will to achieve
- The commitment to be responsible
- The leadership to motivate
— *Thanks to Bob Slater, London, Ontario*

THE GIFT

A boy ought to feel at home in a wood
As any of Nature's children should
If their senses are tuned to the scene;
For security grows with the growing trees
And mystery stalks with the sun and the breeze
Through the patterns of shadow and sheen;
There's a hiding place in the branches on high,
His spirit on wings, to lean from the sky
And to marvel at what it may mean;

Scouter's
Five Minutes

While the undergrowth stirs with the small, secret things,
The twitter, the glitter, the whisper of wings,
And the key to this kingdom of green.

A boy ought to feel at home on the heath
With the wind in his hair and the turf beneath
To set the young animal free;
With the daisies and dandelions starring the grass
And adding their spring to his feet as they pass
Like a cantering colt on a spree;
To run and to jump and to roll on the ground,
To lie and to listen to Nature's small sound,
Like the drone of the bumble bee,
To search in the grass for ants at their work,
Where dragonfly hovers or spiders may lurk,
Just to watch and to wonder — and see.
A boy ought to feel at home with a stream,
At one with the ripple and gurgle and gleam,
For the water's a wonderful toy,
To paddle and dam in the sparkle and splash,
To start with delight at the kingfisher's flash,
And the fish so elusive and coy.

So to marvel at all the Creator has made
Of which we are part, and to offer our aid
To help Him, to love and enjoy;
For the eyes to see and the senses to feel
Are the greatest delights that God may reveal,
And the gifts I would give to a boy.
—*Hazel Addis*

THOUGHTS — *from Jack Dalton, Montreal*
• It is not the lack of an eye, a leg, an arm, or a college degree that makes careers crippled. It is the lack of a positive attitude. We seldom

SCOUTER'S FIVE MINUTES

think of what we have, but what we have not is the greatest tragedy on earth.
• A real friend is one who walks in when the rest of the world walks out.
• What an absurd thing it is to pass over all the valuable parts of a man and fix our attention on his infirmities
• Few people are wise enough to prefer useful reproof to treacherous praise.
• Man is always trying to make something for himself, rather than something of himself.
• Children go wrong, not on account of poverty, overcrowding or lack of recreation facilities, but because they are living with the wrong type of people.
• The most difficult thing youngsters have to do is learning good example without seeing any.

Or, as B.-P more succinctly put it;

". . . boys are critical beggars, and quickly see through the man who does not believe or has not 'been there'."
—*from B.-P.'s Outlook*

20 Steps to Successful Fire-lighting

1. Saw a dead limb into short logs.
2. Bandage left hand, sharpen saw and remind yourself that It could have been worse.
3. Carefully chop one short log into kindling.
4. Bandage left foot, repair boot, sharpen axe and remind yourself that it could have been *much* worse.
5. Very carefully shave one piece of kindling to slivers.
6. Make a small pyramid of all the slivers (including those embedded in your hand).
7. Apply a lighted match to the pyramid.
8. Apply another lighted match to the pyramid. (The greater the need for the fire, the more difficult it will be to light.)

SCOUTER'S FIVE MINUTES

9. Make mental note that 'a Scout is cheerful' and apply yet another lighted match. (A fire will self-ignite if a cold salad is planned for supper.)

10. Add kindling and gently blow into the base of the fire.

11. Stop coughing, dry your eyes and apply ointment to burned nose.

12. Apologize to the Scout who happened to be within earshot and assure him that your remarks were not addressed to him personally.

13. When fire is burning, search for saw and/or axe and collect more wood. (The desire for a fire increases as the supply of wood decreases.)

14. Upon discovering that the fire has gone out during your absence, soak wood with can of lamp oil.

15. Treat face and arms for second degree burns and relabel the can of lamp oil to read 'Gasoline'.

16. Assume an air of superiority and ask which of the watching Scouts noticed your deliberate mistakes.

17. After the sudden torrential downpour, repeat steps 1-18.

18. Observe the phenomena that:

   a) no matter where you locate the fire, you will always be directly in the path of the smoke.

   b) When you move, the smoke will follow you.

   c) The smoke will seek to reach the maximum number of people.

   d) When you move far enough away that you receive no heat or light, the smoke will rise straight up in the air.

19. Pay special attention to the fact that:

   a) A fire is much more difficult to put out than it is to start.

   b) The further you are from a water supply, the more water will be required to extinguish the fire.

   c) Ten minutes before your planned dousing of the fire, someone will add a fresh supply of wood.

20. Give silent thanks for the discovery of natural gas and the invention of the kitchen stove.

— Our many thanks to Colin Wallace

SCOUTER'S FIVE MINUTES

Those who draw inspiration from the tale of B.-P. at Mafeking will be interested in this bit of news from England's *Scouting* magazine. As of September, 1980, Mafeking has become **MAFIKENG**, a Tswana word meaning 'place of stones'. The name change came when the town was incorporated into the independent Republic of Bophuthatswana at midnight on that date in 1980.

We owe thanks for this lesson in procrastination to THE SABLE (Feb. '81), the Scouting magazine from the province of Mashonaland, Zimbabwe.

HE HAD A YEAR TO DO IT IN

He had a year to do it in!
So brushed the thought away;
A chap with half his energy
Might do it in a day.
A year! 'Twas too ridiculous,
As everyone should find;
However, he would get it done
And have it off his mind.

But not today. A few months hence
would suit him better still;
Meanwhile, a far less irksome job
Might occupy his skill.
He would not let the matter pass
Entirely from him, No;
And doubtless he might take it up
In, say a month or so.

He had six months to do it in!
For six long months had flown;
Well, why should that alarm a chap
With talents like his own?
The job, whence once embarked upon,

SCOUTER'S
FIVE MINUTES

Would soon be rattled through;
However, he would think of it,
In, say, a week or two.

He had three months to do it in!
"Oh brother!" was his cry;
The thing hangs on me like a weight,
Each day that passes by.
Let's see: three months? Ah, that's enough;
But, just to clear the doubt,
Make arrangements for a start
Before the month is out.

He had a week to do it in!
And care was in his glance:
"It's hard," he cried, "that flight of time,
Won't give a chap a chance!"
He still delayed; the swift week passed,
As weeks will ever run,
And though a year was given him,
The task was still undone.

BEAVER'S PRAYERS
Opening:
God, I thank you for this day,
In my work and in my play.
Help me to be very kind and good
Help me to act, as your child should.

Closing:
Hear us God, Beavers bright
Keep us safe from morn 'til night
Guide us in your own sweet way,
Bring us back another day. — Amen
— Thanks to Barbara Oxford, 1st S.A. Springdale Colony, Nfld.

Scouter's Five Minutes

CUB PRAYER
God our Father
Bless us as we gather here today
Help us all to understand our promise better
Teach us to love you more
And love all your people
And serve our country faithfully.
— Amen
—from the 31st Capilano Cub pack

Thought for Scouters
"For the boy is truth with dirt on his face,
Beauty with a cut on his finger,
Wisdom with bubble gum in his hair,
And the hope of the future with a frog in
his pocket!"
—from an address by Mike Downes, Victorian Branch Commissioner for Scouts, published in SCOUT magazine, Australia.

October. Harvest time. A time for thanksgiving. Through the ages, people from many different cultures in all parts of the world have celebrated the harvest with music, feasting, laughter, and prayers of thanks to their Great Provider. Grateful for His gifts they offered gifts in return and pledged to work with Him to ensure that the coming year was as plentiful as the year past.

And so it is today in most countries of the world. On a special day each fall we bow our heads in thanks over a groaning table of turkey, fresh garden fruits and vegetables, and pumpkin pie. In England people deck their churches with sheaves of grain, apples, pears, and the colourful harvest of their vegetable gardens, and in Japan they offer thanksgiving bowls of rice and prayer before a candle-lit shrine. Everyone thanks God in his own special way.

SCOUTER'S FIVE MINUTES

A BEAVER'S PRAYER
Thank you, God, for this day
For my friends and for my play,
Thank you for good things to eat
For eyes and ears, and hands and feet
Thank you God, for all You do
And, I will try to help You, too.

THANKSGIVING PRAYER
O God, we thank you for this universe
and for the earth you have given us
    as our home:
for its vastness and its riches,
and for the abundance of life which teems
    upon it, and of which we are part.
We praise you for the arching sky
    and the blessed winds,
for the driving clouds
    and the constellations on high.
We praise you for the salt sea
    and the running water,
for the everlasting hills, for the trees,
    and for the grass under our feet.
We thank you for our senses, by which
we can see the splendour of the morning,
and hear the jubilant songs of love,
and smell the breath of springtime.
Grant us, we pray you, a heart wide open
    to all this joy and beauty ...
—*from* Let's Celebrate, *available at Scout Shops across the country.*

SCOUTER'S FIVE MINUTES

GREAT SPIRIT MAKE ME
(translated from the Sioux)

O Great Spirit. whose voice
> I hear in the winds,
whose breath gives life to the world,
> hear me.
> I am small and weak.
I need your strength and your wisdom.
> May I walk in beauty.
Make my eyes ever hold
> the red and purple sunset.
Make my hands respect
> the things you have made and
my ears sharp to hear your voice.
Make me wise so that I may know the things
> you have taught your children,
the lessons you have hidden
> in every leaf and rock.
Make me strong
> not to be superior to my brothers
but to be able to fight my greatest enemy
> ... myself.
Make me ever ready to come to you
> with straight eyes,
so that when life fades as the fading sunset
my spirit will come to you without shame.
— *printed with thanks to Canadian Camping magazine, the official publication of the Canadian Camping Association.*

> We are the youth of today
We were not born until after the war
> We are able to go to school
Some of us have ten-speed bikes
> We have loving parents

SCOUTER'S FIVE MINUTES

We have never gone hungry
>We don't know what war really is!

What is hunger? What is a concentration camp?
>What is an air raid? What is a bomb?
>What is fear?

I know we are free!
I know who liberated us!
I know what they sacrificed!
>Thanks, soldiers, for our freedom.

—from the London District Council Digest, Nov. 1980.

For those who've supposed that **Warm Fuzzies** *had something to do with Canada's long, cold winters, here's the story that started it all. Originally from the Northwest Territories Council bulletin, it was first printed in* **the Leader***, October 1976.*

Once upon a time there was a tiny village nestled between two mountains. Each person in the village was very happy because at birth he was given a bag of *Warm Fuzzies*. You could reach into your bag and pull out a *Warm Fuzzy* whenever you wanted, and everybody wanted to all the time. *Warm Fuzzies* were given to other people on the street, at home, everywhere. *Warm Fuzzies* made you feel just like they sound; warm, happy and contented. Everyone in the village was happy. Everyone but the bad witch.

Now we all know that bad witches like us to be unhappy. This bad witch was no exception. She tried and tried to make the people stop giving away *Warm Fuzzies*. One day she whispered to little Johnny Brown, "If you keep giving away all your *Warm Fuzzies*, you won't have any left for yourself."

Johnny didn't listen at first, because everyone always had lots of *Warm Fuzzies*. The more you gave away, the more you got. Then the witch said to Johnny, "If you give away **COLD PRICKLIES** you will be able to-keep all of your *Warm Fuzzies*." Well, Johnny got to thinking about this and noticed that his mother was always giving away *Warm Fuzzies*. So was his father and his sister. Soon, he thought, they would have no more for him. So Johnny started saving

SCOUTER'S
FIVE MINUTES

his *Warm Fuzzies* and giving out **COLD PRICKLIES** instead. Soon the whole village was giving **COLD PRICKLIES**. Everyone was gloomy and sad and very grouchy. The village was no longer happy. There wasn't a *Warm Fuzzy* to be found!

This went on for years and years and the wicked witch was very happy. One day an old man came to visit the village. When he spoke to anyone they frowned at him, turned their backs and walked away. But the old man continued to be friendly, polite and pleasant, and one day a very young boy smiled back at the old man. It made him feel good-so good that he patted his dog, and the dog didn't bite him! It was the first *Warm Fuzzy* given in some time. The little boy dug out his bag of *Warm Fuzzies* because they were much nicer than **COLD PRICKLIES**, and he started giving them away. The townspeople grumbled and growled for awhile, but soon they felt like giving *Warm Fuzzies* too. One by one they went home to find their Warm Fuzzies and soon everyone was giving out *Warm Fuzzies*. The bad witch was so upset and disgusted that she left the village and took all of her **COLD PRICKLIES** with her. To this day the village is happy and contented. Maybe, just maybe, if we give out enough *Warm Fuzzies*, our world can be as happy and pleasant as you'd find it there.

...our Saviour's birth is celebrated,
The bird of dawning singeth all night long.
— *Wm Shakespeare*

Simple words; poetic words;
wonder-filled words to sing with joyous music;
words given us by the Man whose birth
    we celebrate.
Peace! Joy! Hope! Love!
These are the words for Christmas.

SCOUTER'S FIVE MINUTES

Fear not: for behold, I bring you tidings
Off great joy, which shall be to all people.
For unto you is born this day in the city
of David a Saviour, which is Christ the Lord.
—*from the Gospel of St. Luke*

Then be ye glad, good people,
This night of all the year,
And light ye up your candles
For His star, it shineth clear.
—*old carol*

What can I give Him,
Poor as I am?
If I were a shepherd
I would bring a lamb,
If I were a Wise Man
I would do my part,
Yet what I can I give Him
    Give him my heart.
—*Christina Rossetti*

YULE LOG PRAYER

May the fire of this log warm the cold;
May the hungry be fed;
May the weary find rest,
And may all enjoy heaven's peace.
—*traditional*

Deep peace of the running wave to you;
Deep peace of the flowing air to you;
Deep peace of the shining stars to you;
Deep peace of the quiet earth to you;

SCOUTER'S FIVE MINUTES

Deep peace of the watching shepherds to you;
Deep peace of the Prince of Peace to you.
— *prayer translated from the Gaelic*

Christmas sometimes brings out the cynicism in us. Christmas words may seem like cheap tinsel trying to hide the shabbiness of honky-tonk commercialism, the signs of bitter suffering, even in our own land of plenty, the horror of thoughtless violence and full-scale war in our careless world.

But the message in the words has its own light and, like Scrooge, we listen despite ourselves, we join the songs, and we hope.

And some Christmas words make us think.

Would you follow the star tonight
If it shone past the Milky Way,
Leave comfortable homes and follow it still
Over the hills and away?
How many would open their doors tonight
For a weary and shabby pair,
Make room at hearths for a Stranger-Child
Though the infant be wondrous fair?
How many would give of their gifts tonight,
The best they possess and more,
For their faith in a star and an angel choir
And a king for evermore?
We censure the folk of a bygone time
For indifference to Mary's plight.
How many would do any better now?
Would you follow the star tonight?
— *Author unknown. Published in* Scouting (U.K.), *November 1974.*

Start the New Year Right
Forget each kindness that you do
    as soon as you have done it;

SCOUTER'S FIVE MINUTES

Forget the praise that falls to you
    the moment you have won it.

Forget each slight, each spite, each sneer
    whenever you may meet it;
Forget the slander that you hear
    before you can repeat it.

Remember the kindness done to you,
    no matter what its measure;
Remember praise by others won
    and pass it on with pleasure.

Remember every promise made
    and keep it to the letter;
Remember those who lend you aid,
    and be a grateful debtor.

Remember all the happiness
    that comes your way in living;
Forget each worry and distress,
    be hopeful and forgiving.

Remember good, remember truth,
    Remember heaven's above you,
And you will find through age and youth,
    true joys, and hearts to love you.
— *author unknown*

SOMETHING TO THINK ABOUT

A **HANDICAP** is something for which society is responsible; a structure, an attitude, a lack of education that interferes with your doing the things you want to do.

A **DISABILITY** is what you can't do; e.g. walk, hear, see.

Scouter's
Five Minutes

An **IMPAIRMENT** is what causes the disability; e.g. paralysis after polio, lack of muscular control because of cerebral palsy, etc. Or try these plain and simple definitions.
- *Impairment:* not having a leg.
- *Disability:* not being able to run.
- *Handicap:* steering a wheelchair to a building and finding there are a dozen steps leading up to the door.

—These thoughts come from YOUTH MAGAZINE, September 1981 issue.

Here's a toast you may find useful for your Parent-Son Banquet. It has been adapted from an unsigned verse found in the January 1961 issue of THE SCOUT LEADER.

TOAST TO PARENTS
Mr. Chairman, parents and sons:
I'm flattered indeed that I'm asked to appear
To give a toast to the parents this year.
To the parents who love us,
    For better or worse,
We'll offer our tribute
    With this wee bit of verse.
They feed us and clothe us
    And send us to school,
They give us a home, and teach us the "rule".
They encourage our sports, but seldom join in
Mom says that's because she's too fat, or
    too thin.
But once in a while, Dads do become boys
For each year at Christmas,
    they play with our toys.
Now let us be honest;
    Without them we'd feel

SCOUTER'S
FIVE MINUTES

Like a boat on the ocean,
> Without any keel.
To the parents about us,
> And the Father above,
We tender our thanks with this token of love.
> ...to our parents.

All of us are always going to do better tomorrow. And we would, too, if we started today!

LOOK WIDE — a 75th Anniversary Poem

So you've just become a Scouter
And you've got a gang of boys,
And you wonder; "Will the trail ahead
Be filled with cares or joys?"

So you've studied up your handbook
And you've learned about each test,
And you've read a bunch of books that tell
Of Scouting at its best.

You're full of plans on ways and means
To build a top-notch troop,
And you're searching conscientiously
For leaders in your group.

There's that skinny lad
> with the missing tooth
And the kid with the squeaky voice,
Or that freckled, chubby guy with the grin,
All regular, fun-loving boys.

Well, at last you've found the leaders,
Red-haired Tim with the crippled hand,
Eager Eric who talks with an accent,
He was a Scout in his native land.

SCOUTER'S FIVE MINUTES

Soon at camps and hikes and meetings
High adventures you have shared,
And you've walked the trail together
Learning skills to "Be Prepared".

There were times you felt like quitting,
When some fellows let you down,
But the stuff you saw in others
Made you smile instead of frown.

And you watched them grow to manhood,
Others came and took their places,
Yet somehow you found among them
All the old familiar faces.

And a stranger's friendly greeting
Often made you wonder. "Why?"
Till he chuckled; "I am Peanuts!"
And you talked of days gone by.

"Skinny is now a policeman
    And Freckles an engineer,
Eric has become a doctor,
Tim sells autos here.

Smoky is now a minister
    And Slugger owns a store.
But Chips, who played his guitar at camp
Didn't come back from the war."

So you've grown old as a Scouter
With memories that you treasure,
And if anyone asks, "Was it worth it?"
You'll say, "In the fullest measure!"

Scouter's
Five Minutes

For the spirit we build
    and the skills we teach
Go forth through the years to be,
And people we've never met will be glad
That Scouting has you and me!
— *by Bud Jacobi*

B.-P's ANNIVERSARY THOUGHTS

Fifty years ago, on Scouting's 25th anniversary, B.-P. spoke with pride about the spread of the movement, the increased understanding of its aims and methods, and the steadily growing numbers of young people who were attracted to Scouting and Guiding.

..."If these numbers continue to grow — and they are growing rapidly — and if that comradeship continues to spread itself among the future men and women of the world, a very potent leaven will have been established of that spirit of goodwill which is the first essential to the foundation of universal peace. Altogether, we may justly look back with thankful satisfaction on our past. and, what is more. we can look forward with high hope to the future."
— *from B.-P.'s Outlook*

This month, when winter seems reluctant to release its icy grip and spring tends to drag its heels in coming, we offer thoughts to lift spirits and the corners of lips.

• *A smile is a curve that can set many things straight.*

• *A merry heart doeth good like a medicine.*

• *An ounce of mirth is worth a pound of sorrow — Richard Baxter.*

SCOUTER'S
FIVE MINUTES

Happy hearts and happy faces,
Happy play in grassy places,
That is how in ancient ages
Children grew to kings and sages.
—*L.K. Frank*

• *The real way to get happiness is by giving out happiness to other people.*
—*B.-P.*

Smiles — A Story
Once upon a time, two brothers decided to leave home and move to the city. Just outside the city, one of the brothers met an old man.

"How are the people here?" he asked.

"How were the people in your town?" the old man replied.

"Oh, all of them were cross. They grumbled all the time," the brother answered. "That's why I decided to leave."

"Well, you'll find the people here are exactly the same," the old man said, and moved on down the street.

A little while later, the second brother met the old man and asked him, "How are the people in this city?"

"How were the people in your town?" the old man answered.

"They were very nice — always cheerful and helpful," the brother replied. "I hated to leave."

Well, you'll find the people here are exactly the same," the wise old man smiled, and the two moved on down the street together.
—*Thanks to Scout magazine, Australia*

• *Nobody ever hurt his eyes by looking at the bright side of things.*

Once life's little ills annoyed me,
When life's little ills were few;
One fly in my pot of ointment
Put me in a dreadful stew.

SCOUTER'S FIVE MINUTES

Since I'm older, life has taught me
The infrequent good to prize;
I now rejoice to find some ointment
In my little pot of flies
— *Thanks to* Notepad, *N.S. Provincial Council, August 1981.*

"Many are the names of God, and infinite are the forms that lead us to know Him. In whatsoever name or form you desire to know Him, in that very name and form you will know Him."
— *B.-P.*

April brings Easter, Passover, spring. Christians celebrate the resurrection of the saviour; Jewish families commemorate the deliverance of Israel's people from slavery in Egypt; and the season, bursting with all the promise and vitality of rebirth, kindles profound spiritual feelings in people of diverse faiths and backgrounds. What better time to share expressions of the many names and forms of God, and the joy we feel in meeting Him.

Thou art the fire, Thou art the sun,
Thou art the air, Thou art the moon,
Thou art the starry firmament,
Thou art Brahman Supreme:
Thou art the waters — thou,
    The creator of all!
Thou art woman, thou art man,
Thou art the youth, thou art the maiden,
Thou art the old man tottering with his staff
Thou facest everywhere.
— *The Upanishads: Svestasvatara*

Behold, the kingdom of God is within you; you and your Father are one, the Father in you, and you in Him.
— *Jesus*

SCOUTER'S FIVE MINUTES

He created the heavens and the earth with truth, and He shaped you and made good your shapes.
— *Qur'an*

All things are the works of the Great Spirit. We should know that He is within all things.
— *Black Elk, The Sacred Pipe*

I believe in God .. who reveals himself in the orderly harmony of the universe. I believe that Intelligence is manifested throughout all Nature...
— *Albert Einstein*

If men wish to draw near to God, they must seek him in the hearts of men.
— *Abn Sa'id ibn Abi 'I-Khayr*

He to whom you pray is nearer to you than the neck of your camel.
— *Muhammad*

The Lord dwells in the heart of every creature... take refuge in Him with thy whole heart.
— *Bhagavad Gita: Krishna*

O Hidden Life, vibrant in every atom;
O Hidden Light, shining in every creature;
O Hidden Love, embracing all in Oneness;
May each who feels himself as one with Thee,
Know he is therefore one with each other.
— *Dr. Annie Besant*

Tonight the earth is crowned with stars,
A soft wind hums a tune, and for a hat
The pinetree wears a slice of saucy moon.
Goodnight world! Goodnight God!
— *a favourite prayer of the 18th Seymour Beavers*

SCOUTER'S FIVE MINUTES

God and I (tune: *Kum Ba Yah*)
God is good, God made me,
If God is good, I am good,
God is love, God made me,
If God is love, I am love.
God and I, together we'll do
The very best, as He wants me to.
God and I, together we'll do,
The very best, all year through.
— *thanks to* Scout *(Australia)*

"There is a God," all nature cries,
I see it painted on the skies
I see it in the flowering spring
I hear it when the birdlings sing.
I see it in the flowing main
I see it on the fruitful plain,
I see it everywhere abroad
I feel, I know, there is a God.
— *Anon*

My Three Years in Cubs
I'm a little Wolf Cub short and thin,
My first year is about to begin,
If you don't help somebody, it is a sin,
When you win a badge, it will make you grin.

In my second year of Cubs I'm tall and lean,
To earn all my stars, that is my dream,
When we're in our six, we work as a team,
And I try to keep my uniform clean.

SCOUTER'S FIVE MINUTES

In my last year of Cubs, I am tall and stout,
I know what Cubbing is all about,
I've had fun and I want to shout,
Hey you guys, I've become a Scout!
— *by Scout Jason Dunning: written in 1979 during his first Cub year with the 52nd Ottawa (Haida) Pack.*

He Was a Scout
The other day I met a lad
Who saw me looking really sad,
I felt so gloomy on that day,
The boy seemed carefree, bright and gay,
He smiled at me, and still I hear
His friendly greeting, meant to cheer.
He had no legs, but with that smile
He had me beat by many a mile,
And in my heart there was no doubt;
The boy I met, he was a Scout!

Some kids were playing in the park,
Just when my dog began to bark,
A bird had fallen from its nest
And vainly fluttered, took no rest.
The boys looked on. Without a word,
One gently grasped the helpless bird.
He found the nest and placed with care
The bird inside, and left it there.
And in my heart there was no doubt,
So kind a lad; he was a Scout!

A child was drowning in the creek,
Some boys were near and heard his shriek,
Through the swamp they made their way,

SCOUTER'S FIVE MINUTES

Mud bogged them down and caused delay,
But one who saw they'd be too late,
Leaped from the cliff and trusted fate,
He broke his leg but, all the same,
Clung to the child till rescue came.
I heard the tale; could there be doubt?
They said the hero was a Scout!
— *by Scouter Bud Jacobi, St. Catharines Ontario*

Thoughts of a Scouter
Being a Scouter is a treasure
That one can never compare
To dollars, gold or silver,
And other material fare.
No, the wealth of which I'm speaking
Comes from a purer source of joy,
It's a being of God's own making
That we often call a "boy".

He's an active little fireball
Well-known by one and all,
I have the chance to be with him
Each week down at the hall.
He knows not of the cynics
And the skeptics of our day,
The whole world is his wonderland
And he invites us out to play.

When I'm with this lad at Cub camp
And he wonders at a tree,
I feel my inner wonderment
Come flowing out of me.

SCOUTER'S FIVE MINUTES

Under mountains, in the twilight,
Looking at the heavens above,
I know why I'm a Scouter,
I'm a Scouter out of love.
— *by "Baloo" Anthony Gurr, 8th Fort Victoria Scout Group, Victoria, B.C.*

I live in a very small house, but my windows look out on a very large world.
— *Confucius*

JUSTICE
For me, that may be
Getting a turn at bat in a ball game
Not walking the dog any more often
    than my brother
Getting my share of the chocolate cake
Being served in turn at the store,
    even though I'm small
Not having to clean up my sister's mess
Being accepted as a friend
    even though I can't talk well.
For others, that may be
Having enough food to eat so there is
    no pain in my stomach
Having water to drink without walking miles
    to get it, and lining up for it
Having a doctor available when ill
Being able to sleep in a sheltered place
    out of cold, or sun, or rain
Having a school to go to
Knowing there may be a future.
— *by "The Special" group at Fort Garry United Church in Winnipeg. Reprinted with permission of the editor of* The United Church Observer.

SCOUTER'S
FIVE MINUTES

"A typical North American home garbage disposal unit eats better than 30% of the people in the world."
— *World Vision Actionews, Sept. '80*

Beaver Prayer
Our God, how good you are.
We thank you for our families and our friends and other Beavers
And for the good times we share together.
Help us to have fun, work hard and help our families and friends.
— *from the 18th Seymour Beaver Colony*

Cub Prayer
We thank you Lord for Scouting
And all it means to us,
We thank you for the fun
    and things we learn to do
We thank you for the chance to help others
Which is our way of serving you.
Make us better able to do the job, we pray,
And give us a better understanding of our promise
For all the strength we have
    to run and jump and play
For all our senses, strong and sound,
We thank you, Lord, today.
— *thanks to* Scout *(Australia)*

Scout Prayer
Thank you for our wonderful world;
    for the miracles of scientific discovery,
Thank you for Scouting; for its ideals
    and for its brotherhood;
Thank you for all the Scouts,
    whatever their nation, colour and beliefs,

SCOUTER'S FIVE MINUTES

Thank you for our homes, our parents,
  and our friends.
Lord, thank you for all your bounty;
  We are truly grateful.
— *thanks to* New Zealand Scout News

Oh Lord, as you touched men on earth to make them spring up and run and leap for joy, so touch us. Help us to remember those who are less fortunate than ourselves. Help us to put aside our grumblings and discouragements. Teach us to use our eyes and ears to see and hear the beauty you have provided for us on earth. Help us to remember our many blessings and the great opportunities which are ours in this wonderful world.

When he died before the turn of the century, a man named Charles Lounsbury left a very unusual last will and testament. Although poor in material wealth, he was obviously rich in spirit, and his legacy is one that all Scouters would wish for boys. "I devise jointly all the useful ideal fields and commons where ball may be played; all pleasant waters where one may swim (all snowclad hills where one may coast) and all streams and ponds where one may fish or, when grim winter comes, one may skate; to have and to hold the same for the period of their boyhood. And all meadows with their clover blossoms and butterflies thereof, the woods and their appurtenances, the squirrels, and birds and echoes of strange noises, and all distant places which may be visited, together with the adventures there found. And I give to said boys each his own place at the fireside at night, with all pictures that may be seen in the burning wood, to enjoy without let or hindrance, and without encumbrance of care."

Rope or Knot?
How sad it would be without rope,
And what could we have in its place?
Sticky tape or tacky glue,
Just couldn't stand the pace.

Scouter's Five Minutes

Can you imagine camping time
Out in the summer sun,
Trying to erect an eight-man tent,
With only paste and gum!

You couldn't fish or make a swing,
Or skip or tie shoe laces,
Or even tie a parcel up,
To send to distant places.

We could use worms or snakes instead,
But you would have to pray,
That when you went to sleep at night,
The tent wouldn't crawl away!

So to Scouters who hate teaching knots,
Fun comes to Cubs by talking,
Of Tarzan using knots and ropes,
To save a lot of walking!
— *by David Purrington from Exeter, England. First published in* Scouting (UK), *in December 1975.*

It's all a matter of how you look at things

Many years ago, a visitor to Liverpool noticed a huge construction site where the cathedral now stands. Curious about what was happening, he wandered over to men at work on the foundations.

"What are you doing here?" he asked one of the men.

"Can't you see? I'm chipping this stone," the workman replied, and resumed his pounding. The visitor shrugged and moved over to another man.

"What are you doing here?" he asked him.

"I'm making $1.50 an hour," the second workman answered smugly.

SCOUTER'S FIVE MINUTES

Well, the visitor agreed that this was probably true, but it still didn't tell him what was going on, so he approached a third workman and put his question to him.

"What are we doing?" the third man beamed, his eyes surveying the site with joy and pride.

"Why, sir, we are building a cathedral!"
— *adapted from* The Scouter's 5 Minutes

• *Some good folks get discovered; others get found out!*

The Manager

From what we've read in magazines
And seen in sundry movie scenes,
The true manager is he
Who delegates authority;
Who resolutely, firmly acts
But only when he has the facts;
Who speaks well, writes a splendid letter,
But also listens even better;
Who cares about his men, their wives,
But doesn't meddle in their lives;
Who knows details, yet keeps his eye
On goals beyond minutiae;
Who works as long as anyone,
And leaves desk clear, tasks all done;
Who keeps his word, although it hurts;
Who never drinks too much, or flirts;
Who, even on the darkest days,
Can summon up a word of praise
And bravely smile amidst disaster.

The true manager, in short,
Is good at work and good at sport,
Resourceful, charming, man of talents,

SCOUTER'S FIVE MINUTES

Possessed of perfect poise and balance;
His words and deeds and aims all mesh...
We'd like to see one in the flesh!
— *Anon*

• *If Columbus had turned back, no one could have blamed him, but no one would have remembered him.*
— *Anon*

A Trux Thought
Xvxn though my typxwritxr is an old modxl, it works quitx wxll. Xxcxpt for onx kxy, that is. Thxrx arx 46 kxys that function wxli xnough, but to havxjust onx kxy not working makxs thx diffxrxncx.

Somxtimxs with pxoplx, likx with my typxwritxr, not all thx kxys arx working propxrly. You may say, "Wxll, I am only onx pxrson. It won't makx much diffxrxncx." But, you should say, and you can sxx, that thx group, to bx xffxctivx, nxxds thx activx participation of xvxrypxrson.

So, thx nxxt timx you think you arx only onx pxrson, rxmxmbxr my typxwritxr and say to yoursxlf, "I am a kxy pxrson, and I am nxxdxd vxry much!"
— *thanks to* The Trailsman, *New Brunswick Provincial Council.*

• *Any Scouter who still thinks the sky is the limit is short of imagination!*
— *thanks to Colin McKay's* A canny crack, **Scouting (UK)**, *May 1982.*

THOUGHTS ON GIVING
For God so loved the world that he gave His only begotten Son, that whosoever believeth in Him should not perish, but have everlasting life.
— *Bible: St. John*

SCOUTER'S FIVE MINUTES

True givers give themselves in friendship, in sympathy, and in service.
— *Anon*

Blessed are those who can give without remembering, and take without forgetting.

Open your minds to look around you, open your hearts to understand and sympathize, open your hands to help.
— *Pope John Paul II*

The Spirit of love for your fellowman is, after all, the Spirit of God working in you.
— *B.-P.*

The way to heaven is to benefit others.
— *Tao*

A camel lent out for milk is alms, good words are alms, and smiling in your brother's face is alms.
— *Muhammad*

Go often to the house of thy friend, for weeds choke up the unused path.
— *Wm. Shakespeare*

He does not live in vain who employs his wealth, his thought, his speech to advance the good of others.
— *Hinduism*

Love and service are the two keys to the door of heaven.
— *Tibetan saying*

Scouter's
Five Minutes

To feel much for others and little for ourselves; to restrain our selfish and exercise our benevolent affections, constitutes the perfection of human nature.
— Adam Smith

Let your light so shine before men that they may see your good works...
— Jesus

Whatever you give to others, give with love and respect. Gifts must be given in abundance, with joy, humility, and compassion.
— words of the Hindu sages

A man's true wealth is hereafter the good he does in this world to his fellow man.
— Muhammad

Ill is easy to do; it is easy to do harm; hard indeed is it to do helpful and good deeds.
— Buddha

There are two kinds of gratitude — the sudden kind we feel for what we take, the larger kind we feel for what we give.
— Edward Arlington Robinson

He that does good to another, does good also to himself, not only in the consequences, but in the very act; for the consciousness of well-doing is, in itself, ample reward.
— Seneca

Lead us from death to life
From falsehood to truth;
Lead us from despair to hope,
From fear to trust;

SCOUTER'S FIVE MINUTES

Lead us from hate to love,
From war to peace.
Let peace fill our hearts,
Our world, our universe.
— *Prayer of Mother Theresa*

To worship rightly is to love each other. Each smile a hymn, each kindly deed a prayer.

For there is a child born for us,
a son given to us
and dominion is laid on his shoulders,
and this is the name they give him:
Wonder-Counsellor, Mighty-God,
Eternal-Father, Prince-of-Peace.
— *Isaiah*

Then let every heart keep Christmas within.
    Christ's pity for sorrow,
    Christ's hatred for sin,
    Christ's care for the weakest
    Christ's courage for right.
Everywhere, everywhere, Christmas tonight!
— *Phillip Brooks*

Raise your hat to the past, but take off your coat to the future
— *Colin McKay*
Mr. McKay's "canny crack" *(Scouting (UK)*, May '82) is an appropriate thought both for the new year and Scouting's anniversary. It's also a good introduction to this editorial from *New Zealand Scout News*, April '82.

SCOUTER'S FIVE MINUTES

A BOY'S GAME

In this, our 75th anniversary year... it is prudent to look back as well as forward. The events of the past do have a bearing on the future and, while many of the practices of the first 75 years of Scouting may not have a place in the next 75, there is no doubt that they must influence us...

One of the things that tends to be forgotten is that it was boys who started Scouting, not Baden-Powell. He certainly wrote the book, but it was a book for boys resulting in a game for boys.

B.-P. had no intention of starting a separate organization. He merely wanted to assist the existing boys' organizations... with a scheme of training that he thought would appeal to them.

Brownsea Island proved him right, but those existing boys' organizations — or was it the adults in charge? — never took up his scheme. It was left to boys (and later girls) to organize themselves into a game that has spread throughout the world...

Needless to say, adults have got into the act and no-one would deny that... their assistance is necessary to keep the game going... But they should never get carried away with their own importance, especially those who no longer work at boy level.

Taking quotations out of context is sometimes dangerous but there is no mistaking the meaning of many of the quotations of B.-P. He wrote on many occasions about Scouting being a game and was concerned that some adults may have been taking it too seriously with all the pamphlets, rules, pronouncements, conferences and training courses.

"First I had an idea," he once wrote. "Then I saw an ideal. Now we have a movement and, if some of you don't watch out, we shall end up with just an organization!"

—*from* ***New Zealand Scout News****, April '82*

THANKS B.-P. *(an anniversary poem)*
I remember camps with tea full of ash,
Eating potatoes too hard to mash,
My stomach received an awful shock,

SCOUTER'S FIVE MINUTES

I always lost at least one sock.
I remember falls from a bridge of rope,
Washing my face with cold water and soap;
I remember a week at Kandersteg,
Mallet on thumb instead of a peg.

I dream of a camp where it rained all week,
We're proud to say our tent didn't leak;
I still feel the sting of smoke in my eyes,
We were told it kept away the flies.

I see again the nightly campfire,
Sparks like glow worms ever higher;
I hear once more songs from the past,
Fond memories like these will ever last.

We dammed the stream and made a pool,
The water was so clear and cool;
I have brothers in Scouting everywhere,
That's millions of us with dreams to share.

I can use an ax and pitch a tent,
Your time for us was all well spent;
Cubs do their best; Scouts are prepared;
Your thoughts with Beavers we have shared.

We thank you for the last seventy-five,
What growth you'd see if you were alive;
You can be proud of what is past,
In our thoughts you'll always last.
— *by Scouter Peter Fergus, Zephyr, Ont.*

SCOUTER'S FIVE MINUTES

How Wrong Can You Be?

Scene: a small public relations office, circa 1907. A man answers the telephone...

"Hello Acme Promotions here. Yeah... Yeah... O.K. Let me get that down on paper.

"Right. Your name is?... Ha, has... I thought you said Bee Pee... You did! Well, it is a kinda cute name, and from the PR point of view....

"No, I'm not being facetious, and I am listening...

"Yeah .... Yeah... O K. hold it right there. You say you are just out of the army and you want to build up your own army of troops — is this some kind of mercenary outfit?... Well you did say troops... Oh, Cubs and Scouts, then, but you did say troops...

"O.K. You surround yourself with kids and they will be dressed up in pointed hats... wear neckerchiefs... carry poles and wear whats? How do you spell that?...W-O-G-G-L-E-S. And they will be led by A-K-E-L-A...

"Say, are you kidding me? It's not April first, is it?.... O.K., O.K., keep your woggle on! ...

"They will learn all about backwoodsmanship and tracking ... I can't see that being particularly useful in town ... Yeah, yeah, I get your point... there sure are some grassy bits in most towns.

"Can you honestly see youngsters going for this kind of malarky?... You can? Hm!.. What's that? ... Some day there will be millions of them in practically every country in the world?... Aw, no... not on postage stamps, too!

"Well, I must say I admire your convictions but, quite honestly, your idea can't possibly work. No way!

"O.K... Give me a ring when you get back from Brownsea Island or whatever and we can... What? What was that?...

"Oh. O.K., and Dib, Dib, Dob to you too!"

Man hangs up phone and wipes brow.

"Now, all I need is for these Wright Brothers to come along and tell me they are starting an airline!"

—*from Clydesdale Scout Look*

SCOUTER'S FIVE MINUTES

Prayers

    Lord, we'll always remember
        our Scouting years,
With the work, fun, and sometimes fears,
The competitions, camps
        and countless weekends
Which we have spent with all our friends;
And as we grow older and go different ways,
These memories will last us
        for the rest of our days.
— *by Scout Gregory Coomer, England. First published in Scouting (UK), Feb. 1982.*

We thank you, Father, for 75 years of Scouting; for the vision of our founder, Robert Baden-Powell, and for the dedication of men and women through the years who have given their time and talents to support generations of boys and young people throughout the world. We thank you for the opportunities of Scouting today, and for the part each of us has been given to play.

Lord, God, I give you my hands,
    to do your work,
I give you my feet to go your way,
I give you my tongue to speak your truth,
that may meet the challenge of
    the Promise and Law,
grow in my love of you, and seek to build
    a better world for all my fellow men.
— *from Scouting (UK), Mar '82 issue*

GOOD IN ACTION

I'd rather see a sermon,
    than hear one any day;
I'd rather one should walk with me,
    than merely show the way:

SCOUTER'S FIVE MINUTES

For the best of all the creatures
    are the men who live their creeds,
And to see the good in action is
    what everybody needs.
— *author unknown*

A good thought is good. A good word is better,
and a good deed is the best of all.
— *Zorastrian philosophy*

PRAYER
God be in my head, and in my understanding;
God be in my eyes, and in my looking;
God be in my mouth, and in my speaking;
God be in my heart, and in my thinking;
God be in my hands, and in all my doing.

A LITTLE BOY
I am a little boy
I paint fearlessly
I hammer loudly
I build restlessly
I read imaginatively
I write originally
I sing rapturously
May man never quell my creativity,
    Just refine it!
— *by Karen Marsh, Calgary, Alberta*

THE CUB CAR SPIN
Whittle and chip,
    Hurry, it's late!
Got to meet
    The Cub Car date.

SCOUTER'S FIVE MINUTES

Paint 'em up,
    Oil the wheels,
Weigh 'em in,
    And go for the deal.
Don't be sad
    If you don't win,
'Cause next year
    We'll be back again.
— *by Cub Jason Brown, 10, 5th Riverview Pack, New Brunswick*

When life gives you lemons, make lemonade!

If you think you are beaten, you are;
If you think you dare not, you don't;
If you'd like to win, but you think you can't
It's almost a cinch you won't.

Life's battles don't always go
To the stronger or faster man;
But soon or late, the man who wins
Is the one who thinks he can.
— *from a poem by Walter D. Wintle*

When you get to the end of your tether, tie a knot and hang on!
— *Colin McKay,* Scouting (UK), *June '82*

"There is no pleasure that comes near to that of preparing your own meal over your little fire of wood embers at the end of the day, and no scent like the smell of that fire. There is no view like that from your lair on the woodland hillside. And there is no sleep like that in the open with a warm blanket or a good thickness of paper beneath you.
— *words of B.-P.*

Scouter's Five Minutes

ON BOATING
(These excerpts come from the American Coast Guard Pamphlet CG-428)

Boat Loading Commandments
Very I say unto thee... Spreadeth out the people and things evenly in the little boat for he that spreadeth the load not wisely bringeth much woe unto the Coast Guard and himself.

Wisest is he that keepeth the whole load in his boat as low as possible. Thy first command to thy people in the boat shall be, "SIDDOWN!"

Suffer thee not the fools who would ride on the bow for they are non-believers and are not long for this world.

Regard not the number of seats in thy boat for oft they mislead and may bring thee to the sin of overloading.

Commit thou to memory these words... for they shall bringeth thee comfort and keep thee from committing a boating "no-no"!

A Boating Fable
Once upon a time a great king had a heavy throne. He also had a little boat. He liked to go out in his boat sitting on his throne. One day, while he enjoyed the boat and the water, a sudden breeze sprang up and rocked the boat. The heavy throne slid to one side of the boat. The little boat tipped over, causing the king to lose a lot of things, not the least of which was his dignity.

MORAL: People with small boats shouldn't stow thrones!

ABOUT TREES
He that planteth a tree
    is the servant of God,
He provideth a kindness
    for many generations,
And faces that he hath not seen,
Shall bless him.
—*Henry van Dyke*

SCOUTER'S FIVE MINUTES

Harm Me Not!

I am the heart of your hearth on the cold winter nights; the friendly shade which screens you from the summer sun; and my fruits quench your thirst as you journey on.

I am the beam which supports your house, the board of your table, the bed on which you sleep and the timber which builds your boat. I am the handle of your hoe, the door of your home, the wood of your cradle and the shell of your coffin.

I am the bread of kindness and the flower of beauty.

You who pass by, please listen to my prayer:

>   HARM ME NOT!

— the forest reserves of Portugal have been posted with this notice for more than 1000 years!

There are two lasting gifts we can give children: one is roots, the other is wings!

There is so much good
>   in the worst of us,
And so much bad
>   in the best of us,
That it hardly becomes
>   any of us
To criticize
>   the rest of us.

THOUGHT FOR EACH DAY

(Inspired by a calendar of daily thoughts by *Bill Stride*, published in the June 1982 issue of Mississauga District's *the scouter.*)

Sunday:

Let me be true, for there are those
>   who trust me;

SCOUTER'S FIVE MINUTES

Let me be pure, for there are those
    who care;
Let me be strong, for there is much
    to suffer,
Let me be brave, for there is much to dare.
Let me be friend to all who are friendless,
Let me be giving, and forget what I give;
Let me be humble, for I know my weakness;
Help me to laugh, and love, and live!

Monday:
I only have this life to live,
I want to taste its every flavour,
To watch sun's set with mind at peace,
And greet each day as gift to savour.

I only live each day but once,
And want to do all I can do
To show a kindness, make a friend;
To touch another passing through.
If I forget, as I go by,
To stop to ease another's pain
Or smell a rose, remind me, Lord,
I'll never pass this way again.
— *Linda Florence*

Tuesday:
Take time to think, it's the source of power;
Take time to play, it's the secret
    of perpetual youth;
Take time to laugh, it's the music
    of the soul;
Take time to love and be loved,
    it's a God-given gift.

SCOUTER'S FIVE MINUTES

Wednesday:

God grant me the serenity to accept the
 things that cannot be changed,
The courage to change the things that
 can be changed,
And the wisdom to know the difference.

Thursday:

Begin the day in friendliness,
Be friendly all day long,
Keep in your soul a friendly thought,
In your heart, a friendly song;
Have at the ready a word of cheer
For all who come your way,
And they will greet you too, in turn,
And add smiles to your day.

Friday:

For everything there is a season, and a time
for every matter under heaven:
• a time to be born and a time to die;
• a time to break down and a time
to build up;
• a time to weep and a time to laugh;
• a time to cast away stones, and a time
to gather stones together;
• a time to mourn and a time to dance;
a time to keep and a time to cast away.
— *paraphrased from Ecclesiastes 3:1-8*

Saturday:

Give me a good digestion, Lord
And also something to digest;
Give me a healthy body, Lord,
With sense to keep it at its best.

SCOUTER'S FIVE MINUTES

Give me a sense of humour, Lord,
Grant me the power to see a joke,
To get some pleasure out of life
And pass it on to other folk.
— *prayer found in Chester Cathedral and attributed to Michael, Bishop of St. Albans. Printed originally in **The Scout Leader**, March 1960.*

THOUGHTS ABOUT CHILDREN

If a child lives with criticism
    he learns to condemn;
If a child lives with hostility,
    he learns to fight;
If a child lives with ridicule,
    he learns to be shy;
If a child lives with shame,
    he learns to feel guilty.

If a child lives with tolerance,
    he learns to be patient;
If a child lives with praise,
    he learns to appreciate;
If a child lives with fairness,
    he learns justice;
If a child lives with security,
    he learns to have faith;
If a child lives with approval,
    he learns to like himself;
If a child lives with acceptance
    and friendship,
He learns to find love in the world.
— *author unknown*

SCOUTER'S FIVE MINUTES

Think about it!

...when the adult is reinforced for behaving appropriately, we call it *recognition* but, if a child is reinforced for behaving appropriately, we call it *bribery*! If an adult laughs, we call it *socializing* but, when a child laughs at something funny in school, we call it *misbehaving!* If an adult writes in a book, we call it *doodling* but, if a child writes in a book, we call it *destroying property.* If an adult sticks to something, we call it *perseverance* but, if a child sticks to something, we call it *stubborness.* If an adult seeks help and asks questions, we call at *consulting.* When a child sometimes asks for help, we call it *whining.* If an adult forgets something, we call it *absent-mindedness* but, if a child forgets, we call it *retardation.* If an adult hits a child, we call it *discipline* but, if the child hits another child, we call it *fighting.* And finally, if an adult behaves in an unusual way, we call it *unique* but, if a child behaves in an unusual way, we often refer him for *psychological evaluation.*
— *Tom Acheson: comments made at a workshop on* The Creative Child: *Promise of the '80's (May, 1980).*

If you find you don't much care for one of your patrol leaders, try to bear in mind that he probably has reservations about you, too
— *John Sweet*

Boys want noise: let them have it. When they play, let them play heartily.
— *B.-P.*

Canny Wisdom
Youth is never satisfied with the past; pushing beyond its leaders of yesterday, it endlessly seeks new heroes.

For every boy with a spark of genius, there are a dozen with ignition trouble.

SCOUTER'S FIVE MINUTES

The kids of today answer you back before you've said anything.

Adolescence, like snow, eventually disappears if you ignore it long enough.

Bear in mind that youngsters have one thing in common; they close their ears to advice and open their eyes to example.
— *thanks to Colin McKay and his A canny crack which, regularly appears in* Scouting *magazine (UK).*

It's no good trying to force a boy from his mother's apron strings if you merely tie him to your own belt!
— *unknown*

It is easier to bend a boy
  than to mend a man.
—*B.-P.*

New Season Inspiration
Coming together is a beginning;
Keeping together is progress;
Working together is success.

Prayer: Lord, as we start a new Scouting season, we have hopes and dreams. Help us to get along with each other so that we can fulfill those hopes and dreams. Do not let us lose track of our goals in the newness of these people, this place or this time. Help us to make a new start today, leaving behind yesterday's problems and troubles.
— *Ontario Council Provincial Notes*

A New Member
I see you at the meetings,
But you never say, "Hello,"
You're busy all the time you're there
With those you already know.

SCOUTER'S FIVE MINUTES

I sit amongst the people
Yet I'm a lonesome guy,
The "new members" are all strangers too,
And the "old timers" pass me by.

But, darn it, you people asked me in,
And you talked of fellowship;
You could just step across the room,
But you never make the trip.

Why can't you nod and say, "Hello,"
Or stop to shake my hand,
Then go and sit amongst your friends?
Now, that I'd understand.

I'll be at the next meeting,
Perhaps a nice evening to spend;
Do you think you could introduce yourself?
I want to be your friend.
—*Thanks to Jo Brygider, ADC Beavers, Maple Ridge, B.C.
Author unknown.*

Fantasy Island
Many will be shocked to find,
When the day of judgement nears,
That there's a special place in Heaven
Set aside for Volunteers.
Furnished with big recliners,
Satin couches and footstools,
Where there is no committee chairman,
No group leaders or car pools,
No eager team that needs a coach,
No bazaar and no bake sale,
And nothing at all to staple;
Not one thing to fold or mail.

Scouter's Five Minutes

Telephone lists will be outlawed,
But a finger-snap will bring
Cool drinks and gourmet dinners
And rare treats fit for a king.
You ask, "Who'll serve these privileged few
And work for all they're worth?"
Why, all those who reaped the benefits,
And not once volunteered on earth!
— ***The Logo***, *South Saskatchewan Region*

For Thanksgiving

Last fall, *Veldlore* of South Africa included an authentic Indian feast and grace you might try for a special Thanksgiving. Sit in a circle with the meal in the centre: a cooking pot filled with *Wohanpi* (meat stew) and baskets of *Wigli Aguyapi* (fried bread) and *Wojapi* (fresh fruit, nuts and berries).

O Great Spirit,
Who sends the sun and the rain,
The trees and the birds,
The buffalo and the corn,
And all the gifts of the earth;
We thank Thee, O Great Spirit,
For Thy bounty;
For this food;
For shelter;
And for the friendship among us
That grows like the evergreen leaves. Amen.

SCOUTER'S FIVE MINUTES

Gleanings from 60 years of the Leader

The Scouting Man
Let me live my life like a Scouting man,
With Scout friends good and true;
Let me play the game on the Scouting plan,
And play it all the way through.
Let me win or lose with a Scouting smile,
And never be known to whine;
For that is the regular Scouting style,
And I want to make it mine.
— *March 1929*

Necessary materials for a hike are cooking utensils, food, matches, an axe and a few Scouts.
— *April 1943*

The Best
If you can't be the pine
    on the top of the hill,
Be a scrub in the valley, but be
The best little scrub by the side of the rill;
Be a bush if you can't be a tree.

If you can't be a bush,
    be a bit of the grass
And some highway happier make;
If you can't be a muskie then just be a bass,
But the liveliest bass in the lake.

If you can't be a highway,
    then just be a trail;
If you can't be the sun, be a star:
It isn't by size that you win or you fail;
Be the best of whatever you are.
— *Jan. 1926*

SCOUTER'S FIVE MINUTES

No one could tell me where my soul might be;
I sought for God, but God eluded me;
I sought out my brother and found these three,
My soul, my God and all humanity.
—Apr, 1964

If (with apologies to Rudyard Kipling)

If you can light a fire with soggy matches
While standing in a steady stream of rain,
And see it fizzle out before it catches,
And hold your tongue,
    and light the thing again;

If you can fix a brew for all your brothers,
When they are in their blankets warm and dry,
And rather you got wet than all the others,
And laugh when you are tired enough to cry;

If you can tie a knot that never fails you,
And trust it if the worst comes to the worst,
To save your life
    when nothing else avails you,
But put the other fellow's safety first;

If you can give first aid
    to those who need it,
And treat for shock when you are shaken too,
And though you suffer badly, never heed it,
Until you've done the best that you can do;

If you can go on working when you're weary,
And go on singing till your throat is dry;
If you can meet with sadness and be cheery,
And when you fail, just have another try;

SCOUTER'S FIVE MINUTES

If you can trust your friends
    and those about you,
And yet forgive them if they should forget,
And though the whole world sometimes seems
    to doubt you,
Be loyal to the task which you are set;
If you don't put yourself before the others,
And never your patrol before your troop:
If you salute all races as your brothers
In one united, universal group:

If you can see the aim and help to win it,
And never falter till the job is done;
Yours is the earth and all that's in it,
And, what's more, you'll be a Scout, my son!
— *M. Hill, December 1949*

Lord of the far horizon,
Give us the eyes to see,
Over the verge of sundown
The beauty that is to be.
— *May 1941*

The 23rd Psalm — An Indian Translation

The Great Father above is a Shepherd Chief,
    and I am his, and with Him I want not.
He throws out to me a rope,
    and the name of the rope is Love.
He draws me, and He draws me and He draws
    me to where the grass is green
    and the water is not dangerous,
And I eat and lie down satisfied.
Sometimes my heart is very weak
    and falls down, but He lifts it up again,
    and draws me into a good road.

SCOUTER'S FIVE MINUTES

His name is wonderful.
Sometimes, it may be very soon,
>   it may be longer,
>   it may be a long, long time
He will draw me into
>   a place between mountains.
It is dark there, but I will not draw back;
I will not be afraid, for it is in there
>   between these mountains
>   that the Shepherd will meet me,
And the hunger I have felt in my heart
>   all through this life will be satisfied.
Sometimes He makes the Love rope into
>   a whip, but afterwards He gives me a staff
>   that I may lean on.
He spreads a table before me
>   with kinds of food.
He puts His hand upon my head,
>   all "tired" is gone.
My cup He fills it till it runs over.
What I tell you is true. I lie not.
These roads that are a way ahead
>   will stay with me through life
And afterwards I will go to live
>   in the Big Teepee,
And sit down with the Shepherd Chief
>   forever.

Let peace encircle all the world
Let men walk hand in hand
A living bond of Brotherhood
A voice from land to land.

Scouter's Five Minutes

The Meaning of Christmas
To some, Christmas means presents,
To others a Christmas tree;
To some it may mean a party —
That's not what it means to me.
To some it may mean brand new clothes,
Or candy and cake and tea;
To some it may mean another good time —
That's not what it means to me.
We do receive presents on Christmas,
We have a Christmas tree, too
But to me Christmas means
    the Christ child's birth.
Is that what it means to you?

Like silver lamps in a distant shrine
    The stars are sparkling bright,
The bells of the City of God ring out,
    For the Son of Mary is born tonight.

Tonight
The door is on the latch tonight,
The hearth-fire is aglow,
I seem to hear soft passing feet
    The Christ child in the snow:
My heart is open wide tonight
For stranger, kith or kin;
I would not bar a single door
Where love might enter in.

A Christmas Wish for Everyone
Something to do;
Someone to love;
Something to hope for.
— *Kant's **Three Rules for Happiness***

SCOUTER'S FIVE MINUTES

A Cub's Meditation during Prayer

Well, God, here we are again and we've all taken our caps off. I don't know why — Akela's never told us. All I know is that if you forget, Bagheera knocks it off the back of your head. Akela keeps her hat on — I don't get it.

First we are told to concentrate and think about talking to You, and then we're told to shut our eyes. I don't get that either. I find it easier to concentrate if I can see what's going on. When I asked, I was told you just *had* to close your eyes.

We always have to stand up, too. We listen to all the notices sitting in the circle and then, for some reason, we have to stand up. As soon as we stand up and shut our eyes, Jimmy starts trying to pinch my cap with his foot. I have to watch him all the time. Last week, Akela shouted because we were spotted moving during prayers.

At least it isn't for long. Akela usually reads a quick prayer about being good and then we chant the Lord's Prayer. Jimmy always tries to reach the end before the rest of us. We say the Lord's Prayer at school every day, too. I don't understand the middle bit. I don't think I've ever trespassed.

We always do it at the end, too — just when I'm tired out and ready for a cup of cocoa and tied. I don't mean to be rude when I hop from foot to foot. It's just that I'm tired and I can hear the cars arriving outside.

Sometimes Akela says there isn't time to talk to You because there are too many notices. But we always fit the Grand Howl in somehow.

What! Sorry Akela, I didn't realize. I was just thinking — no, not daydreaming. I was talking to God in my own way.

Well, cheerio, God. We'll be here again next week doing the same thing I suppose. I want to do my best for You but I don't know how. I want somebody to help me. Please.

— *Scouting (UK) June 1983*

SCOUTER'S FIVE MINUTES

Alas, Poor Scapegoat, Thy Name is Leader
If a leader writes a letter... It is too long.
If he sends a postcard ... It is too short.
If he sends a bulletin ... It is too expensive.
If he calls a meeting... He is wasting time.
If he does not call a meeting.
> He is a "know it all".

If attendance at the meeting is slack ...
> He should have phoned all the members.

If he does telephone them. He is a pest.
If he asks where the money went ...
> He is insulting.

If he does not ... He is not interested.
If a function is a huge success ...
> The Committee gets the praise.

If it is a failure ... He is to blame.
If he asks for advice ... He is incompetent.
If he does not. He is trying to run the show.
> Ashes to ashes, dust to dust,
> If the others won't do it,
> The leader must.

— *thanks to Jo Brygider & 1st Laity View*

If God is for us,
then who can be against us?

Promise & Prayer
We found these ideas, used for a Scout-Guide ecumenical church service in Southern Alberta, in *Scoutlook,* the region's bulletin. A Venturer and a Ranger alternately spoke the lines of the promise, and all representatives of the two movements joined in for the prayer.

V: We have promised
R: As Brownies, Beavers, Cubs, Guides, Scouts, Rangers, Venturers and Rovers

Scouter's Five Minutes

V: To do our best
R: What we are able to do, whenever we can and in the best way that we know
V: To love and serve God
R: To be active daily in our religion
V: To do our duty to our Queen and our country
R: To be truly loyal in our thoughts and actions
V: To help other people
R: To be of service and to aid other peoples in need of help
V: To keep our laws
R: To understand and try to keep our standards of life.
V: Would everyone join in this prayer...
All: O Father, we pray for Thy blessing on those whom Thou has joined together in the brotherhood of Scouting and sisterhood of Guiding. Grant that we may all so work and play, think and pray together, that we may be more perfectly fitted to serve Thee in the daily calls of duty. Help us to look wide: fill us with high ideals: inspire us with love and good will to all mankind.
Amen

If

This poem was written by Guide Vanessa Scolt of Calcutta, India. We thank Scouter Noshir S. Wadia, also of Calcutta, for sharing it with Canadian Scouters.

If all the folk alive today
    Be either Guide or Scout,
The world would be a better place,
    Of that, I have no doubt.
In trust we'd live as one big clan
    Where truth shall reign supreme,
Deceit an alien word to man,
    Of it he'd never dream.

SCOUTER'S FIVE MINUTES

Friends we'd be to one and all,
    To the poor, the sick, the old,
Castle and creed no obstacle,
    On us, they'd have no hold.

Love for each four-footed friend
    Would certainly increase,
All brutal cruelty would end;
    These friends, too, would be at peace.

If all the folk alive today
    Be either Guide or Scout,
The world would be a wonderful place —
    Of this, do you have a doubt?

Prayer

God of my brother across the sea,
God of the stranger next to me,
God of a world-wide brotherhood —
Grant me the grace to cast aside
The differences that but divide,
And see in all the true and good.

The House with Gold Windows

Once upon a time, a young boy named David lived in a small cottage on top of a hill. Most of the time, David was very happy as he herded the family's goats or gathered fuel or helped in the garden. His parents were very poor and had to work hard, but they loved him very much. From them he'd learned to love the sights and smells of the mountain meadows, the music of the wind and the birds, and the silent companionship of shy wild creatures.

But sometimes David was lonely, and wished he had a friend to play with. Sometimes he didn't want to do his work, and wished his parents were richer. At these times he'd remember the trip to the village he'd made with his father a long time ago. He'd remember the shops filled with toys, books and puzzles and the well-dressed boys

SCOUTER'S FIVE MINUTES

he saw playing with colourful balls and hoops and toy boats and balloons. Why can't I be like other boys, and have store-bought toys and lots of time to play with them?" he'd grumble.

One evening, after a long day's work, David sat on top of his hill looking down into the valley and feeling very sorry for himself. The sun was setting behind him when he noticed, far down in the valley, another house a marvellous house with gold windows which glittered and glowed as the sun settled lower and lower in the sky.

"The boy who lives in a house with gold windows must be very rich," thought David.

Right then and there he decided that, the very next day, he would go down into the valley to meet such a boy. Maybe they would become friends, and the boy would invite David to stay in the beautiful house, and the two of them would play with toys all day long.

Very early the next morning, David started to walk down into the valley. But the house with gold windows was farther away than he thought, and he walked and walked all day. Finally, as evening was falling, he reached the house. His heart sank.

Now that he could see it, he found the fine, rich house was only an abandoned shepherd's cottage. When he peeked through the door, he could see that, more recently, animals had used it for shelter. And the beautiful gold windows were rain-streaked and grey with dust and cobwebs.

Feeling foolish and very tired, his mouth dry and his tummy growling, David curled up on the stoop and cried himself to sleep.

When he woke up, cold and stiff, the morning sun was rising behind him. Hungry and a little scared, he looked out across the valley and up the hill to remind himself how far he would have to walk that day. And there, at the top of the hill, he saw his house a marvellous house with gold windows which sparkled and winked at him as the sun climbed higher and higher into the sky.

David rubbed his eyes and looked again at his house. He began to smile. With a bit of a skip and a happy grin, he started towards home.

— *a story by C.L. Paddock, retold by Linda Florence*

SCOUTER'S FIVE MINUTES

Beaver Cheer

Beavers, Beavers
(clap hands twice behind back)
One, Two, Three,
(hold up one, two, three fingers)
Sharing, Sharing (outstretched arms)
With you and me (point to you & me)
Yea (squat in chopping position)
Beavers! (jump up, arms stretched high)
— *Rainbow Mary McCarroll, 1st Dundalk Beavers, Ontario*

Handshake

The universe is so complex,
The brightest intellects admit,
They cannot see the full design
Nor where the varied pieces fit:
But this I know; one human hand,
Whether of stranger or brother,
Dark or light, old or young,
Fits beautifully into another.
— *Thanks to* ***The Outlook,*** *B.C./ Yukon*

Trees

I have the dream of the whole earth made green again, an earth healed and made whole through the efforts of children: children of all nations planting trees to express their special understanding of the earth as their home; children of all races holding hands, circling the earth, expressing and celebrating their special understanding of all children as their brothers and sisters.
— *Dr. Richard St. Barbe Baker, founder of the Men of the Trees movement (1922) and friend of B.-P.*

SCOUTER'S FIVE MINUTES

Ten Little Campers: or Safety Pays
Ten little campers walking in a line,
One found some poison ivy,
And then there were nine.

Nine little campers,
   running 'cause they're late,
One ran too far too fast,
And then there were eight.
Eight little campers looking up to heaven,
One tripped on a rock,
And then there were seven.

Seven little campers,
   fishing just for kicks,
One fell overboard,
And then there were six.

Six little campers poking 'round a hive,
One stirred up a hornet's nest,
And then there were five.

Five little campers
   watching their kites soar,
A kite fell on a hydro line,
And then there were four.

Four little campers, stopping off for tea,
One poured gas onto the fire,
And then there were three.

Three little campers
   swimming somewhere new,
One dove into the lake,
And then there were two.

Scouter's Five Minutes

Two little campers lying in the sun,
One stayed out too long,
And then there was one.

One little camper had many happy days,
His vacation was the best,
    'Cause safety always pays!

I love to think of nature as an unlimited broadcasting station through which God speaks to us every hour, if we only will tune in.
— George Washington Carver

The New Pathfinders
Far away from the avenues of asphalt,
From the city smog and the spewing, sooted smoke-stacks,
There runs a rutted gravel road;
A wooded winding trail no wider than a cowpath
Breaks away from the road off toward the forest.
It meanders over meadow, glen and river valley.
Often losing itself entirely in the trees
Or piles of glacial rock:
It re-emerges at the base of a crashing waterfall
Or on a bluff overlooking a rapids-chiseled gorge.

Chipmunks dart from a hollow log along this
    weed-choked track
And disappear in a forest of fiddlehead ferns:
Cottontail, box-turtle, partridge —
All stop to stare
At an odd, noisy procession marching along.
Dressed in uniform of sylvan green.

Like a perky little family of bob-white
They zig-zag and hop and skirt around tangles of briar,
Stopping to inspect rotting logs festooned with scaly fungi;

SCOUTER'S FIVE MINUTES

Rosy-cheeked and chattering, they're small replicas of their guide
Who breaks trail and leads them in happy song.

Deeper in they go, until the noises of settlement are forgotten,
Until time and place can only be told in the stars overhead.
Then, in a ritual as ancient as the caves of Folsom,
A spark is ignited, cheeks grow red, eyes widen in wonder;
Small, pudgy hands link in the dark:
Laughter chases away, for a time, all the old fears;
Voices unite, vows are sworn, friendships sealed.

These are the new Davy Crockets, David Thompsons, Thompson Setons;
The blood of the red man and the pioneer runs through their veins;
The forest is their New World; the streams their Nile:
They're the new map-makers, the trail-blazers;
So, as they pass in a file, cheer them on their way.
They're looking for old answers; they're hunting for the truth:
They're us and not us: they're everything we ever hoped to be;
They'll clear a path through to morning:
They'll conquer the heights;
They'll carry their spirit to the farthest ends of the earth:
And if we let them, they'll poke their stubby little fingers
Into the very eye of the universe itself.
— *Leslie D. Bachmeier, Leamington, Ont.*

The Crow Man Who Stole Fire

This legend from eastern Australia has a lot of possibilities as campfire fare. It not only tells how the world learned the secret of fire but also includes creepy things a good storyteller can play up (the snakes, for example); an origin legend about the Pleiades (Seven

SCOUTER'S FIVE MINUTES

Sisters constellation) you can relate to summer star-gazing at camp; and a story about the crow and his harsh voice — often a familiar sound around the campsite.

In early times, the only people who knew how to make fire were seven women, and they refused to share their secret. The Crow Man, Wakala, very much wanted to know the secret. He made friends with the women, and joined them as they moved about to gather food.

As he travelled with the women, Wakala learned that they carried their fire in the ends of their digging sticks. He also learned that termites were one of their favourite foods. Most important, he learned that they were terrified of snakes.

Knowing this, he came up with a plan. He buried a nest of snakes in a termite mound, and then told the women he'd found termites for them. When the women poked into the mound, they disturbed the snakes and, terrified, thrashed wildly at them with their digging sticks. They managed to kill many of the wiggling reptiles but, as they swung their sticks, they sent sparks flying from the tips.

This was just what Wakala had expected and he was ready. He quickly caught some of the sparks between two pieces of bark, then fled to his own camp and kindled a fire with them. The women, furious at losing their exclusive ownership of fire, rose into the sky where they became the constellation called the Seven Sisters.

But Wakala was no better than they. He refused to share the fire with anyone. If people approached to ask for some fire, he mocked them with a harsh, "Wah, wah!" They pleaded and argued with him, and he became more and more quarrelsome and evil-tempered.

One day, when men once again bothered him for his fire, Wakala completely lost his temper. In a fit of rage, he threw some coals at the men. Although he hit none of them, he started a raging bushfire that raced through his camp and burned him to death.

When the fire burned down, the men sombrely returned and, as they gazed at Wakala's charred body, were surprised to see it tremble

Scouter's Five Minutes

and come to life. In a flick of an eye, it changed into a crow and flew to the upper branches of a tree. There it sat, mocking them with Wakala's harsh call:

"Wah! Wah! Wah!"

Campfire Cheers
Desert Fruit Cheer — YUCCA, YUCCA, YUCCA!

Seal of Approval — Put forearms together from elbows to wrists and flap hands together while yelling, "Urk, Urk, Urk!" like a seal.
— *Thanks to Sandy Bard, Edmonton, Alta.*

Campfire Closing
Whatever you are, be noble;
Whatever you do, do well;
Whenever you speak, speak kindly;
Spread happiness, wherever you dwell.

• • • • • • • • • • • • • • • • •

Thoughts for Thanksgiving
As we bow heads in thanks for the bounty of our land and lives, it's important to remember that we truly are the fortunate few. Thank you for friendship and Scouting, which offer hope that, one day, all people will find God's world good.

"There are at least 600 million people worldwide who still go to bed hungry every night of their lives. About 800 million people — one in five — now live in 'absolute poverty' ... About 40 percent of them are children. We are told that food consumption will rise faster than output over the next decade and the number of people starving will double.

"We need to ask ourselves how much longer we can seriously believe that two-thirds of the world's people will sit hungry with

SCOUTER'S FIVE MINUTES

folded hands and endure their suffering, while the remaining third of us worry about how we can lose 10 pounds and where we can park our car."
— *Albert Watson, in the **United Church Observer**, June 1983.*

A Beaver Thank You

Thank you for Beavers; we learn how to share
Thank you for leaders who show us they care;
Help us to learn to have fun at our play,
And how to work hard for our family each day;
The world will be much better, we know,
For the love and the friendship we learn how to show.
— *Mary McCarroll, 1st Dundalk Beavers, Ontario*

A Cub Thank You

Heavenly Father, we ask for your blessing
For loved ones and friends who are near,
We thank you for food and for love and for life
And the spirit of Scouting that's here.

Two Special Prayers

*In the March '82 issue of **Scouting (UK)** magazine, we found some prayers written by Cub Scouts in Co Down, England. We think two of them are particularly appropriate.*

God bless Cubs and Scouts all over the world, especially those in troubled countries who cannot get to Cub meetings because of this trouble. God bless those who are short of food. Help all Cubs to be honest and truthful in all their tasks, and help them to keep the Cub Promise.
— *Gavin Dickson, 3rd Newtownards*

Dear God, thank you for my friends who stand by me when I am sad and lonely. Please bless them and lead them through their years on

SCOUTER'S FIVE MINUTES

this earth. Oh Lord, bless all the Cub packs around the world and help them be friendly and considerate to each other.
— *Richard Kelly, 4th Bangor*

Don't walk before me...
I may not be able to follow.
Don't walk behind me...
I may not be able to lead.
Just walk beside me...
And be my friend.
— *Motto of Troop 26, Oklahoma, U.S.A.*

And Then the Rainbow
They came,
Pride in their colours;
Their faces showed expectation:
They came,
The eyes full of wonder
Gleaming, sparkling.
They came,
The smiles — open, sincere;
I saw oneness in our fellowship,
Friendships that no boundary can contain;
A symbol tied us together,
A handshake bound our belief,
A song joined us in spirit,
A promise joined us in our God:
We stood together as one body
Sharing that moment,
Thinking our thoughts,
Meeting our minds.
And God's promise brightened the sky,
Showing hope for the future.
— *by Jeannette to commemorate the opening ceremony, XV World Jamboree. Sent by Catherine Held, North Delta, B.C.*

SCOUTER'S FIVE MINUTES

Looking at Conflict

As we remember those who died in two world wars, the degree of conflict in today's world is a painful reminder that we've made little progress towards lasting peace. Perhaps, in this collection, you'll find ideas to help your young people look at and learn from their own natures and relationships so that they *can* find the way to peace when they take charge.

Nobody knows the age of the human race, but all agree that it is old enough to know better.

The Poppy

The poppy is red and the poppy is green.
The poppy remembers the tragic scene
Of men and women who died at war,
And how they suffered in blood and gore.
And how they fought and risked their lives
To bring us peace throughout our lives.
In Flanders Field the poppies bloom
Where many people met their doom;
On Remembrance Day, we wear with pride
The poppy red for those who died.
— *Scout Timothy MacTavish, 12, Coleville, Saskatchewan.*

You've seen it in your section — a couple of boys who've become enemies. Put this limerick on a card and, when you notice the two "going at it" give them the card to read together.
There once were two cats of Kilkenny
Each thought there was one cat too many;
So they fought and they fit,
And they scratched and they bit,
'Til, excepting their nails and the tips of their tails
Instead of two cats, there weren't any!

SCOUTER'S FIVE MINUTES

See the worst, but look at the best. Don't expect to find any man perfect. He is bound to have defects. Any ass can see the bad points in a man. The thing is to discover his good points and keep these uppermost in your mind so that they gradually obliterate the bad ones.
— *from B.-P.'s Outlook*

Small boys throw stones at frogs in jest. The frogs do not die in jest; they die in earnest. — *Aristotle*

Prayers
I'm a Beaver, God, still little yet,
But I'll try with all my might and main.
If I get mad at a friend some time,
Please help me make things right again.

Dear God, give me the patience to hold my temper when nothing goes right. When my friends put snow down my back or a frog in my bed, help me remember that there will be days when I'll look back at these special times with longing. Help me remember these golden times when my friends are there when I need them. Help me repay them with all the kindness they have given me; presents to treasure, tears and laughter to remember. Thank You God for bringing these people into my life. May they be as happy to know me as I am to know them.
— *Author Unknown*

Our prayer is that men everywhere will learn finally to live as brothers, to respect each other's differences, to heal each other's wounds, to promote each other's progress and to benefit from each other's knowledge...
— *Adlai E. Stevenson*

SCOUTER'S FIVE MINUTES

Young People and God
*From Peter Ball, the Bishop of Lewes and Anglican religious consultant to the Scout Association in the United Kingdom. Excerpted from an article in the August, 1984 issue of **Scouting (UK)** magazine.*

"If we are to try to teach spiritual awareness, or the opening of the eyes of the young to God, the first thing that needs to be said is that we must learn from them.

"I visited a Primary School for their harvest festival. I had a sermon all lined up but, as I processed into the school hall in cope and mitre, I knew that my sermon was all wrong. Instead, surrounded by all those simple gifts, I simply asked the children to pick up the fruit".

"First we looked intently at a tomato, then an orange followed by an apple and a potato. We experienced the colours and the shapes. Then we felt each one and enjoyed the varieties of their taste. We then smelled each one and the children began giggling and shifting around in sheer delight. We shook each item and tried to hear the rattling of the ripe pips in the apples and, inevitably, the tomatoes could be heard squelching! But, by this time, the children were beginning to wonder and their eyes were beginning to open to where worship, the reverence and loving regard of God begins".

"When I was a curate...I was sent into the Church school to teach. I used to play a game that I called, 'The Prayer Game' with the 10 year olds. We would read a Gospel story, perhaps the feeding of the five thousand, and I would ask the children to close their eyes for 30 seconds and 'see' the scene in their imaginations. They could all see Jesus on a mound and the Galilean lake below, next to the colourful crowd. I then asked them to close their eyes again and discover what they could hear. They could hear the swish of the women's dresses or the sound of the sea. One young lad said, 'I can hear the sound of crusty brown bread being broken.' That was good. Finally, they closed their eyes to find out what they could smell.

SCOUTER'S FIVE MINUTES

Three-day old fish were always a favourite discovery and one small boy whispered that he could smell grass that had been crushed by being trodden on or sat on".

"These are just a few thoughts and ideas. The first thing is for us to realize that, by doing these things, we are allowing the young to know about God Himself, who is the source and the centre of life — the God of prayer and of love... In this way we shall have imparted the best gift of all."

Merry Christmas Around the World

In Germany, it's *Fröehliche Weihnachten;* in Denmark *Glaedelig Jul*. In the Netherlands, they say *Hartelijke Kerstroeten* in Sweden *Gud Jul* and in Finland *Jauskaa Joulua*. You'll hear *Gledelig Jul* in Norway and *Hristos Razdajetsja* in Russia. In Mexico and Spain it's *Feliz Navidad*. Italians wish each other *Buon Natale* while, in Greece, it's time to say *Eftihismena Christougenna. Happy Christmas* in England: *Joyeux Nöel* or *Merry Christmas* in Canada — no matter what the words, the meaning is the same: warm wishes to all in this season of joy and hope.

Fingers & Hands — Working Together

A Game

Give everyone five or six toothpicks each. Ask them to pick up the first toothpick between two thumbs; the second between the pointer fingers; the third between the middle fingers; the fourth between the ring fingers and the fifth between the little fingers. They'll have some fun accomplishing the trick, and you'll have an opening to your story.

SCOUTER'S FIVE MINUTES

A Story
To start, hold up a Bible on the tips of the fingers of one hand. Keep the other hand quiet at your side until it pops up for its part at the end of the story. Set down the Bible and begin.

A bunch of fingers were arguing amongst themselves one day. The first finger said, "I am the most important. I'm the First Finger. I point." *(Point at someone)*

"I'm the most important," said the Second Finger "I'll prove it! Come on all of you, stand up beside me. There now. Who's the tallest? See — I am, so that proves I must be the most important!"

"You're both wrong," said the Third Finger. "I'm the most important because I'm the best looking. I wear the ring, so I'm the most important.

"Oh no, you're not," the Little Finger piped up. "I may be little, but I know I'm the best because I can get into all the awkward places." *(Point to ear, then nose)*

The thumb had been listening carefully to all of this and finally stood up. "If you're as important as all of you say you are, then try this," the thumb said. "Pick up this book." *(Each finger tries to pick up the Bible, with predictable results and appropriate moans and groans. You might get the boys involved here.)*

"I'll tell you what," said the thumb, finally. "Let me help." *(The thumb helps each finger in turn, and each makes a comment: e.g. "See — I knew I could do it!", etc., to which the thumb replies quietly, "Yes, with a little help.")*

"Now," said the thumb. "Isn't that better? If, instead of arguing, you all joined together, just think what you'd be. Why with God's help, you'd be a Hand! And then you'd be able to do anything." *(Pick up Bible in one hand. Suddenly, the other hand comes to life.)*

"Hey, I'm a Hand," cried the other hand. "That's a great story, but it isn't over, yet. There are a lot of things one hand can do, but some things can only be done by two!" *(Set down Bible, clap hands and get everyone clapping. Then offer your left hand to a boy for the Scout handshake. End with all shaking hands).*

SCOUTER'S FIVE MINUTES

A Prayer
Dear God,
I see Your Hand in everything around me,
I feel it in the touch of my family and friends,
I know the paths you show aren't always easy,
I need Your Hand to guide me:
Please help me use my hands wisely
To take care of Your world and help other people,
To reach out in friendship, every day of my life.
Amen

Laws For Me When I Grow Up
"I will have the poor people to be rich as we are, and they ought by rights to be happy as we are, and all who go across the crossings shall give the poor crossing sweeper some money and you ought to thank God for what He has given us and He made the poor people to be poor and the rich people to be rich and I can tell you how to be good. Now I will tell you. You must pray to God whenever you can but you cannot be good with only praying but you must try very hard to be good."
—B.-P., Feb. 26, 1865

The Spirit Lives On
Oh where are all the knobby knees,
The mushroom hats, things built of trees?
The strangled bugle bands that beat
For marching Scouts with two left feet?
Oh where are all the howling packs
That Dybbed and Dobbed with crouching backs?
Akela's wild and screaming horde
Who never thought to say, "I'm bored."

Scouter's Five Minutes

Are all these gone like morning dew
Burned up when sun breaks forth anew?
Has our great Founder's dream been lost?
Have modern times blunted its thrust?

Not so! reverberates the shout
From smallest Cub to senior Scout.
From all four corners of the globe.
From many nations new and old.

To do our best is still our aim.
Personal achievement, that's the GAME:
No need to ask, "Who lost? Who won?"
B.-P.'s spirit still lives on!
— *by Peter Murphy, 1st Kanata "B" Troop, Ont.*

Prayer
"Give us, O God, the vision which can see Thy love in the world in spite of human failure. Give us the faith to trust Thy goodness in spite of our ignorance and weakness. Give us the knowledge that we may continue to pray with understanding hearts, and show us what each one of us can do to set forward the coming of universal peace."
— *Astronaut Frank Borman while on his moon orbiting mission*

International Campfire Ideas — Australia

Opening
When the sands of the desert are burning
And the billabong's dusty and dry,
Then, cobbers, the tribes will all gather
For coroboree under the sky;
So lay down your boomerangs, cobbers.
For coroboree under the sky.

Scouter's Five Minutes

Closing
Now coroboree's over, but friendship
Will bind us as brothers: and though
The Abbos will scatter, our council
Is strong, wherever we go.
While love, peace and brotherhood bind us.
As we gather beneath the stars,
Walkabout, coroboree, friendship.
To the dreamtime, will always be ours.

Songs
Waltzing Matilda: Tie Me Kangaroo Down: Ging Gang Gooli

Words & Phrases
beaut: lovely, fine
billabong: large pool in a dry river bed
billy: covered cook pot
cobber: friend, buddy
coroboree: council, jamboree
crook: no good, spoiled
damper: soda bread cooked on a stick over the fire
Pommie: English
squatter: station owner, boss
My word!: expression of surprise (Golly!)
swagman: tramp
walkabout: migration, hike, trek
swag: blanket roll
abbo: short for aborigine
jumbuck: sheep
didgeree do: musical instrument
too right: right on
Proper muck-up/Fair cow: terrible mess

SCOUTER'S FIVE MINUTES

Italian Campfire

Opening
O Drummer, summon the Legions;
Send the call o'er valley and hill,
For council we take round our campfire
And friendship; listen, who will:
Let friendship be our clear watchword,
Let us join in the campfire's light
Our hands, to show we are brothers
Forever, as we are tonight.

Closing
The legions have marched and then vanished.
The travellers journeyed afar,
But we in the twilight have gathered,
Our lodestone a twinkling star;
We have friendship, firelight and laughter.
And flames that are both warm and bright,
So that song and story and worship
Will make us feel safe through the night.

Songs
On Top of Spaghetti: Papa Picallino: Que Sera, Sera

Phrases
Giovane Esploratore (Boy Scout); *amici* (friend); *fuoco* (fire); *pasto* (meal); *pranzo* (dinner); *campeggio* (camping); *nuotare* (swim); *nuotaore* (swimmer); *viaggio* (journey); *vagabondare* (hike); *e ora di andare a letto* (time for bed); *arrivederci* (be seeing you).
—*Many thanks to Joan Kearley, Thorburn, Nova Scotia*

SCOUTER'S FIVE MINUTES

Grab Bag

For Leaders: Calorie Counter

To find out how easy it can be to get in shape for summer, check this chart showing the number of calories burned in these common activities.

Beating around the bush	75
Climbing the walls	150
Passing the buck	25
Dragging your heels	100
Bending over backwards	75
Running around in circles	350
Climbing the ladder of success	750
Jumping to conclusions	100
Swallowing your pride	50
Throwing your weight around	50-300
Pushing your luck	250
Making mountains out of molehills	500

Nothing to it, eh'? No wonder we all look so good!
— *With thanks to KIN magazine.*

For Cubs

The next time the pack has company, try this lead in to the Grand Howl.

We're members of the Wolf Cub pack.
And this is our night to howl.
When the moon shines bright
On the hills so black *(point upwards)*
You'll find us out on the prowl: *(lean forward; make prowling motion with paws)*

SCOUTER'S FIVE MINUTES

Our claws are sharp *(hold up hands, crook fingers)*
Our fangs are clean, *(point an index finger at each corner of mouth and grin)*
Our fur is brushed, as can be seen; *(remove caps, bow to show hair)*
Our ears are cocked for every sound, *(wiggle two fingers at each ear)*
We put our noses to the ground.
And Howl... Howl... Howl! *(Take Grand Howl position heads low; raise heads and howl three times.)*
— *Rev. Don Hester, Naicom: from* **Northern News,** *North Saskatchewan Region.*

For Scouts: Our Flag
(Stand by the Canadian flag holding two pieces of cloth: one red, one white.)

What is our flag? Simply a Piece of cloth? Sure, these pieces of cloth could make a Canadian flag, but would they then be simply pieces of cloth? Think of our flag flying from a tall staff— a symbol of our country and the principles for which we stand.

Our flag took the white background of the two original flags planted on our land to remind us of our history and our two founding nations. Bordering the white that represents our great land are two bands of red, symbol of the rising and setting sun and a reminder of our national motto: *From Sea to Sea*. The single red maple leaf in the centre is our country's emblem, symbol of valour, sacrifice and unity.

Red for valour; white for truth — may our flag make us conscious of the greatness of our land and the unconquerable will of its people. As it reflects our past, may it help us realize our duty and obligation to our future.

Do you see anything in these pieces of cloth by themselves to demand your respect? You could make them into an apron just as easily as a flag. You could mop the floor or wipe your shoes with them. But, make them into our flag and they represent our great nation and everything we stand for.
— *Guy Mandeville, Kingston, Ont.*

SCOUTER'S FIVE MINUTES

International Youth Year Prayer
May men, with the help of God, build up throughout 1985, united communities of participation, development and peace.

Think Truly
Think truly, and thy thoughts
Shall the world's family feed;
Speak truly, and each word of thine
Shall be a fruitful seed;
Live truly, and thy life
thall be a great and noble creed.

Prayer from the West Indies
Oh God, who has made the earth so varied and cast the races of man in so many different molds, we who live in these lovely islands of the western sea pray for all your children. Grant that we, ...with all men everywhere. may enter into the full joyous life of Your Kingdom.
—*from **Scouting (UK)** magazine, Jan. '82.*

Lord's Prayer for Beavers
Our Father who art in heaven, and who art very near to us,
Help us to keep thy name holy, and never to use it in wrong ways;
Help us to do what you want us to, as the angels do in heaven;
Give us this day the food we need, and may we help to feed the hungry;
Forgive us when we are naughty as we forgive those who are naughty to us;
Keep us from wanting to do wrong and help us to do right;
For thine is the kingdom and the glory and the power, forever and ever Amen.
—*A favourite from Jack Adair, B.C.*

SCOUTER'S FIVE MINUTES

Friendship: from India
There is beauty in the earth,
The mountains high, the valleys green,
The rippling brook, the waterfall,
The wild sweet rose so oft unseen;
The song of birds, the smell of spring
Autumn colours bright and gay,
A thousand treasures we can find
If we but look about each day;
Yes, gracious is the bounty
That God to man does send;
Then, as a crowning glory.
God gave to man — a friend.

Closing Ceremony Thoughts
May I grow in character and ability as I grow in size.
May I be honest with myself and others in what I do and say.
May I always honour my parents, my elders and my leaders.
May I develop high moral principles and the courage to live by them.
May I strive for health in body, mind and spirit.
May I always respect the rights of others.
May I set a good example so that others may enjoy and profit from my company.
May I give honest effort to my work.
May I learn things that will help me make life better for every living thing in God's beautiful world.

Around a Canadian Campfire
Opening
Near the waters, near the reedbeds,
Near the wigwam, O my brothers,
We will light our evening campfire,
Light the red flower of the forest,
That her leaves and petals rising
Call us to our friendly council.

SCOUTER'S FIVE MINUTES

Closing
As we watch the red flower dying,
Red and golden petals fading,
Grey of ashes in our campfire,
Grey of evening close our council.
— *Joan Kearley, Thorburn, N.S.*

Three Closing Benedictions
Great Chief of the Universe, guide us till we meet again. (Arms and faces up-raised; lowered slowly)

May the Great Spirit of all good spirits be with you now and forever more.

May the Great Spirit bring sunshine and happiness into the hearts of all big and little braves now and forever in great measure.

Lord's Prayer *(Translated from Chinook)*
Our father who stayeth in the above
Good in our hearts be Thy name,
Good Thou Chief among all people
Good Thy will upon earth
As in the above.
Give us every day our food;
If we do evil,
Be not Thou very angry, and if
Anyone evil towards us
Not we angry towards them
Send away far from us all evil.

A Scouter's Legacy (Tune: *The Rose*)
When I joined the game of Scouting
And some friends were at my side;
Dreams came true at every outing,
With the Scout Law as my guide.

SCOUTER'S FIVE MINUTES

For B.-P. gave inspiration,
"Be Prepared" and to "Look Wide";

Brotherhood with many nations
Filled my heart with joy and pride.
Till my boyhood days were over,
Found adventures on the trail;
From a Beaver to a Rover
With a trust that did not fail.
I remembered all the pleasure
That the Scouters brought to me:
I resolved to share this treasure
As a leader yet to be.

Then one night a boy was speaking.
Promised me to do his best,
And I knew that he was seeking
What had been my cherished quest;
I would help him find his way
Through the years that he might roam,
So I'll live in him each day
After God has called me home.
— *by Bud Jacobi, St. Catharines. Ont.*

A World of Insight
Things change so fast these days, you can't be wrong all the time even if you try.
— *Colin McKay,* **Scouting (UK)**

If Scouting is to remain stable, we've all got to work like horses.
— **Scouting in New South Wales**

A leader is a person who finds out where everybody is heading, then shuffles around to get in front!
— **Scout**, *Australia*

Scouter's Five Minutes

All things come to him who waits, but if you go after them, you get the pick.
— *Scouting in New South Wales*

Why God Made Boys

God made a world out of his dreams
Of magic mountains, oceans and streams.
Prairies and plains and wooded land;
Then paused and thought, "I need someone to stand
On top of the mountains, to conquer the seas,
Explore the plains and climb the trees;
Someone to start out small, and grow
Sturdy, strong like a tree: and so
He created boys, full of spirit and fun.
To explore and conquer, to romp and run
With dirty faces, banged-up shins,
Flashing eyes and great wide grins.
When he completed the task He'd begun,
He surely said. "That's a job well done!
— *from Jean Layman, North Halton Region, Ont.*

Gilwell 84

As strangers we together met
But friends we soon became,
And finally we were brothers,
Our concern for youth the same;
More than forty under training,
And fun was had by all,
Under sunny skies and in the rain
On Gilwell in the fall;
Beaver Lions, Beaver Mushrooms,
The Red Six, Green and Blue,
The stars of Orion's Company,
Patrols Haida and Hagar II;
Canoeing in the dark of night,

Scouter's Five Minutes

Trips up and down the hill,
The lodge, the campfires, the trainers,
Memories our only bill.
I pray the Lord remind us
In the years that are to come,
The reason we came together
Was more than just for fun;
And if our shadow should cross the path
And help to mold one child,
Then my friends, it will be worth all
And we'll see it in his smile.
— *by Venturer Advisor Rob Rogers, Greater Victoria Region, B.C.*

Needs
You need enough happiness to keep you serene;
Enough troubles to make you strong;
Enough suffering to make you human;
Enough hopes to keep you optimistic;
Enough failures to keep you humble;
Enough success to keep you confident;
Enough friends to give you comfort;
Enough enthusiasm to make you dare boldly;
Enough faith to banish depression;
Enough love to keep you young in heart;
Enough time to sing your joy;
And enough peace to keep you happy.
— The Needs of Human Beings, *Dr. Klies,* ***Scouting (UK)****, Jan. '85.*

A Thought
Freedom is not worth having if it does not include the freedom to make mistakes.
— *Mohandas Gandhi*

SCOUTER'S FIVE MINUTES

Prayer

Our Father, who art in heaven and who art on earth, even journeying with your people, thank you for being faithful and for never abandoning us. When we are in the wilderness, guide us through and out. When we are lost, please find us. When we cry out, please hear us — in the name of the One who said. "Lo, I am with you always." Amen

—from Meditation *by Bruce Miles,* ***Presbyterian Record****, Mar. '85*

A Tribute

At camp on July 13, 1985, long-time contributor, Scouter Bud Jacobi of St. Catharines, Ontario, was called home. A dedicated Scouter for 35 years, Bud made his first **Leader** contributions to the Jan. '54 issue. One was a letter suggesting topics it might be helpful for the magazine to cover — topics he then helped it cover with his many submissions over the years, most recently *When Kids Become a Pain* and the song *A Scouter's Legacy* (J/J'85). The other was his poem *Look Wide* which we felt captured the spirit of Scouting's 75th anniversary and printed again in the Feb. '82 issue.

In June, Bud sent us a brand new song — his words set to an old German folk tune. Shortly after his death, his wife Wendy invited us to share it with you. "He used this song at his last camp and was very proud of it." she said. "The children enjoyed it tremendously."

Thanks to Mrs. Jacobi, we are pleased to share *The Magic of Camp Life* in memory of a valued contributor, a good man and a very fine Scouter. God bless and keep you, Bud.

SCOUTER'S FIVE MINUTES

The Magic of Camp Life

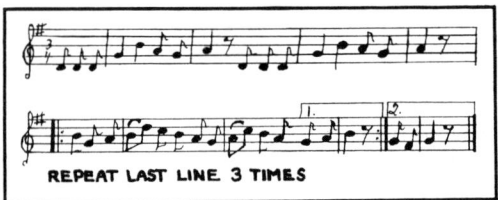

**The Magic of Camp Life
by Bud Jacobi**

From far and wide to camp we roam
To find a home away from home;
We camp together
In every weather
And share our dreams.

We meet in friendship through the years,
We talk about our hopes and fears;
But with each other
We soon discover
A sense of peace.

In spite of country, class or creed
We're campers all in thought and deed:
The joy, of sharing
The love of caring
Brings harmony.

As nature's wonders soon we know,
Then very close to God we grow;

SCOUTER'S FIVE MINUTES

Among our pleasures
Are cherished treasures
As memories.

Prayer
God's light surrounds us.
God's love enfolds us,
God's power protects us,
God's presence watches over us;
Wherever we are, God is.

A Special Christmas Closing
Christingle Oranges are a craft Cubs make along with you as you tell a short yarn for your closing ceremony at the meeting just before Christmas. Ask everyone to bring an orange and a birthday candle from home. When they gather in the circle, give each several colourful jelly candies, four toothpicks, a piece of sticky tape and a strip of foil. Ask them to watch what you do as you talk and do the same with their materials.

Hold up the orange and look at it. It's round with bumps and depressions — like the earth. Your opening words might be: "A long time ago on a winter's night in a lowly stable in Bethlehem, Jesus was born to the world." Push a birthday candle into the top centre of the orange. Then talk about the earth's riches while you are poking a few candies onto the ends of each tooth- pick. Stick these "fruits of the world" into the orange, positioning them evenly around the candle, and say Jesus taught people to love each other, to love God, and to share. He knew this was the way to peace and to ensuring all the world's people enjoyed the fruits of God's good earth. Then, put the foil ribbon around the orange and secure with sticky tape as you tell how Jesus' wise teachings and influence quickly encircled the world.

SCOUTER'S FIVE MINUTES

Ask everyone to place his finished Christingle orange on the floor in front of him. Make a solemn ceremony of lighting the candles (Jesus' shining influence), dim the lights and sing *Silent Night* before sending the Cubs home with their special symbols of Christmas.

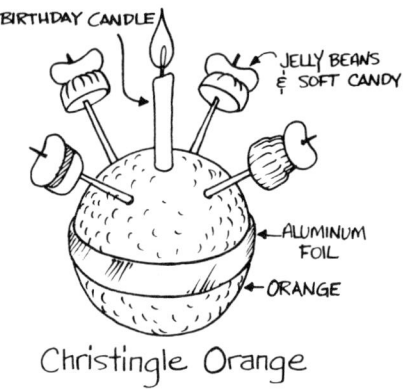

Christingle Orange

Beavers' Christmas Prayer
Thank you Lord for sending us your son Jesus on that first Christmas. We ask for your blessing on all our friends and on all your children throughout the world.

The Scouting Gift
The greatest gift to each and all
Is not a book, a bat or ball,
But love we have for one another;
To call our fellow Scouts our brother.
Whether they are far or near
To show we need them, and make it clear;
To have a neighbour who's a friend
And hope this friendship never ends;
The love of families around us,

SCOUTER'S FIVE MINUTES

The hope of peace and joy surround us.
No — not the gifts in parcels gay.
But a handshake, the Scouting way.
— *by Cub A. Adams, England: written for a Christmas carol service. From* ***Scouting*** *(U.K.)*

Because
Because God is, we are called to be.
Because God is love, we are called to be loving.
Because God is there, we are called to be there for others.
— *from* ***Youth & Adults Together***, *The United Church of Canada*

A Prayer for Beginning
For what we are about to do, may the Lord make us truly responsible;
For what we are about to think, may the Lord make us truly wise;
For what we are about to say, may the Lord make us truly sensible;
For what we are trying to achieve, may the Lord accept and bless our efforts.
— *Thanks to Colin McKay,* ***Scouting*** *(U.K.)*

A Happy Life
A happy life is not built on tours abroad and pleasant holidays, but of little clumps of violets noticed by the roadside, almost hidden away so that only those can see them who have God's peace and love in their hearts: it is one long continuous chain of little joys; little whispers from the spiritual world; little rays of sunshine on our daily work.
— *from the diary of Edward A. Wilson, with Scott's Expedition to the Antarctic*

SCOUTER'S FIVE MINUTES

On Neutrality
If you are neutral in a situation of injustice, you have chosen the side of the oppressor. If an elephant has his foot on the tail of the mouse and you say you are neutral, the mouse will not appreciate your neutrality.
— *Bishop Desmond Tutu*

A Thought
Getting an idea is like sitting down on a tack: it should make you get up and do something about it.

Farewell to a Scouter
For all your time and trouble,
Dedication to our cause,
For your care and understanding,
Selfless giving without pause;
You have set the best example
For our Scouters and our boys.
And have always stood to help us.
Through both tragedies and joys:
We may not have given credit
Always when it was due,
But we hope you know our feelings
As we give our thanks to you;
Though goodbyes are now upon us,
May we wish for you, our friend,
That your time away be shortened.
And your way lead home again.
— *by Carol Jordan, 2nd St. Albert Group Committee, Alta.*

The 23rd Psalm for Busy People
The Lord is my pace setter, I shall not rush;
He makes me stop and rest for quiet intervals;
He provides me with images of stillness, which restores my serenity;
He leads me in ways of efficiency, through calmness of mind,

SCOUTER'S FIVE MINUTES

And His guidance is peace:
Even though I have a great many things to accomplish each day,
I will not fret, for His presence is here;
His timelessness, His all importance will keep me in balance;
He prepares refreshment and renewal in the midst of my activity
By anointing my mind with his oils of tranquillity;
My cup of joyous energy overflows:
Surely harmony and effectiveness shall be the fruits of my hours.
For I shall walk in the pace of my Lord
And dwell in His house for ever.
— *by Toki Miyashina, Japan. Thanks to* **New Zealand Scout News**

The Spirit Lives
The Spirit lives, there is no doubt,
Within the heart of every Scout,
The hope lives on, the dreams survive,
The Scouting spirit is alive!

In England, many years ago,
There lived a man who sought to sow
The seeds of brotherhood of man,
And there the spirit first began.

The Scouting spirit spread about
To nations east, west, north and south,
And soon, on every land and shore,
Young men were taught the Scouting law.

We camped and learned of nature's ways,
We gloried in our youthful days,
We ventured where all others feared,
Because we knew we were prepared.

The world has changed as years went by,
Society's values went awry,
And many ask, "What is the worth
Of Scouting on this wretched earth?"

SCOUTER'S FIVE MINUTES

But each new Scout who learns our law
Brings with him hope, and much, much more;
Each generation of Scouts gives
The proof that Scouting's spirit lives.

The treasured values of the past
Still guide Scouts of today; they last
In spite of changes that we see
Around us in society.

And still, adventures filled with fun
Await today's Scouts, every one;
In them that spirit, born of old
May yet transform this sorry world.

And so we say without a doubt,
That in the heart of every Scout
The hope lives on, the dreams survive,
The Scouting spirit is alive!
— *by G.K. Sammy, former Scout of 31st Trinidad: dedicated to the Naparima District Scouts who attended the XV World Jamboree, 1983.*

Inspiration
Good, better, best,
Never let it rest,
Till your good is better,
And your better's best.
— *from W.K. Wolstenholme, Rivers, Man.*

To Pack Scouters
The man stood by the Pearly Gate,
His head was bent and low,
He asked the angel standing there
Which way he had to go.
"What have you done," the angel asked,

Scouter's Five Minutes

"To gain an entry here?"
"I've run a Cub pack," he replied,
"For years, and years, and years."

The Pearly Gates flung open wide
And proudly tolled the bell;
"Pick up your harp and enter in,
You've had your years of hell!"
—*by the Hessle Venture Scout Unit: from* ***Scouting (U.K.)*** *magazine.*

Prayer

God of the universe, help us to see the hope of a better future for all people. Help us to rise above our own likes and dislikes when there are more important things to consider, and to play our part in achieving some great good for our country and for the world. Amen.

Getting the Message Across

Brother William was very nervous about having to give his first sermon before all his fellow monks. On the appointed day, Brother William mounted the pulpit and peered over the top of it at the rows of inquisitive faces. He cleared his throat and began, "Brothers, do you know what I am to say to you today'?" The monks looked at each other and all slowly shook their heads.

"Well, neither do I!" said Brother William, and left the pulpit and fled from the church.

Later, the Abbot called Brother William into his office and told him, in no uncertain terms, that his performance was not good enough and that he was to give his first sermon the following day.

As directed, Brother William again mounted the pulpit and peered over the top at the rows of inquisitive faces. He began: "Brothers, do you know what I am to say to you today?" Now the monks had been discussing this possibility and decided, to a man, to nod their heads in response to Brother William's question.

Scouter's Five Minutes

"Then," replied Brother William, "there's no need for me to tell you!" And once again, he fled from the pulpit and out of the church.

As you may imagine, the Abbot was unimpressed with Brother William's performance and ordered that he return to the pulpit the very next day.

So, knowing this was his final chance, Brother Williams lowly climbed the steps to the pulpit and peered over the top at the rows of inquisitive faces. Once more, he cleared his throat and began, "Brothers, do you know what I am to say to you today?" Now, the monks were ready for this and one half nodded and the other half shook their heads.

"In that case," said Brother William, "those who do know can tell those who don't know!" And he descended the steps of the pulpit and fled from the church.

Contrary to his expectation, the Abbot was all smiles when next Brother William faced him in his office.

"Well done, Brother William," he said. "your sermon had a fine message for us all to learn."

And indeed it did, for is this not the Scout method of training: those who do know help those who don't know.
—*Thanks to* **Scouting** *(U. K.) magazine*

Be At Peace
You are a child of the universe, no less than the trees and the stars. You have a right to he here. And whether or not it is clear to you, no doubt the universe is unfolding as it should.

Therefore, be at peace with God, whatever you conceive Him to be and, whatever your labours and aspirations in the noisy confusion of life, keep peace with your soul.

With all its sham, drudgery and broken dreams, it is still a beautiful world...
—*from an inscription in St Paul's Church, Baltimore, dating to 1692.*

SCOUTER'S FIVE MINUTES

Gaelic Prayer

Be Thou a bright flame before me,
Be Thou a guiding star above me,
Be Thou a smooth path below me,
And be a kindly shepherd behind me,
Today, tonight and forever.

The Friendship Stick

When God created this wonderful earth, He made it a place filled with brilliant colours — the flowers, the trees, the birds and animals.

"But," said God, "my world is not complete. I need to create a higher being, one who can think and who will take care of the earth. I will call him man. He will have a wife and children and I will call this a family."

God thought, "I have many colours in my world. I must have colour in my people as well. I will create people who are yellow — the colour of the glowing sun which gives warmth and light. I will make people who are black — the colour of the deep starry night which gives quiet and peace. Some of my people will be brown — the colour of the warm earth where seeds grow to feed my people. Lastly, I will make some of my people white like the cool crisp snow of winter.

"All of my people must have eyes to see the beauty around them," God thought. "Some eyes will be brown like the many small birds that sing in the trees, and some eyes I will make blue — the colour of the beautiful sky".

On each Friendship Stick are six circles. The two at the top represent eyes — one brown and one blue.

Below are four circles. The top one is yellow, which represents the yellow-skinned people. There are more yellow skins in the world than any other.

SCOUTER'S FIVE MINUTES

The next circle is black. The second greatest number of people in the world have black skin.

The third circle is brown for the brown skins of the world.

The last circle is white. This is the colour of the fewest people of the world.

When your stick is complete, you must not keep it, but instead exchange it with someone else as a sign of friendship.

What You Think
What you think of me,
I will think of me,
What I think of me.
Will be me.
—*Thanks to Hazel Tagg, Kootenay Boundary Region, B.C.*

Isn't It Funny?
When the other fellow takes a long time to do something, he's slow. But when I take a long time to do something, I'm thorough.

When the other fellow doesn't do it, he's too lazy. But when I don't do it, I'm too busy.

When the other fellow goes ahead and does something without being told, he's overstepping his bounds. But when I do something without being told, that's initiative!

When the other fellow states his side of a question strongly, he's bull-headed. But when I state my side of a question strongly I'm being firm.

When the other fellow overlooks a few of the rules of etiquette, he's rude. But when I skip a few of the rules, I'm being original.

When the other fellow does something that pleases higher-ups, he's polishing the brass. But when I do something that pleases them, that's cooperation.

When the other fellow gets ahead, he sure had the lucky breaks. But when I manage to get ahead — well, man! it was hard work that did it.'

Funny, isn't it? Or is it?
— *thanks to* ***New Brunswick Scouting News***

SCOUTER'S
FIVE MINUTES

It Makes a Difference
In a world that seems to be increasingly filled with trouble, crime, pain and war, how can one Scout make any difference?

A young boy walking the beach one morning noticed an old man picking up starfish and tossing them back into the sea. He caught up to the man and asked him why he was doing this.

"Because the stranded starfish will die when the sun comes up. They dry out," the man explained.

"But the beach goes on and on, and there are zillions of starfish," countered the boy "How can what you do make any difference?"

The oldster looked at the starfish in his hand. "It makes a difference to this one," he said, and tossed it to safety in the waves.
— *an adaptation by T. Gray, Sunnybrook, Alta.*

Measurements
When God measures man, He puts the tape measure around the heart, not the head.

How Fire Came to the Earth
Long ago, there was no fire on earth. Only the Sky People had fire. The Earth People had to eat their food raw, and in winter they were very cold.

"This is not right," said Coyote. "I will go and take some fire from the Sky People." He had a plan, which he told to his friends. So Coyote and his friends Rabbit, Blue Jay, Fox, Bear, and Salmon journeyed to the land of the Sky People.

"They have come to steal our fire," said the Sky People when they saw Coyote and his friends.

"No, we haven't," said Coyote. "We have only come to play games and have contests with you." And to prove his words, Coyote and his friends danced and played games and held contests for three days and three nights. Then Coyote sent his friends away, according to their plan.

SCOUTER'S FIVE MINUTES

"You have come to steal our fire." the Sky People said again.

"No, I haven't," said Coyote, and he began to dance wildly around the bonfire. Then he grabbed a piece of the fire and ran as fast as he could with it. The Sky People ran after him.

When he could no longer run and the Sky People were about to catch him, he gave the fire to Blue Jay, who flew as fast as he could. When Blue Jay's wings became too tired, he gave the fire to Fox, who had been stationed behind another tree. Fox ran until he collapsed and the Sky People caught up with him. As they grabbed him, Rabbit jumped out from behind a tree and took the fire from Fox. Rabbit ran and ran, but when he came to a river, he could not cross. He gave the fire to Salmon, who put the fire in his mouth and swam with it to the other side and gave the fire to Bear. Bear carried the fire hack to the camp of the Earth People.

And that is why, thanks to Coyote and his friends, we have fire on the Earth to this day.

— an adaptation of a North American Indian legend that, with some variations, appears in the mythology of many tribes.

A Thought for Closing
May the road rise to meet you;
May the wind be always at your back:
May the rain fall softly upon your face;
May the Lord hold you in the hollow of His hand.

A Camper's Ten Commandments
Thou shalt do thy share and more;
Thou shalt keep thy sense of humour;
Thou shalt do thy camp duties to the best of thy ability:
Thou shalt not cry over burnt food;
Thou shalt treat other people as you would wish them to treat you;
Thou shalt not pollute or destroy;
Thou shalt not giggle all night;

Scouter's Five Minutes

Thou shalt not forget about personal cleanliness;
Thou shalt spread thy friendship to someone new;
Thou shalt listen to thy leaders, for they are wise in the ways of
 making camp a happy time for everyone.
—*from the Columbia Valley District, B.C.*

Jamaican Camp Grace

Lift up your hearts:
Hearts and minds and voices all give thanks
For this our bread;
Hearts and minds and voices all give thanks
For these our friends;
Hearts and minds and voices all give thanks
For this our camp;
Hearts and minds and voices all give thanks
For this our world;
Hearts and minds and voices all give thanks
We thank the Lord:
Hearts and minds and voices all give thanks.

Give Thanks

Give thanks for sun and sky around.
And all the riches of the ground.
For all our blessings and this food.
For life and friends and all that's good.

Campfire Opening

Let the music cheer us;
Let the laughter bring us together;
Let the spirits rise with our songs;
Let the Great Spirit lift us again;
Let the happy fellowship of our campfire circle
Go out into all the world.
—*from Linda Kish, Lethbridge, Alta.*

SCOUTER'S FIVE MINUTES

Campfire Closing
May the sun be warm and kind to you.
May the darkest night bring a star shining through.
May the dullest day bring a ray of light for you,
And when you leave here tonight.
God's hand to you.
—*from Linda Kish*

Prayer
Lord, we will be canoeing today;
We shall be very busy;
If during the course of the day
We forget about you,
Please don't forget about us.
—*from South Saskatchewan Region's **Loop***

Beaver Prayer
Thank you God, who loves us,
For every happy day,
For trees and grass and flowers and sun,
For friends to share our games and fun,
Thank you God, we love You. Amen

Some Thoughts
If you can't see the bright side, polish up the dark one and look at that.
*(Colin McKay, **Scouting U.K.**)*

Remember that it takes both sunshine and rain to make a rainbow.

The Lord asks of you only this: to act justly, to love tenderly, and to walk humbly with your God. (Micah 6:8)

SCOUTER'S FIVE MINUTES

Giving Thanks
We do not see the wind,
We only hear it sigh;
It makes the grasses bend,
Whenever it goes by.
We do not see God's love,
But in our hearts we know,
He watches over us,
Wherever we may go.
We do not have to see
To know the wind is here;
We do not have to see
To know God's love is near.
— *author unknown*

The Traveller & the Tracker
Once a Traveller and a Tracker set out to explore the world together. As they wound their way through the wilderness, the Traveller was amazed at the Tracker's habit of pausing several times a day to pray.

"Why do you pray to something intangible?" the Traveller asked. "How do you know there is a God?"

Now the Tracker was very skilled in noticing things and, through the years, had gained much insight reading the smallest signs. And he answered the Traveller this way:

"I know there is a God when I see the leaves turning yellow. I know there is a God when a trout jumps at a fly, and when grass waves in the dry wind. I know there is a God when clouds shade my head and the stars wink at night "

"So you see, said the Tracker, "I know there is a God, for I can find his footprints throughout the Universe."
— *by Ben Kruser, Regional Field Executive, Calgary, Alta.*

SCOUTER'S FIVE MINUTES

Let us give thanks to God upon Thanksgiving Day. Nature is beautiful and fellowmen are dear, and duty is close beside us, and God is over us and in us. *(Phillips Brooks)*

Beaver Prayer
Now, before I run to play,
Don't let me forget to pray
To God who keeps me through the night
And wakes me up with morning light;
Help me, Lord, to love you more
Than I have ever loved before,
In my work and in my play;
Thank you, God, for another day.
— *8th Belleville Beavers, Ont.*

We Thank You Lord...
...for the lives of Lord and Lady B.-P.
...for all the fun and adventures we have in Scouting
...for the worldwide brotherhood of Scouts
...for the beauty of the world and all the marvellous things You have made in nature
...for keeping us fit and well and happy
...for our homes, our parents, and all who look after us
Please help us. . .
..to be good sportsmen, fair and honest in work as in play and in everything we do
..to find ways of serving You by helping other people as best we can
..to be worthy of our uniform and loyal to our promise, behaving as true brothers to all mankind
..to look after Your creation and keep this world as lovely a place as You intended it to be
..to help all children who are not so lucky as we, especially those who are hungry or lonely, sick or sad

Scouter's
FIVE MINUTES

..to be loving and caring as we grow older and to do our best to repay your blessings in every way we can.
— *Thanks to Hazel Addis, **Scouting (U.K.)***

• • • • • • • • • • • • • • •

Footprints
One night a man had a dream. He dreamed he was walking along the beach with God while, across the sky, flashed scenes from his life. For each scene, he noticed two sets of footprints in the sand — one belonging to him and the other to God.

When the last scene of his life flashed before him, he looked back at the footprints in the sand. He noticed that, many times along the path of his life, there only one set of footprints. He also noticed that it happened at the very lowest and saddest times in his life. This really bothered him, and he questioned God about it.

"Lord, you said that once I decided to follow you, you'd walk with me all the way," he said. "But I have noticed that, during the most troubled times in my life, there is only one set of footprints. I don't understand why, when I needed you most, you left me."

"My precious child," the Lord replied, "I love you and I would never leave you. During your times of trial and suffering, when you see only one set of footprints in the sand, it was then that I carried you."
— from *Scouting (U.K.)* magazine's *A Canny Crack*

Boys have a thousand muscles to wiggle with and only one to sit still with.

Good Day Vitamins: A Beaver Yarn
Rusty left the house very early that morning with his fishing gear and a determined look on his face. His father had told him the best time for fishing was at sunrise, when everyone was still sleeping and the animals hadn't yet had a chance to disturb the fish.

SCOUTER'S FIVE MINUTES

He went through the woods to the cove where a small stream emptied into the pond and the fish would find plenty of food. As he came to his fishing spot, he saw Silver Beaver sitting quietly by the pond with his eyes closed.

"Keeo, are you all right"" he whispered quietly, afraid his friend was hurt.

Keeo opened his eyes and looked at Rusty."Good morning, Rusty,," he said. " Beautiful day, isn't it?"

"Yes," said Rusty, "but what are you doing by yourself at this time of the morning,?"

"I come here often to think good," Keeo replied.

It seemed his beaver friend still had much to learn about speaking human, Rusty thought."You mean you come here to think well."he said.

"No. I come here to think Good," Keeo said."When things are not going too well or I feel alone and scared, I come here and think of the good things that can happen. And then I feel better."

"I do that in my room when my parents get angry at me," said Rusty. "But what happened this morning to make you upset?

"Sometimes I just come here to feel good for the day," Keeo replied. "You could call it Good Day Vitamins."

With a big smile, Rusty sat down next to Keeo, took out his fishing pole, and got his own kind of Good Day Vitamins.
— *by John Risdon, Gloucester, Ont.*

An Irish Blessing
May the blessed sunlight shine upon you and warm your heart until it glows like a great fire, so that a stranger may come and warm himself at it, and also a friend.
— *thanks to Anne Barbour Essex, Ont.*

SCOUTER'S FIVE MINUTES

Clear Morning

My will slowly forces my resting eyes
to peer into the land of the awake
The orange light through the tent
shatters
the work of my will
by slamming my eyelids together.
I try again
Now, I am prepared
The morning is fresh and crisp
clear
The sun dawns over the mountains reaching for the sky
The snow
white
clean
glistens and shines
I walk to meet nature
The reunion lasts. . .
—*by Venturer Gavin de Lint, Regina 21st, Sask.*

A Scout's Christmas

Gobots, dinobots and Christmas tree lights,
Everything looks so shiny bright;
Dolls with curls for little girls,
Robot toys for little boys:
A little boy gets big — no doubt,
And sometime soon becomes a Scout;
The Christmas gifts he wishes sent
Are hatchets, knives and sleeping tent;
All Scouts know what Christmas means,
And they all love the manger scenes,
So let's not worry about what we get
Because what we give is better yet.
— *by Scout Aaron Andrews, 2nd Westmount, Nova Scotia, Christmas 1985*

Scouter's Five Minutes

Gifts

The best thing to give to your enemy is forgiveness; to an opponent, tolerance; to a friend, understanding; to a child, a good example; to your father, deference; to your mother, conduct that will make her proud of you: to yourself, respect: to all men, charity.
— *Arthur James Balfour*

Love

Love all God's creation, both the whole and every grain of sand. Love every leaf, every ray of light. Love the animals, love the plants, love each separate thing. If you love each thing, you will perceive the mystery of God in all; and when once you perceive this, you will thence-forward grow every day to a fuller understanding of it, until you come at last to love the whole world with a love that will then be all embracing and universal.
— *Fyodor Dostoevski*

If fun is good, truth is still better, and love best of all.
(William Makepiece Thackeray)

Declaration

The world is my country,
The human race is my race,
The spirit of man is my god,
The future of man is my heaven.
— *F.R. Scott*

Good News

Everyone has inside himself ... a piece of good news. The good news
   is that you really don't know....
How great you can be,
How much you can love,

Scouter's Five Minutes

What you can accomplish, or
What your potential is.
How can you top good news like that?
—*Anne Frank, from her diary*

We Can Do It!

Give the new year an enthusiastic start with the chorus of this Panama Canal workmen's song. Maybe your section or group will want to adopt it as a theme chant.

Got any rivers they say are uncrossable?
Got any mountains you can't tunnel through?
We make a specialty of the impossible.
Got any job that you want us to do?

A Toast to the Boys

Here's to the membership,
Here's to the boys,
Creators of havoc and
Makers of noise:
They scream and they holler
And batter our ears;
They run and they tumble
And drive us to tears;
But still, in the end,
They grow and they learn;
They show off the skills
And the badges they earn:
We guide them and teach them

SCOUTER'S FIVE MINUTES

Because, in the end,
they're what it's all for—
We do it for them.
To the Boys!
— *by Greybeard: an excellent toast for a February parent/son banquet.*

Everybody's Canoe

A young Indian brave was busy at work carving a canoe out of a log. As he worked, members of the tribe passed by. Everybody had a piece of advice to offer the young man.

"I think you are making your canoe too wide," one of them said. The young brave, wishing to show respect for the advice of an elder, narrowed down the canoe.

A little later, another warrior stopped by. "I'm afraid you are cutting the stern too full," he said. Again, the young brave listened to his elder and cut down the stern.

Very soon, yet another member of the tribe stopped, watched for awhile, then said. "The bow is too sheer." The young brave accepted this advice as well and changed the line of the bow.

Finally the canoe was complete and the young brave launched it. As soon as it hit the water, it capsized. Laboriously he hauled it back onto the beach. Then he found another log and began his work anew.

Very soon, a member of his tribe stopped by to offer some advice, but this time the young brave was ready.

"See that canoe over there?" he asked, pointing to the useless craft on the beach. "That is everybody's canoe." Then he nodded at the work in progress "This one," he said, is *my* canoe.
— *Author Unknown*

A Thought

For every complex and difficult issue, there is always an answer that is simple, easy, and wrong.
— *H.L. Mencken*

SCOUTER'S FIVE MINUTES

A Scout's Prayer

Lord, we are camping in the snow today;
We may fear the cold,
But we trust that your Spirit
Will guide and warm us.
—*from the* **South Saskatchewan Loop**

Beaver Prayer

The air we breathe, the friends we meet,
The walk to use our eyes and feet,
The things around us make us say,
Thank you, God, for each new day!
—*from* **Scouting (U.K.)** *magazine*

Prayer for Peace

God, make me an instrument of Your Peace;
Where there is hatred, let me sow love;
Where there is injury, pardon;
Where there is doubt, faith;
Where there is despair, hope;
Where there is darkness, light;
And where there is sadness, joy:
That I may seek to console, rather than to be consoled,
To understand rather than to be understood.
To love rather than to be loved:
For it is in giving that we receive,
In self-forgetfulness that we find our true selves,
In forgiving that we are forgiven:
God, make me an instrument of Your Peace.
—*from the organizers of* **A Million Minutes of Peace**

SCOUTER'S FIVE MINUTES

Sioux Prayer

Ho! Great Spirit, Grandfather, you have made everything and are in everything. You sustain everything, guide everything, provide everything, and protect everything, because everything belongs to you I am weak, poor and lowly; nevertheless, help me to care, in appreciation and gratitude to you and for everything.

I love the stars, the sun and the moon, and I thank you for our beautiful mother, the Earth, whose many breasts nourish the fish, the fowls and the animals, too. May I never deceive Mother Earth; may I never deceive my people; may I never deceive myself; and above all, may I never deceive you.

On Spirituality

The common misunderstanding is to think spirituality means "religion", and sometimes, a specific religion. At its heart, spirituality has to do with meaning.

Why am I here?
What am I going to become?
What is creative; what is destructive?
What do I have to do in order
to get along happily with other people,
and to enjoy God's creation and God's friendship?

All people ask spiritual questions, and those who are younger tend to look to those who are older for help in finding answers. We cannot necessarily give them the answers for their lives, but we can help them as they try to sort out their meanings. We can listen to their concerns, and we can ask questions and make suggestions based on our own experience.

— *Scouter Rob Brown, Saskatoon, Sask.*

Scouter's Five Minutes

A True Friend
A true friend is one to whom you can tip out all the contents of your heart, chaff and grain together, knowing that the gentlest hands will take and sift it, keep what is worth keeping and, with the breath of kindness, blow the rest away.
— *an Arabian definition of a friend*

Thanks Be to God
Thanks to God for things we see,
The growing flower, the waving tree,
Our mother's face, the bright blue sky
Where birds and clouds go floating by;
Thanks be to God for seeing.

Thanks to God for things we hear,
For sounds of friends who laugh and cheer,
The merry bells, the song of birds,
For stories, tunes, and kindly words;
Thanks be to God for hearing.
— *from Hazel Tagg, Red Deer, Alta.*

Take Time
Take time to work;
This the price of success:
Take time to think;
It is the source of power:
Take time to read;
It is the foundation of knowledge:
Take time to give to others;
It will bring you happiness:
Take time to love;

SCOUTER'S FIVE MINUTES

It is the sacrament of life:
Take time to dream;
It hitches the soul to the stars;
Take time to laugh;
It lightens the highway to eternal life:
Take time to plan,
And you will have time for all the rest.
— *from Jo-Anne Wood, Grandora, Sask.*

All great ideas need wings to fly: but, above all, they need landing gear.
— *thanks to South Waterloo's* **Notes 'n News**

Rainbow
Rainbow, rainbow,
The heavenly miracle of —
Rainbow, rainbow,
A rainbow coloured with love.

Gem conjured out of the shadows,
Miracle wrought in the rain,
We see in each shimmering rainbow
Life's colours again;
Like poppies ablaze in the cornfield,
With midsummer blue skies above,
Like butterflies' wings and all living things,
The rainbow is coloured with love.

Rainbow, rainbow,
That sunshine caught in the rain;
Rainbow, rainbow,
A sunshine caught in the rain.

The Lord made mankind in His image,
To dwell on the earth in His place,
And just as He coloured the rainbow,

SCOUTER'S FIVE MINUTES

He coloured the folk of each race;
So children are brothers and sisters.
Whatever the language, they prove.
With eyes shining bright and face black or white,
They radiate friendship and love.

Rainbow, rainbow,
You tell us the sun's close by;
Rainbow, rainbow,
A smile in our troubled sky.
— *words by Jack Macfarlane. with thanks to* **Scouting (U.K.)** *magazine.*

B.-P. on Scouting

What we need and what, thank God, we've got in most places in our movement, is not merely the spirit of good-natured tolerance but of watchful sympathy and readiness to help one another. We not only need it but we've "got to have it" if we are going to teach our boys by the only sound way, that is through our own example, that greatest of principles — goodwill and cooperation.
— *from* **B.-P.'s Outlook**

The Blessing of St. Francis of Assisi

May the Lord bless thee and keep thee; may He show His face to thee and have mercy upon thee; may He turn His countenance to thee, and give thee peace. May the Lord bless thee. Amen.

Campers

Campers are very special people:
They have felt the cool wind of dawn;
They have known the slow march of the stars along the milky way;
They have reached out their hands to new friends;
They have stood tiptoe to the meaning of life, and found it good:

SCOUTER'S FIVE MINUTES

Their eyes have caught the vision of the shining future,
Their hearts have encompassed all the bounds of earth,
And their minds have listened to God.
—*from **Campfires, A Collection of Favourites** compiled by Linda Kish, Lethbridge, Alta.*

Dear God

During a Cub Day in Dumfriesshire, Scotland, leaders asked Cubs to write short prayers to attach to a Prayer Tree featured on the site. Try the idea at a Cub day or camp, and harvest prayers like these to remind you just how very many things we have to be thankful for.

Thank you, God, for this wonderful day I am having.
Dear God, thank you very much for inventing Cubs.
Dear God, thank you for not letting me get chickenpox.
Dear God, thank you for this day out because I will have fun, and I can't wait to try out the death slide.
Dear Lord, thank you for this marvellous day, and we hope the Cubs will last forever.
Dear God, thank you for the fresh taste of tooth-paste.
Thank you God for all good things. Thank you God for life itself.
   Thank you God for everything.

Dear God, thank you for everything — parents, pets, and everything you made.
—*from **Scottish Scout News***

No Heroes?

"There are no heroes in Scouting," declared Akela. We were discussing the low membership in our sections compared with the high attendance in the local hockey leagues. "Every kid in town wants to be Wayne Gretzky. Nobody wants to be Baden-Powell. There's no glamour in Scouting. And besides, there's no money in it!"

Argue as I might, I had to concede the strength of hockey's pull. Yet I still feel Akela is wrong. Scouting is full of heroes, from B.-P.

SCOUTER'S FIVE MINUTES

on down. If the boys are unaware of them, perhaps we — you and I, Akela — are at fault.

For 80 years throughout the world, Scouts have been helping at natural disasters, fighting poverty and ignorance, assisting in war zones, saving lives. By the nature of the movement, Scouts tend to be quiet heroes. There is no one to announce, "He shoots! He scores!" when a Scout does a good turn, but that doesn't mean the heroes don't exist.

And glamour! An international jamboree, with thousands of Scouts in their distinctive national uniforms! White water canoe trips! Camping on mountain crags, on salt-scorched deserts, by placid lakes. The countless dramatic challenges of Scouting! Perhaps, if our troop offered more of these, Scouting would have more appeal in this town.

But still, Akela is right on one point. There's no money in it!
— *by Greybeard, Sunnybrook, Alta., from **The Arrow**, Central Alberta Region's newsletter*

From the Inside

I live in a body labelled "handicapped",
Stunted legs and arms askew;
I live in a body I wouldn't have chosen,
But then, few of us do.

People say I am brave,
As though bravery were a choice;
I learned early not to scream.
For mine is an unheard voice.

The world is competitive.
And I'm ill-equipped to compete,
But I'm no less of a person,
Because I am not complete.

Scouter's Five Minutes

I live in a body labelled "second rate",
Though I feel second to none;
When society knows the difference,
Then my battle is won.
— *Thanks to* ***Scouting (U.K.)***

Basic Definitions

Impairment: the loss of a function because part of the body is defective or missing: e.g. an eye that does not see, a missing leg, a brain with a memory that doesn't work.

Disability: the lack of ability to perform a function or activity most other people can perform; e.g. difficulty in seeing, walking, hearing, thinking, speaking. A disability is caused by an impairment.

Handicap: the limitation of a person's ability to lead a regular life. A disability becomes a handicap when society's attitudes and physical obstacles make it difficult for someone to do things; e.g. people in wheel chairs are handicapped when stairs prevent them from entering a building; blind people are handicapped in reading if they are not taught Braille.

Beatitudes to Friends of People with Disabilities

Blessed are you who take the time to listen to my difficult speech, for you help me to know that, if I persevere, I can be understood.

Blessed are you who never bid me to hurry, or take my tasks from me and do them for me, for often I need time rather than help.

Blessed are you who stand beside me as I enter new and untried ventures, for my failures will be outweighed by the time I surprise myself and you.

Blessed are you who ask for my help, for my greatest need is to be needed.

Blessed are you who understand that it is difficult for me to put my thoughts into words.

Blessed are you who, with a smile, encourage me to try once more.

SCOUTER'S FIVE MINUTES

Blessed are you who never remind me that, today, I asked the same question twice.

Blessed are you who respect me and love me as I am — just as I am, not as you wish I were.

A Prayer: Grant me, I pray,

Quickness of eye to perceive my brother's handicap and insight to understand him;

Wisdom to appreciate my brother's needs and strength and skill to help him;

Sensitivity to discern my brother's feelings and openness to accept and value him;

Joy in my brother's achievements and a cheerful spirit to encourage him;

Appreciation of my brother's worth and gracious words to express it to him;

Thankfulness for all my brother teaches me, and gratitude for the opportunity to serve him.

— *Thanks to* **Scouting (U.K.)**

The Taming of Fire
by Steve Elson

Before the age of transformers, the Bill Cosby Show and Lego, there was a time when fire-lighting ceremonies were held. On these special occasions, people from all over the community came together to celebrate the Taming of Fire. Before this time, fire was a wild force that burned forests, shot down from the sky in lightning bolts, and frightened everyone. This is how it all began...

Long ago there was a young girl named Sarah who lived in a small village. Just beyond the village was a thick wood where, even in the middle of the day, it was hard to see. One day Sarah went out to

SCOUTER'S FIVE MINUTES

pick blueberries. Now, everyone knows how good blueberries are, and wild blueberries that you pick yourself are very delicious indeed.

Well, as you might have guessed, Sarah got lost. Soon night came and she was all alone — hungry and very frightened. She found a hollow log just small enough for her to crawl into and finally fell asleep.

In her sleep, she had a dream. She was still cold and hungry and alone but, out of the darkness, came a wise old man. In her dream, he saw Sarah huddled in the log and woke her up.

"I can see, little girl, that you are cold and hungry," he said. "Perhaps I can help you."

He took a gleaming red coal out of his pocket, placed it on the ground, put some leaves on it, and blew. Soon the leaves began to smoke, and then to burn. He added small twigs and more dry grass. Before long, there was a fire — a gloriously bright fire that gave heat and comfort to Sarah and the old man. Sarah began to feel all warm and snuggly inside.

By this time, it was near morning and the damp cold woke Sarah up. She realized, sadly, that her warm cozy feeling had been nothing but a dream. But there beside her on a bare patch of earth was a glowing red coal. Remembering her dream, Sarah did just what the old man had done. Soon she had a good fire burning.

Thanks in part to the smoke of her fire, by the time she was warm, the people from her village found her. They stood around amazed at the sight they beheld, for never before had fire been tamed. It was a miracle, a gift given to a lost and frightened young girl deep in the woods. Rejoicing, the village people took the hot coals home with them and learned to use fire for many, many things.

To celebrate and remember this event, every year in October when the nights began to grow longer and colder, the village people gathered around in a large circle and, from a hot red coal, started a fire that grew into a huge bonfire. The celebration reminded them of the taming of fire, the warmth and pleasure it brought, and the special gift given to a young girl on a cold dark night.

SCOUTER'S FIVE MINUTES

For us, the fire-lighting ceremony symbolizes a gift from God who gave us fire and the power to tame it.

We thank Steve Elson, advisor of the 9th Welland Venturers, Ont., who wrote the tale for a campfire held in Oct. '86. He tells us that, during the dream portion of the story, the fire-master lit the campfire with a hot coal (a stick with a red hot end). "It was quite effective" he says.

Giving Thanks
He who thanks but with the lips
Thanks only in part;
The full, the true Thanksgiving
Comes from the heart.

Thanksgiving Prayer
We thank thee for the world so large,
The land, the sea, the lakes, the sky,
And for the stars that shine above;
We thank thee Lord for everything.

We thank thee for the birds that fly,
The gardens, the blossoms, the flowers, the bees,
And for the trees with leaves so green;
We thank thee Lord for everything.

We thank thee for creatures large and small,
The wild ones, the tame ones, we cherish them all,
And for the fish that live in the sea;
We thank thee Lord for everything.

Scouter's Five Minutes

We thank thee for the gentle winds,
The rain that falls to fill lakes and streams,
And the warming sun that helps things grow;
We thank thee Lord for everything.

We thank thee for the food we eat,
The clothes we wear, the friends we meet;
For our families and the gifts of living;
We thank thee Lord for everything.
— *by William Fraser, Dartmouth, N.S.*

World Wonders
Often I think there is little left in the world
That is wondrous to see;
Then I have to pause and watch
A group of Scouts growing up around me.
— *thanks to the S. Saskatchewan **Loop**.*

I Asked...
I asked God for strength that I might achieve;
I was given weakness that I might learn to obey:
I asked for health that I might do greater things;
I was given grace that I might do better things:
I asked for riches that I might be happy;
I was given poverty that I might be wise:
I asked for power that I might have the praise of men;
I was given weakness that I might feel the need for God:
I asked for all things, that I might enjoy life;
I was given life that I might enjoy all things:
I received nothing I asked for,
But everything I wished for, despite myself;
My prayer was answered:
I am among all people most richly blessed.

SCOUTER'S
FIVE MINUTES

Gifts

From western skies the colours slowly die,
The stars above the pines their watches keep:
Another joyous day goes swiftly by,
Another night bestows her gift of sleep.
— *thanks to the Odawa Beaver Service Team, National Capital Region, Ont.*

A Time to Celebrate

Christians devote much of December to the celebration of the birth of Jesus. Other faiths also mark religious holidays in December. Catch the join-in spirit of the 16th World Jamboree's theme "bringing the world together" by getting together with people from different faiths to share some of your traditions.

Dec. 8 is *Bodhi Day,* the celebration of Buddha's enlightenment. Buddhist scriptures describe the moment:

"Pleasant breezes blew softly, rain fell from a cloudless sky, flowers and fruits dropped from the trees out of season as if to show him reverence ... At that moment, no one in the world was angry, sick, or sad, no one did evil, no one swelled with pride. The world became quiet, as if it had reached perfection . . . All living things rejoiced.......

Buddhists also celebrate *Joye-E* (New Year's Eve) on Dec. 31 and *Shusho-E* (New Year's Day) on Jan. 1.

From late Nov — end Dec, Jews celebrate *Hanukkah,* the Festival of Lights and Dedication in memory of their victory over the Syrians and the rededication of the temple of Jerusalem. An important symbol of Hanukkah is the Menorah, the candelabrum that holds the Hanukkah candles,

SCOUTER'S FIVE MINUTES

Eight little candles shining so bright,
One candle for each Hanukkah night,
There to remind us of eight holy nights,
When one little candle shone so very bright.

On Dec. 26, members of the Zoroastrian Faith mark the anniversary of the death of the faith's founder, Prophet Zarathustra. Dec. 31-Jan. 4 is *Ghambar Maidyarem,* the Zoroastrian festival celebrating the creation of animals.

Christmas Wishes

"And he shall judge among many people and rebuke strong nations afar off; and they shall beat their swords into plowshares and their spears into pruning hooks; nation shall not lift up a sword against nation, neither shall they learn war any more. But they shall sit every man under his vine and under his fig tree, and none shall make them afraid...."(Micah 4: 3-4)

Jesus' birth, foretold with this promise, is a time of hope, joy and wishing people well. The blessings of peace and joy are wishes expressed in the writings of many religious traditions and we've chosen a few examples that might well be wishes for the holiday season. Perhaps, if we increase our understanding by sharing our beliefs with each other, one day the world truly will realize the promise of Christmas.

"May the wicked become virtuous. May the virtuous attain peace. May the peaceful be free. May the free make others free." — Hinduism

"May all become happy. May all remain radiant in health. May all see beneficence. And may not any one feel miserable." — Jainism

"The Lord bless you and keep you; The Lord make His face to shine upon you and be gracious unto you; The Lord lift up His countenance upon you and give you peace." (Numbers 6: 24-26 — Jewish tradition)

Scouter's Five Minutes

"Great Spirit, bless our children, friends, and visitors through a happy life. May our trails lie straight and level before us." (North American Indian tradition)

Christingle Hymn

In the Dec. '85 issue, we described Christingle oranges and their meaning. In a more recent issue of *Scouting* (UK) magazine, we found further information about the Christingle tradition and a hymn.

The first Christingle services were special children's services held in Moravia, Czechoslovakia, over 200 years ago. The Christingle orange represents our world and the candle in the top symbolizes the light of the world, Jesus. Four toothpicks poked into the orange to mark the four major compass points show the light of the world shining in all directions. The pieces of fruit and sweets on the picks represent both the good things that come to people through Christ and the bountiful fruits of the earth. A red ribbon tied around the centre of the orange symbolizes the blood Jesus shed to save the people of the world.

To explain the symbolism of the Christingle orange, the 1st Goring Cubs, England, set these words to the tune *The Holly and the Ivy*.

The orange of Christingle,
The world reminds us of,
And how our God created us,
And on us shed His love.

Chorus: O sing about Christingle,
Your voices loud employ,
Your praises sing to God our King
For Jesus and His joy.

SCOUTER'S FIVE MINUTES

The candle of Christingle,
With shining flame so bright,
Reminds us of our loving Lord,
Who is the world's true light. *(Chorus)*

The red band on Christingle,
Which plainly we can see,
Reminds us of how Jesus Christ,
Was killed upon that tree. *(Chorus)*

The four sticks of Christingle,
With which the orb we spear,
Remind us how God cares for us,
All seasons of the year. *(Chorus)*

The fruits of the Christingle.
They have a special worth,
As symbols of the Spirit's fruits,
As well as fruits of earth. *(Chorus)*

The whole of the Christingle,
It is a joy to see,
It shines to show how Father God.
Loves even you and me. *(Chorus)*

A Quiet Hero
by Greybeard

Wayne Gretzky probably scored again last night. Now, I know I'm going to ruffle a few feathers when I say this, but big deal. Another point, yawn, hooray, ho-hum. It'll be in the papers and discussed on sports talk shows and all that. The guy's a real hero, right?

SCOUTER'S FIVE MINUTES

A couple of summer's back, I met another hero. Only 11, he wasn't very big. And he was a very homesick Scout.

"Big deal," I hear someone out there echoing my comment, "a little wimp who can't stand to leave his mommy."

That's a pretty insensitive thing to say about a kid whose feelings are tearing him up to the point of crying in front of his friends — a kid who probably hates himself for being "weak" and feeling homesick. To make things worse, we were at the base camp for our canoe trip on the rain-swollen North Saskatchewan River and more than one boy (and leader) was having second thoughts. The homesick Scout came to me that morning as we were loading the canoes.

"Greybeard, I don't think I want to go. I think I want to go home," he said. When he'd made similar comments the night before, the other Scouts and the leaders had joked and tried to distract him. But there comes a time when a boy has to go either forward or back.

We walked away from the bustle and I put my hand on his shoulder. "In five minutes we'll leave," I said. "You can be in the canoe or you can be in the truck going back. I hope you'll come, but it's up to you." And then-oh, how hard it was to do — I walked away and left him to his thoughts.

He came on the trip. A couple of his buddies gave him a friendly punch on the shoulder, but nobody cheered. His accomplishment wasn't printed in the papers or discussed on talk shows. Now Gretzky — he's okay. But to me, that Scout is a special kind of hero. The quiet kind.

Thoughts about Symbols

Similar symbols can have different meanings around the world. Take a star, for example. There's the star associated with Christ's birth, the Jewish Star of David, and the Muslim star and crescent. To the people who use it each star symbol has great meaning. The owl symbol is yet another example. An owl is considered wise in the western world but foolish in India.

SCOUTER'S FIVE MINUTES

All people react to colour, as well, and often use it to express ideas, as in the North American expressions. "He's feeling blue" or "I saw red!" But colours, like symbols, can have different meanings in different cultures. Red can mean anger or passion in the west, but signifies joy in China and the Ukraine. In India, it is the colour for a bridal gown. Yellow can signify wisdom or the harvest to a Russian, joy to a European, fear or cowardice to a North American, and spirituality to a Buddhist. Green is a holy colour to Muslims and a colour of hope in the Ukraine. In the English language, it is used as an expression for tranquility, envy, or naïvity.

It's something to think about. How many different cultures are represented in your section or group?
— *thanks to North Waterloo District's **Scouting News**.*

Racism is man's greatest threat to man — the maximum of hatred for the minimum of reason (Abraham Joshua Heschel)

The Promise of the Rainbow
by Dorothy Kinlock

In the Red of the fire, we see energy and warmth, the eternal flame of the Olympics, the ashes of Soweto and the horrors of Chernobyl.

May we, in Scouting, douse the terrible flames of fear and nurture only the sparks of good which are in all of us.

In the Orange of the earth, we see the fruits of the earth spilling from the horn of plenty, but we are also well aware of the desolation and devastation of drought-stricken lands which we have never seen.

May we, in Scouting, feed the spirit which fills the hearts and minds, and so the bellies, of children everywhere.

The Yellow of light fills the whole world with happiness, peace and joy. It is people who destroy these things.

Scouter's Five Minutes

May we, in Scouting, light candles which will become beacons of trust throughout the nations of the world.

In the Green of plants, we have the beauty and majesty of the natural world.
May we, in Scouting, encourage our youngsters to appreciate and respect the dangers of the rock face, the intricacies of the spider's web, the wonders of birth and the healing power of a plant.

In the Blue of water, we are reminded of the cruelty of the open sea but also the thrill of a sail in full flight and the sheer joy of children splashing on a beach.
May we, in Scouting, so train our youngsters that each activity, whether simple or arduous, is seen as a challenge to be met and, ultimately, enjoyed.

In the Indigo of infinity and space we realize the vastness of the universe and, whatever humanity's achievement, we know, too, the neatness of God — if we only have faith.
May we, in Scouting, help others to experience that faith by our work and by our example.

And, in the Violet of people, we remember the love of God and the promise of the rainbow.
May we, in Scouting, fulfil the promise of the rainbow by starting afresh and working towards making the world a better place in which to live.
— *with many thanks to* ***Scouting (UK)*** *magazine.*

The Spirit of B.-P.
Gone Home — a simple sign to mark his passing:
Gone Home — a worldwide family grieves the loss;
Gone Home — the spirit keeps on living;
Gone Home — to live forever in the hearts of youth.

Scouter's Five Minutes

Left hands stretched around the world, we greet each other,
We know that deep inside we have a lot to share;
We have all been touched by the same spirit;
We pass it on to others because we care.

Three fingers in salute, we made a promise
To God, our country and to all who live;
This bond joins us through all generations.
As we face the challenge and adventure life can give.
— *by Jean Buydens, Greater Victoria Region, B.C.*

Three Trees: A Story for Easter

We all have dreams. At one time, everyone has been a race car driver or a doctor in his dreams. But time and opportunity often change our early dreams, like they did long ago for three trees who had dreams.

The trees grew on a quiet hillside forest in sunny land by the Mediterranean Sea. They talked together about how they would like to be used when, eventually, they were cut down.

"I'd like to be a cradle for a young baby," said the first tree. "I would rock him gently and soothe him to sleep. My sides would be very smooth so I would not hurt his tiny hands."

"I'd like to be part of a great ship," said the second tree. "I'd sail the oceans, see adventure in other lands, and provide sailors a safe place in raging storms.

"I'd like to be something beautiful, something carved with love so that it brings joy and hope to everyone who sees it and fame to the artist who carved it," said the third tree.

Gently blessed by the sun and refreshed by the rain, the trees grew. Then, one day when they were ready, a woodsman came, cut them down, and carried them away.

The first tree went to a carpenter's shop where he heard he was to become a manger. So much for his dream of becoming a cradle, he

SCOUTER'S FIVE MINUTES

moaned. Instead of being in a house, he'd be out with cattle brushing their hot, damp bodies against him and hay scattered everywhere.

The second tree was excited when he was taken to a boat builder. Was his dream coming true? To his horror, he found that he would become part of a fishing boat. All he could look forward to was having smelly fish tossed into him and the same weary, boring journey every day. Some adventure!

The third tree was filled with shame when, instead of being carved into a thing of beauty, he was made into a rough wooden cross.

And so, the destiny of the trees was not what they'd imagined, but it was their chance to serve the Lord — one as a manger. the other as a fishing boat, and the third as a cross.

May we also dream dreams. but never miss the opportunities that come our way.

— *Many thanks to **Scouting (UK)** magazine.*

My Brother
You are my brother because you are a human, and we both are sons of one Holy Spirit; we are equal and made of the same earth. You are a human and, that fact sufficing, I love you as a brother. I love you whether worshipping in your church, kneeling in your temple, or praying in your mosque.
(Khalil Gibran)

Little Bits
Let us endeavour to live that when we come to die, even the undertaker will be sorry. *(Mark Twain)*

The human body is remarkably sensitive. Pat a man on the back often enough and his head swells.

SCOUTER'S FIVE MINUTES

God gave us two ends; one to think with and one to sit on. Our success depends on the one we use the most. Heads, we win: tails, we lose.
*(Ida Clarkson. Thanks to **Mamook Papah**)*

When you have a difficult job to tackle, ask God to help you to tackle it. and He will give you strength. But you must still do the tackling yourself. *(B.-P.)*

The More You Put In...

The chaplain and his young son were camping just outside a small seaside town. Not far away was a tiny church that had no minister, so the chaplain offered his services for the Sunday. No fee was payable.

As the chaplain and his son were passing out of the door after the service, the son noticed a small box which had on it the words "For Contributions".

"Father, don't you think you should put something in the box?" the son asked.

"Certainly," the chaplain said. He dug into his pocket, pulled out a dollar, and put it into the box.

The two had gone a little way back to the camp when a man came running after them.

"It's our custom to give the minister whatever is dropped into the box," he said when he caught up with them. "I found this dollar and here it is. " And he handed back the money the chaplain had donated.

After the man had left, the boy looked up at his dad. "Father," he said, "if you had only put more into the box, you would have got so much more out."

SCOUTER'S FIVE MINUTES

And isn't that true about everything — Scouting, living? The more you put in, the more you will get out.
— *by the Rev. Bill Sutherland, from **Scottish Scout News**, with thanks.*

Responsive Reading for Camp

Leader: Lord, we know that this world we live in doesn't belong to us: it is Your creation.
All: But sometimes we don't take care of it as well as we should.
Leader: We forget that animals and plants are living things that belong here too
All: And they also have a right to some space on this planet.
Leader: Help us to be wise in the use of our resources
All: by planting trees for those we cut down; by putting on a sweater instead of turning up the heat; by shutting off lights in empty rooms; by recycling instead of throwing away: by walking carefully through the woods to disturb as little as possible.
Leader: Help us, Lord, to respect nature and her needs, and to remember that what we take from nature was placed there by Your hand.
— *from Anne Barbour, Essex, Ont.*

To Open and Close a Campfire

Come, come, light up the fire,
Come, come, join in the ring,
Here find dreams to inspire,
Stories to tell, music to sing.

The stars shining over us,
Their light shines before us,
Oh God of nature,
Grant to us a perfect peace.
— *from the campfire booklet put together by the Odawa Service Team, National Capital Region, Ont.*

SCOUTER'S FIVE MINUTES

The Runners
We're hopeless at racing,
Me and my friend;
I'm slow at the start,
He's slow at the end:
He has the stitch,
I get sore feet,
And neither one of us,
Cares to compete:
But cooperation's
A different case;
You should just see us.
In the three-legged race!
—*from Scouting (**UK**) magazine*

If the Earth...

If the Earth were only a few metres in diameter, floating a few metres above a field somewhere, people would come from everywhere to marvel at it. People would walk around it, marvelling at its big pools of water, its little pools, and the water flowing between the pools. People would marvel at the bumps on it and the holes in it, and they would marvel at the very thin layer of gas surrounding it and the water suspended in the gas. The people would marvel at all the creatures walking around the surface of the ball and at the creatures in the water.

The people would declare it as sacred because it was the only one, and they would protect it so that it would not be hurt. The ball would be the greatest wonder known, and people would come to pray to it, to be healed, to gain knowledge, to know beauty, and to wonder how it could be. People would love it and defend it with their lives

SCOUTER'S FIVE MINUTES

because they would somehow know that their lives, their own roundness, could be nothing without it. If the Earth were only a few metres in diameter...
— *from Scouting (UK) magazine*

Nature & I
I am part of Nature.
I am part of everything that lives.
I am bound together with all living things in air, in land, in water.
My life depends on Nature — upon its balance, upon its resources
    and upon the continuity of both.
To destroy them is to destroy myself
As a member of the human race, I am responsible for its survival.
I am a part of Nature.
I will not destroy it.
— *from Scouting (UK) magazine*

Campfire Openings
As our music cheers us, so be the melody of our lives;
As our mirth unites us, so be the harmony of our hearts;
As our spirits rise to the lilt of our song, so may the Great Spirit uplift
    us to renewed endeavour;
And may the happy fellowship of this circle go out into all the world.
— *thanks to John Lockie, Ottawa, Ont.*

Mosquito: Try this at a closing campfire. Each of the eight speakers holds up a large card showing his or her letter. You can spell out just about any word that has meaning to the people at your campfire.

M is for the memories we share tonight — the memories of camp.

O is for the opportunities we have to grow together, to learn new skills, and to share fellowship around this campfire tonight.

SCOUTER'S FIVE MINUTES

S is for the super things we have done here and the super people we have met and made our friends.

Q is for the quiet times we experience together — times to reflect and give thanks.

U is for the ultimate peacefulness of the outdoors.

I is for the inspiration we receive from nature and from our friends.

T is for the terrific leaders who have been with us at camp.

O is for "On with the Show!'
Put them all together, and what do you have?
MOSQUITO!
— *thanks to Linda Kish, Lethbridge, Alta.*

God of the Open Air
The Spring '87 issue of Canadian Camping Magazine *included two prayers and a benediction the editor kindly gave us permission to reprint. They were submitted by Madelene Allen, St. Donat, Quebec.*

God of the open air, we rejoice that we can live in touch with sunshine and rain and growing things. The drumbeat of a shower on the tent roof, the fragrance of fresh, cool forest trails, an evening under the stars — all speak to us of You. No one but You could ever supply such beauty. No one but You could ever provide the inner strength which comes from sleeping under the stars, or singing together around a campfire, or paddling down a sleepy river...

The trees stand tall and straight above us, and we feel that we want to grow to be like them. The wind sings in the trees, and we try to remember that sound forever. The stars sparkle in a dark night sky, and we fall asleep wondering. Oh God, keep us good campers, we pray, throughout all our lives striving to uphold all that is pure and ideal. God of the open air, this is our prayer today.

Good Morning, God
Dear Father, this is me talking.
Of course, You know I'm at camp.
I'll try to be good today, and I sure am having a good time:
Swimming and paddling that canoe, and going fishing are such fun.
I'm glad You thought of making cool blue water, and sunshine, and silvery fish,
But, God, what about that fish that got away yesterday?
Where did he go?
You make such pretty things, God.
I like the way the pine trees stand up on the hill.
I like the red flash of the wing of a red-winged blackbird,
The funny feel of the milkweed pod I picked,
The big golden moon,
And the feel of wiggling my toes in the cool, wet, sand.
Thank you, God, for making all these things.
Oh, and please bless everyone and help me be a good camper all day today.
Good morning, God.

A Benediction
May the silence of the hills,
The joy of the wind,
The music of the birds,
The fire of the sun,
The strength of the trees,
And the faith of youth,
In all of which is God,
Be in our hearts now and evermore.

SCOUTER'S FIVE MINUTES

Jesus, A Camper

Jesus would make a good camper.
He loved the out-of-doors —
Mountains and sparkling blue waters,
A campfire on sandy shores,
Hikes along dusty brown roadways
A friend or two at His side,
Talks when the cool shadows lengthened
And the sun melted into the tide.
Jesus would make a great camper
Because He loved people, too;
Campers of all kinds and all races
Would find Him a comrade true;
He had a way that was thoughtful,
Courageous and glad and free;
Should He appear on these campgrounds,
An all-round camper He'd be.
—*from Linda Kish, Lethbridge, Alta.*

World Hunger Grace

For food in a world where many walk in hunger;
For faith in a world where many walk in fear;
For friends in a world where many walk alone;
We give thee humble thanks, O Lord.

A Scouter's Thanks

I give thanks for all the fun in Scouting,
For all the friends I've made;
For the time I've had to pass to others
The things I've learned and made.
I give thanks for joyful hours of camping,
For every bush and tree,

SCOUTER'S FIVE MINUTES

For all the dawns and sunsets
That you have given me.
— *William Fraser, Dartmouth, N.S.*

Working Together
Kind hearts, kind words, kind deeds
Come easy with our friends;
Can we with strangers do the same
And happier hours spend?
The fire is lit, the gloom is chased,
And friendship now takes its place.
—***The Grapevine***, *Niagara Region, Ont.*

There is enough in the world for everyone's need, but not enough for everyone's greed. If everyone cared enough and everyone shared enough, wouldn't everyone have enough? (Dr. Frank N.D. Buckman, *Scouting (U.K.)* magazine)

Promise — A Prayer
Scouter Andrew Robertson of the 219th Toronto writes, "One day, we were looking for a prayer to use in our annual Scout Week church parade. As we talked, the idea came to use the promise and turn it into a litany. A litany is a prayer made into a series of verses and responses and involves the boys in the process of talking to God. The promise was the perfect start to the conversation. We hope you can use this idea at a regular meeting, a campfire, or as part of your church parade.

LEADER (L): Oh God, help all of us to think about our promise and law. Be with us at all times while we try to live up to them.

PEOPLE (P): On my honour, I promise

L: Help us, good Lord, to keep our word.

Scouter's Five Minutes

P: To do my best,

L: Help us, good Lord, to keep on trying, even when it seems very difficult.

P: To love and serve God,

L: Help us, good Lord, to love and serve you as we should and to know that, whatever we have done to displease you, you still forgive and love us, and that you have a place for us.

P: To love and serve my queen and my country,

L: Help us, good Lord, to strive for peace, to obey the laws of our country, use its resources wisely, and care about and appreciate its many different peoples.

P: To love and serve others,

L: Help us, good Lord, to be concerned about each other, even if others don't always show concern for us; and help us to be grateful for all we have and to do a good deed each day.

P: And to live by the law laid down by our founders.

L: Help us, good Lord, to be helpful and trustworthy, kind and cheerful, considerate and clean, and wise in the use of our resources.

P: Help us, oh God, by your love and strength, to do all that we promise.

Scouter's Five Minutes

When the Night Ends

"How can we determine the hour of dawn — when the night ends and the day begins?" the rabbi asked his students.

"When, from a distance, you can distinguish between a dog and a sheep?" one of the students suggested.

"No," the rabbi answered.

"Is it when you can distinguish between a fig tree and a grapevine?" another student asked.

"No," he replied.

"Please tell us the answer then," said the students.

"It is when you can look into the face of a human being and have enough light to recognize in him your brother," the wise teacher replied. "Up until then, it is night, and darkness is still with us."

A Persian Proverb

God will not ask thy race,
Nor will He ask thy birth;
Alone He will demand of thee,
What hast thou done on earth?

Peace cannot be kept by force. It can be achieved only by understanding. (Albert Einstein)

Sweet Grass and Candle

*This material is used with permission from **Canadian Camping Magazine**. Written by Rev. John W. Oldham after an ecumenical worship service for native and non native people, it is dedicated to Canada's Original Peoples.*

Sweet grass and candle, the peace pipe and bible
The stories of elders and beat of the drum;
They are the symbols of true faith and justice:
We gather in circle, affirming we're one.

Scouter's Five Minutes

Welcome the stranger, for he is our brother,
And she is our sister, of mother earth:
Care for creation, for all life is sacred,
And we are united by vision's rebirth.

Join in the circle that will have no ending,
For we are all equal and loved in God's sight;
Praise the Great Spirit! We gather as family
To sing of love's freedom and dance with delight!
Welcome the stranger, for he is our brother,
And she is our sister, of mother earth.
Care for creation, for all life is sacred,
And we are united by vision's rebirth.

All the flowers of all the tomorrows are in the seeds of today.

On Wings of Love
The priceless gift of life is love.
For with the help of God above
Love can change the human race
And make this world a better place:
For love dissolves all hate and fear
And makes our visions bright and clear,
So we can see and rise above
Our pettiness, on wings of love.
— *The Beaver's Bark, northern B.C.*

He who can no longer listen to his brother will soon be no longer listening to God either. (Dietrich Bonhoeffer)

Scouting's Prayer for Peace
As December brings hope for love, understanding and peace, we open with a linked-hands group prayer from the World Scouting organization and up with material from several Scouting publications, prime among them South Africa's *Veld Lore*.

SCOUTER'S FIVE MINUTES

O God, we join with Scouts throughout the world to pray for peace. Grant that, through Scouting, we may come to understand each other better and learn to live together in harmony.

All the World is Our Neighbour

Give us vision, Lord, to see this world as You would have it be. Give us strength of purpose and courage to do Your will, whatever difficulties come our way.

Give us healthy bodies and strength and the joy of living. Teach us to love the open road, the fresh air, the hills, the lakes, the rivers and all the beauties of nature created by You.

Above all, O Lord, give us that wonderful gift of love. May we realize that all the world is our neighbour. Give us the strength and will always to help each other.

Sometimes our light goes out but is blown again into flame by an encounter with another human being. Each of us owes the deepest thanks to those who have rekindled this inner light. (Albert Schweitzer)

Heavenly Treasures

In the days of the Second Temple, King Monobaz became a convert to Judaism. At a time of famine, he unlocked his ancestral treasures and distributed them among the poor. His ministers rebuked him, saying, "Thy fathers amassed; though dost squander."

"Nay," said the benevolent king. "they preserved earthly but I heavenly treasures: theirs could be stolen, mine are beyond mortal reach: theirs were barren, mine will bear fruit time without end: they preserved money. I have preserved lives. The treasures which my fathers laid by are forth is world: mine are for eternity." *(The Talmud)*

Scouter's Five Minutes

What's Christmas?

Christmas is fir trees, spruce trees and pine,
Strung with bright balls and bright lights that shine,
Icicles hanging and "snow" on the boughs,
With more gifts beneath than the space allows.

Christmas is fridges, fur coats and clothes,
(Depends on the bait to which Santa Claus rose)
Right down to hankies and gadgets for shelves,
And trinkets the donors could well use themselves.

Christmas is homecoming: train tracks and road
Bring back the wanderers, load after load;
Hand-clasps and kisses, joy-founded tears,
Uniting old friendships parted by years.

But back of it all, there is peace and good will;
A star over Bethlehem, silent and still,
Yet spreading the word on the wings of the morn,
The Christ Child this day to the world has been born.

Give Us Courage

Give us courage, O Lord, to stand up and be counted;
To stand up for those who cannot stand up for themselves;
To stand up for ourselves when it is needful for us to do so.
Let us fear nothing more than we fear You.
Let us love nothing more than we love You, for in this way we shall
    fear nothing else...
Let us seek no other peace but the peace which is Yours:
Make us its instruments, opening our eyes and our ears and our hearts

SCOUTER'S FIVE MINUTES

so that we should know always what work of peace we may do for You.
— Alan Paton, author of *Cry the Beloved Country.* Thanks to *Scouting (U.K.)* magazine.

Let's Look After It

"This land belongs to many people, some of whom are dead, some of whom are living, but most of whom have yet to be born."
— *wise words of an African chief quoted in the **New Zealand Scout News.***

Self-Respect

Self-respect cannot be hunted:
It is never for sale,
It cannot be purchased:
It comes to us in quiet moments
In quiet places,
When we suddenly realize that
Knowing the good, we have done it;
Knowing the beautiful, we have served it;
Knowing the truth, we have spoken it.
— *A. Whitney Griswold, with thanks to **Hai-Etlik,** Islands Region, B.C.*

Loving & Serving God

God, I give you my hands to do your work;
I give you my feet to go your way;

I give you my tongue to speak your truth,
That I may meet the challenge of the Promise and Law,
Grow in my love for you,
And seek to build a better world for everybody.

SCOUTER'S FIVE MINUTES

Grace

The bread is on our table,
Bless those who have no bread,
And give us grace in sharing
This bounty round us spread.

- - -

If I Had a Kid

If I had a kid, I would want him to be a Scout in this world today. I would want his Scouter to be somebody who could accept that people can disagree without being disagreeable. I would want him to be somebody who could discuss things and accept other people as human beings even if he didn't agree with them. I would want him to be kind. I would want him to be somebody who would teach my kid that democracy is a good thing and works if we listen, work together, look at both sides and, yes, sometimes compromise.

I wouldn't want him to think he was the only one in the world who tried hard. If he didn't, he couldn't help my kid to be any different from a lot of other people who walk the streets today and try to tear down the world around them. How many of those kinds of Scouters do we have? How many do we need?
— *author unknown: thanks to the **Sarnia Pacemaker**, Ont.*

My friend is not perfect, nor am I. We suit each other admirably!

- - -

If Only...

Won Lee was a stone cutter who lived in ancient China. He cut large stones and he cut small stones. He made them into ornaments

SCOUTER'S FIVE MINUTES

for gardens. Some he cut to build houses. He was proud of his work, but sometimes he would think, "If only I had more money" or "If only I had less work."

One day, Won Lee was walking home from work. The sun was very hot and he was tired, so he sat down at the side of the road. He felt the heat of the sun and thought, "It's the sun that gives us the daylight, the warmth to grow our crops. Surely the sun must be the most powerful of all things.

Won Lee said quietly to himself, "God, if only I could be the sun. I would love to feel what it is like to be the most powerful, the greatest of all things."

God answered Won Lee. "You may become the sun," He said. And Won Lee became the sun. He felt wonderful; so strong and powerful. He shone down on the world far below.

After a few days, a puffy white cloud appeared in the sky. It drifted about and, when it came near Won Lee, it blotted out his rays and cast a shadow on the world. Won Lee was sad. Surely this cloud was more powerful than he? "If only I were the cloud. That would make me the greatest of all things," he said.

God heard, and again He answered: "Won Lee, you may become the cloud." So Won Lee floated about the sky feeling very grand.

One day, Won Lee saw a great black cloud coming his way. Soon it surrounded him, and he saw the black cloud dripping droplets of water. The drops fell on the earth and made a mighty river.

Won Lee thought that this black cloud must be very powerful to swallow up a cloud and turn itself into a river, so he said, "If only I were the river. How mighty I would be. Then I would be truly happy."

Again God heard and answered: "Okay. You may be the river."

So Won Lee flowed along, feeling the mighty rush of water. Then he came to a bend in the river. There was a great boulder jutting out into the river. The great boulder held the river, swirling it back onto itself.

Won Lee thought, "The rock! The rock! At last I have found the mightiest of all things. If this rock can hold back the raging river, then it is the greatest. If only I were this great big rock, I would be happy.

SCOUTER'S FIVE MINUTES

So God made Won Lee into the boulder and he stood there, holding back the water and feeling very great and happy. Then, one day, along came a man who cut a large piece off the boulder. Won Lee was sad. No longer was he the greatest if this man could come along and cut him up.

"If only I could be the man who cut up the stone, I would surely be the greatest," Won Lee thought.

And God said to Won Lee: "But you are the Stone Cutter!"
— *with thanks to **Australian Scout** magazine.*

Prayer

Thank you, God. It is a grey day, yet I am happy. Not because some special thing is going to happen, but because I am at peace within.

I do not wish I were someone else: I am glad to be me. I do not wish I were someplace else: I am happy being where I am. I am learning to savour the present moment, and to be glad to be alive and living in it. Thank you, God.
— *from Linda Kish, Lethbridge, Alta.*

When You Walk Through Woods

When you walk through woods, I want you to see
The floating gold of a bumblebee,
Rivers of sunlight, pools of shade,
Toadstools sleeping in mossy jade,
A cobweb net with a catch of dew,
Treetop cones against the blue,
Dancing flowers, bright green flies,
And birds that put rainbows in your eyes.

SCOUTER'S FIVE MINUTES

When you walk through woods, I want you to hear
A million sounds in your eager ear;
The scratch and rattle of wind-tossed trees,
The rush as a timid chipmunk flees,
The cry of a hawk from the distant sky,
The purr of leaves when a breeze rolls by,
Brooks that mumble, stones that ring,
And birds that teach your heart to sing.
When you walk through woods, I want you to feel
That no mere human could make this real,
Could paint the throb of a butterfly's wing,
Could teach a wood thrush how to sing,
Could create these wonders of earth and sky;
There's something greater than you or I.
When you walk through woods and the birches nod,
Please, meet a friend of mine named God.
— *Anon*

God is always present in the formless form and speaks to us in the soundless sound. Blessed is the person who is able to see Him and listen to Him everywhere and in everything. (Swami Nirmala-nanda)

Evening Prayer

Lord, in the quiet of the evening, come into our hearts as we lie down to rest, and help us to know that, in camping outdoors, we need not fear. You are with us.
— *The Outlook,* B.C./Yukon

Camp Closing Prayer

God, we thank you for this beautiful weekend. The smiling faces we see and the laughter we hear echoing through the trees fill our hearts with gladness and remind us that, in this fast-paced world of ours, there are times when we all need to pause and refresh ourselves in nature's calm and beauty.

Scouter's Five Minutes

You Know It Was a Great Camp When...
- the Scouts fall asleep on the way home;
- everybody is too tired to complain, and you're too tired to care if they do;
- you have managed to bring back most of the troop gear, and none of the dishes are mouldy:
- you introduced the visiting assistant district commissioner to your assistant and you couldn't remember his name;
- you introduced yourself to the assistant district commissioner and you couldn't remember your name;
- you have half a dozen new jokes to tell at work;
- your head count finally comes out right just as you get back to the hall;
- the troop critic looks up at you and says, "How come we never did this last year?"
- your spouse (mother, friend) refuses to come close to you because of the way you smell;
- your dog thinks you smell wonderful.

—*Greybeard, Sunnybrook, Alta.*

The things that count most in life are usually the things that cannot be counted. (Bernard Meltzer)

Our Spiritual Compass

For Scouts on a hike or canoe trip, a compass is an important tool. Because it gives you a stable reference point (magnetic north), you can set a course and follow it. As long as your compass is accurate and you don't damage it, it will serve you faithfully. If you trust it.

SCOUTER'S FIVE MINUTES

Our faith or spirituality is something like that. We have a point of reference that does not change, God. And we have a compass, so to speak, in our relationship with God. It's something we have learned and continue to learn about, just as we learn to use a compass properly.

We use our spirituality and faith to get us through this grand journey we call life. If we are prepared to trust the things we have learned about God and creative living, our spirituality can guide us through the joys and temptations of life. We can use it to show us what service we may give and what potential dangers to stay away from. We can use it to guide us in our friendships, in our work, in what we say to people and about people, and in how we treat our natural world.
— *Scouter Rob Brown, N. Saskatchewan Region*

From "Roots & Wings"
In this fragile age, it is more important than ever that youth be given the opportunity to interact and to experience to look through the diversity and multiplicity of cultures, religious beliefs, ideologies and systems around them and discover workable principles and elements common and sacred to all... In this lies the hope that, through youth's natural affinity to find in each other elements that transcend the traditional barriers of nationality, class, religion and cultural differences, this generation will discover the answers that have eluded those before them. *(Jeanne Sauvé, Governor General of Canada and Chief Scout, from an address at the University of Alberta, Sept. '87)*

Patience
An aged man, whom Abraham hospitably invited to his tent, refused to join him in prayer to the one spiritual God. Learning that the old man was a non-believer, Abraham drove him from his door. Later that night, God appeared to Abraham in a vision. "I have borne with that ignorant man for 70 years," he said. "Could you not have patiently suffered him one night?" *(The Talmud)*

Scouter's Five Minutes

A Beaver's Spring Prayer
Thank you, God, for the wind that dries and warms the earth so that seeds may grow, giving us food to eat and flowers to see and smell. And thank you for fun outdoors on windy days.

Campfire Opening
May this fire touch us with the magic of its mystery;
May we see in its dance the ever-changing beauty of the world;
May this fire be good medicine
Where fellowship, adventure, and fun sit side by side;
May this fire tonight remain forever in our hearts,
Even as the first fire kindled by our ancestors
Has remained alight through the ages.

Campfire Closing
As darkness creeps into our circle of light,
Embers that glow and sigh
Draw our friendship circle closer,
Whisper memories that will not die:
God's magic danced in our fire's flames,
And fills the gathering night
With mystery and a wondrous peace,
That bids safe sleep 'til morning's light.

A Man on a Hill
by Scouter Shanie, 902nd Toronto Cubs

A time ago, a man on a hill had a thought. What could he do to help his country, his world? The thought became a plan, and 20 boys sailed off to Brownsea Island. By 1909, those 20 had become thousands of boys and girls, men and women. The plan was now a course of action.

SCOUTER'S FIVE MINUTES

Years later, in the midst of battle, a soldier spares his enemy and tends his wounds, because both are Scouts. The course of action is something more. Wells are dug, schools are built. Many people share, help without-fanfare, because that thought is now a way of life.

From that one thought stretches a web of hands, young and not-so-young, male and female, all faiths, all peoples. We are an important link in the encircling net. What will we do with our small share of the thought? Whose hand will we, in turn, grasp?

Only One

I am only one person, so I can't change everything in this world. But, I *am* one person and I can change some things.

Creator Spirit, Come

O God, Creator of lakes and dunes,
Help us to feel your spirit
In the beauty of nature around us:
Make us calm and,
In the quiet, speak to us:
Help us to listen;
We have so much to learn from you
And also from one another:
Help us to share
Our plans and our decisions,
Our dreams and expectations:
Help us to celebrate
Your presence among us,
And to work together in your name.
— *Martha Koenig, from* ***United Church Camping****, Spring'85*

A Grace a Day

When a Pack Scouter in the U.K. found his Cubs always mechanically repeated "For what we are about to receive..." before camp meals, he decided to try a different grace each meal. He

SCOUTER'S FIVE MINUTES

prepared some cards with a short grace on each side and, at meals, placed a card on each table. The person asked to say grace picked up a card and chose the one he wanted. The Cubs were always eager to read the cards, he says.

You might ask each of your Cubs to create his own two graces and prepare such a card to bring to camp. These examples are some of the graces our Scouter used to start the idea.

This happy meal will happier be
If we, O God, remember Thee.

We thank you, God, for happy hearts,
For fine and sunny weather;
We thank you, God, for this our food,
And that we are together.

For every cup and plateful,
God make us truly grateful.

As we enjoy this earthly food
At this table you have spread,
We'll not forget to thank you, God,
For all our daily bread.

Zulu Farewell

Go well and safely, go well and safely,
Go well and safely, the Lord be ever with you.
Stay well and safely, stay well and safely,
Stay well and safely, the Lord be ever with you.

RECIPES

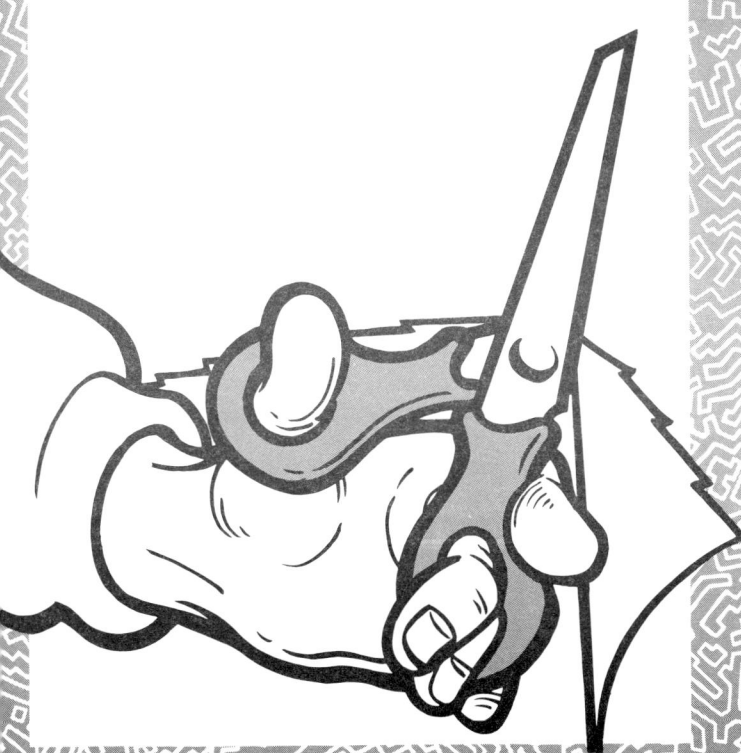

RECIPES

THANKSGIVING

At this season of plentiful rich foods it might be timely to read the following menus printed in a wartime issue of "The Scouter". At a time when many basic foods, such as meat and butter, were severely rationed, leaders still planned weekend camps and shared hints on stretching the rations to satisfy hungry Scouts.

Here is the menu of a patrol which camped Saturday afternoon till Sunday afternoon in April at a cost of 1s.3d. a head, and they had, if anything, more in quantity than was necessary.

Saturday — Tea-supper: Bread, margarine, jam, cocoa.
Sunday — Breakfast: Porridge (1 1/2 tablespoons for each boy), egg and fried bread, bread, margarine, tea (1 teaspoon each).
Dinner: Boiled fresh haddock and sauce, potatoes, rhubarb and custard.
Tea: Bread, margarine, jam, tea.

Here is the menu of another patrol, and it also cost 1s.3d. a head.

Saturday — Tea-supper: Sardine fritters, bread, margarine, cocoa.
Sunday — Breakfast: Porridge, eggs and fried bread, bread, margarine, tea.
Dinner: Stew, boiled rice and syrup.
Tea: Bread, margarine, jam, tea.

• You would be wise to consult your butcher about what kind of meat is not rationed, and what cuts are cheap. Certain cheap cuts, if stewed very slowly for a very long time, are quite as good as the expensive parts. The patrol who had the second of these menus started the stew on the supper fire, left the billy in the embers at night, and put it on the fire again directly after breakfast on Sunday. It was never allowed to boil and, although a cheap cut, was very tender owing to the amount of slow simmering.

RECIPES

- It is always wise to make porridge on the supper fire and leave the billy on the ashes at night, because porridge — real oats, not the packet stuff — needs to cook for a long time and it saves a lot of trouble in the morning.

- For fritters of any kind (sardine, bacon, bananas, etc.) take flour, break an egg into it, mix and then beat milk in, to a thick creamy consistency. Get some fat boiling in a frying pan, pour in the batter, and wrap it round the sardine or other filling.

- To cook and make sauce for cod, fresh haddock, etc., put the fish into a billy with just enough water to cover it. (If the billy is at all old and the quality of the tin has suffered, it is wise to stand the fish on a plate in the billy or it may taste unpleasant.) Boil the fish slowly until cooked. In another billy put a lump of margarine (1 oz. is enough for a patrol), melt it over the fire, mix in a tablespoonful of flour very slowly and stir until the flour forms a dry lump which does not stick to the tin. Then very slowly pour in the fish stock (water in which the fish has been boiled) and stir continuously over the fire until you have a sauce.

(We've come a long way from the days when kids at camp could be fed for approximately 17 cents a head! But the article also suggests bulk buying through your group committee, to save on funds, an idea worth considering.)

BIBLE CAKE

Here's an unusual approach to baking a cake. The recipe is believed to be for the cakes from which hot-cross buns originated, and therefore is most appropriate for the Easter month. Because you will have to look up Bible references *(King James version)* to discover the ingredients, a little organization can make this a challenging study and cooking activity.

RECIPES

Ingredients

1. 250 g Judges v. 25, (last clause)
2. 250 g Jeremiah vi. 20
3. 1 tablespoon 1 Samuel xiv. 25
4. 3 Jeremiah xvii. 11
5. 250 g 1 Samuel xxx. 12
6. 250 g Nahum iii. 12, chopped
7. 2 oz. blanched Numbers xvii. 8, chopped
8. 500 g 1 Kings iv. 22
9. Season with 2 Chronicles ix. 9
10. A pinch of Leviticus ii. 13.
11. 1 teaspoon Amos iv. 5
12. 3 tablespoons Judges iv. 19, (second ingredient mentioned in the verse).

The ingredients the boys should find are: butter, sugar, honey, eggs, raisins, figs, almonds, flour, spice, salt, yeast and milk.

Procedure

Cream together 1, 2 and 3.
Add 4, one at a time, beating well.
Beat in 5, 6 and 7.
Sift together 8, 9, 10 and 11 and stir into first mixture.
Stir in 12. Bake in a slow oven (160°C) for 1 1/2 hours.
Eat while still warm.

MONSTER (Sour Dough)

Sour dough at camp makes biscuits, pancakes, jackets for 'pigs in a blanket', etc. The possibilities are unlimited, once you have established your Monster.

RECIPES

Sour dough starter
500 mL milk
500 mL flour
Pour milk into a glass or ceramic bowl and cover with cheese cloth. Let stand, preferably outdoors, for one day. Stir in flour and re-cover bowl. Leave outside for two days. Bring it inside and allow it to sit until it begins to bubble and sour. Refrigerate in a large plastic container with a good fitting lid. Monster has been born.

Never touch Monster with metal! Feed once a week if you are kind. When you begin to use Monster regularly, you must feed twice weekly. Always feed 24 hours before use. Diet is: 250 mL whole milk, 250 mL flour and 1/3 cup white sugar, well stirred in. To make sure you'll always have starter, put a cup of Monster in a plastic container with a tight lid, label and freeze.

Basic Monster Biscuits
To 250 mL Monster, add 250 mL flour, 1/3 cup vegetable oil, 2 tsp. baking powder, 1/2 tsp. baking soda and 1/8 tsp. salt. Mix well in plastic or glass bowl. Turn out on floured surface and knead lightly 8 to 10 times, or until stickiness is gone. Flatten with hands to 3 cm thickness, cut into biscuits, cover with cloth and let stand in pan for 10 minutes. Bake 10 to 15 minutes (longer in a reflector oven) at medium-high heat (400 degrees F). Don't forget to feed Monster when you're done!
— *Thanks to Gene Refausse, Trenton, Ont.*

Among other things, Christmas is a time for goodies, and boys will have fun learning to make sweet things to eat. Recognizing that few meeting places are equipped with ovens, we offer a number of no-bake sweet recipes. One of them requires a hotplate or other source of surface heat, and we did include a "cookie paint" recipe for lucky groups who have access to an oven.

RECIPES

Cubs will certainly want to sample their products, but they also can gift-package goodies for friends, serve them at a party, or wrap them in foil and hang them on the tree as special treats for visitors.

PEANUT BUTTER BALLS
- 250 mL peanut butter
- 250 mL (or a little less) liquid honey
- 250 mL milk powder
- Chopped dried fruit (apples, dates, raisins, apricots) and nuts
- Toasted coconut or sesame seeds

Combine peanut butter, honey and milk powder and mix well. Stir in dried fruit and nuts. Form into balls and roll in coconut or sesame seeds. Chill.

FONDANTS
- 8 oz. icing sugar
- 2 tbsp condensed milk
- peppermint, vanilla or fruit flavouring
- food colour appropriate to flavouring shredded coconut, chopped nuts or grated chocolate
- walnut or almond halves

Sift icing sugar. Blend in milk until creamy. Add chosen flavour and colour. Form into balls and roll in coconut, nuts or grated chocolate. Press half nuts into balls and let set.

CHOCOLATE BITES
- 1 can chow mein noodles
- 12 oz. chocolate chips
- 12 oz. butterscotch chips
- 1 lb. peanuts

In a saucepan, melt together the two kinds of chips. Mix in noodles and peanuts. Drop by spoonful onto waxed paper and let set.

RECIPES

PEPPERMINT CREAMS
- 1 egg white
- 500 g icing sugar
- peppermint flavouring to taste

Whip egg white until fluffy. Stir in a third of the icing sugar. Beat well. Continue to beat while adding the rest of the sugar, but don't let the dough become too dry and stiff. It should be soft and pliable when you add peppermint flavouring and knead well. Form into balls, roll in icing sugar and let set.

If you have a portable oven, bring it and some refrigerator cookie dough to a meeting, then let your boys cut and paint Christmas cookies. Make "cookie paint" by beating together:
- 3 egg yolks
- 1 tsp water
- 1 tsp sugar

Pour portions of this mixture into three or four separate containers and tint each portion a different colour with food colouring. After the boys have rolled, cut and placed the dough on baking sheets, they can use clean paint-brushes to paint faces or designs on their cookies. Bake as per cookie recipe.

If an oven is simply out of the question, bring along a batch of pre-baked cookies, ingredients for a simple icing, and food colouring.

Have the boys make up the icing, tint portions different colours and, using clean brushes, paint the cookies with coloured icing.

The return of the hiking season means it's time to sift through recipes for nutritious, high energy foods that you can prepare ahead and carry along.

RECIPES

NIBBLERS
500 mL salted peanuts
375 mL large-flake rolled oats
500 mL raisins
125 mL shredded coconut
500 mL sunflower seeds
60 mL honey
15 mL cooking oil
2 mL vanilla
Combine first 5 ingredients in a large bowl. You can vary the proportions to taste. In sauce pan, heat honey and oil to boiling. Boil one minute, remove from heat and add vanilla. Pour over ingredients in bowl and toss to coat evenly. Spread mixture out on flat pan and dry for several hours. Seal in zip-lock plastic bags and carry in pocket for on-the-trail munching.

FRUIT LEATHER
Use ripe apples, pears, peaches, etc. Cover a potful of fruit with water and bring to a simmer. Simmer until fruit is soft, then drain off juice and press the fruit through a sieve. Add honey or sugar to taste. Pour the mixture onto a greased baking sheet and put into a 120°C oven until dry. Cut into strips and roll. Store in an airtight container, and repackage in a plastic bag on hiking day. Carry in a spot you can easily reach when the hiking "hungries" hit.

WALKING SALAD
Cut off the top of a large apple and core. Scoop out most of the flesh of the apple and chop finely. Add raisins, nuts, sunflower seeds, and cottage cheese or plain yogurt to the chopped apple. Mix well and stuff the mixture back into the apple shell. Replace the top of the apple, wrap in plastic or foil, and carry along to eat while walking.

RECIPES

THERMOS TREAT
2 tablespoons peanut butter
2 tablespoons honey
425 mL milk
5 mL vanilla
5 mL wheat bran
5 ice cubes
sprinkle of cinnamon
Put ingredients in blender and blend at high speed. Pour into chilled thermos, wrap with newspaper, and carry in pack. Serves four tired, thirsty hikers.

MID-DAY MEALS
• Cut a large Spanish onion in half and scoop out the middle of each portion. Fill one half with seasoned hamburger meat. Sprinkle on some grated cheddar, cap with the other onion half and wrap in heavy duty foil. Seal well and, when lunch time comes, put package directly on the coals to cook.

• Cook chicken dinner while you walk. Early in the morning, wash, dry and season a whole chicken. Cover it with barbeque sauce if you like. Wrap several stones in foil, and heat them until very hot. Quickly put a large heated stone in the chicken cavity and tuck others under wings and around thighs. Wrap chicken in heavy duty foil, then wrap the whole parcel in several insulating layers of newspaper. Put into a plastic bag, tie closed and load into your pack.

Tell one of your hiking buddies to bring along carrot and celery sticks, and have others bring bread and drinks. Hot chicken should be ready to unwrap and eat by noon.

COLD WEATHER DRINKS
Chai — Hot Spicy Tea
Cries of *"Chai, gurram chai!"* — tea, hot tea — are welcome sounds to many a weary traveller in India. Tea sellers and tea stalls or shops

RECIPES

are found at frequent intervals beside the busy roads. Try some for yourself.

You need: tea leaves
        sugar
        milk
        a pinch of cinnamon powder
        1 or 2 cardamom seeds

In a saucepan, heat a pint of water. When water is boiling, add 4 or 5 teaspoons of tea leaves. Boil for a few seconds, remove pan rom heat and stir in milk, sugar and spices. Return to heat just until boiling, then pour through a strainer into cups.
— *thanks to Jim Sharp, Montreal*

Campfire Hot Chocolate
Just thought I'd send a note describing the production of the best large batch of campfire hot chocolate I ever tasted. We boiled a measured volume of water and added powdered milk as per the directions on the box. We then added an instant powdered chocolate of the kind you can mix with either hot or cold milk, again using quantities suggested on the box. It eliminated the need for someone to stand over the milk to make sure it didn't overheat, and the results were so good we couldn't fit enough in the pot to satisfy 15 people.
— *thanks to David Butt, St. John's, Nfld.*

HOT TRAIL BREAKFASTS
Porridge
Pre-mix oatmeal, raisins (to taste), brown sugar, powdered milk, salt, and a touch of cinnamon if desired, Apportion mix in plastic bags. At breakfast time, simply add water and cook.

Wheat Germ & Apple Pancakes
175 mL whole wheat flour
175 mL all purpose flour
30 mL wheat germ

RECIPES

15 mL baking powder
2 mL salt
2 mL cinnamon
150 mL dry egg powder
15 mL brown sugar
170 mL powdered milk
125 mL dried apples, chopped

Package in plastic bag with these instructions: Melt 4 tablespoons margarine in frying pan. Add enough water to the dry ingredients to make a thin batter. Add melted margarine. Fry pancakes in greased pan. Mix makes 8-10 pancakes.
— *thanks to Helen Singh, Little Fort, B.C.*

SWEET FUN

Mock Angel Cake
Cut white bread into large fingers and spear on toasting fork. Dip fingers into condensed milk and then into coconut. Toast over the fire.
— *thanks to Bob Lamarche and Petawawa District Scouters' News*

Fruity Bits — Candle Cooking
Peel fresh fruit and cut into chunks. Spear with skewers. Dip fruit pieces first in orange juice and then in brown sugar. Heat over candles, taking care not to burn.
— *thanks to Scout (Australia), July '81*

Donut Balls
Beat 125 mL water into 250 mL biscuit mix to make stiff, sticky dough. Drop small spoonfuls into hot oil in pan. When nicely browned, remove and put into a paper bag containing a sugar/cinnamon mixture. Shake to coat.
Makes 12 donut balls.

RECIPES

Recipes from the Kitchens of the Officer's Quarters, Historic Fort York

We thank Alistair McLaren of Bramalea, Ont., who obtained these historic recipes in response to a reader's request, and the Toronto Historical Board for supplying them.

"I am advised that most of these recipes can be made, with slight changes, at camp," Alistair writes. The Toronto Historical Board explains some of the "slight changes":

"In keeping with the ingredients available to the pioneer housewife in Upper Canada, the ingredients used in these recipes include brown sugar and pearlash. Baking powder may be substituted for pearlash."

Of course, you can also substitute margarine for butter and powdered for whole milk. The candied cranberries recipe may inspire you to try something similar with other fruits or berries. It also seems an ideal dish to try in an improvised solar oven. If the oven doesn't work or the sun disappears while you're cooking, just pour on milk and you'll still have a delicious dessert.

Welsh Cakes

2 small cups flour	1 tsp. pearlash
pinch salt	1/2 cup sugar
1/2 cup butter	1/2 cup lard
1 egg	1 cup currants

Mix well, roll thin, cut into circles. Flour griddle and brown. Turn with knife and brown on other side.

Candied Cranberries

Wash approximately 750 mL cranberries. Grease an oven dish well. Put cranberries in, sprinkle with about 375 mL brown sugar and bake in a moderate oven for about 40 minutes. Test to determine if sugar should be increased. Allow to cool for serving.

RECIPES

Dried Apple Cake
3 cups dried apples, soaked overnight in water. Chop slightly, let simmer for 1 1/2 hrs in 2 cups syrup or molasses. Add 2 eggs, 1 cup sugar, 1 cup milk, 1/2 cup butter, 1 tsp. soda, and enough flour to make a stiff batter. Bake in a quick oven.

Forcemeat
Combine about 250 mL of bread crumbs, 1 onion minced in mortar and pestle, and leftover meat, also minced. Add whatever seasonings are on hand — salt, pepper, parsley, tarragon, etc.

Bind the mixture with one or two eggs, as needed. Shape into balls and brown on the griddle.

Forcemeat balls are served in soups, as dressing in fowl and fish, and as a savoury in the fingers.

Currant Scones

2 scant cups flour	1/2 c. cold butter
2 tablespoons sugar	1/3 c. currants
3 teaspoons baking powder	1 egg
1/2 teaspoon salt	1/2 cup milk

Combine flour, sugar, baking powder and salt in a bowl. Using two knives, cut in butter until mixture has consistency of coarse corn meal.

Stir in currants. Pour egg and milk over surface of flour mixture; stir quickly and lightly with a fork to form a soft dough. It will be quite moist.

Turn dough onto lightly floured board and knead gently about 15 times. Shape dough into a ball; pat or roll out ball into an 8 inch circle about 1/2" thick. Cut circle of dough into 8 even pie-shaped wedges. Place on ungreased baking sheet, arranging so that they do not touch. Brush with lightly beaten egg. Bake in hot oven about 10 or 12 minutes.

RECIPES

Chefs Outdoors (J/J '83) included a lot of mouth-watering descriptions of the kinds of treats prepared by Venturers during an outdoors cooking contest in Toronto, but it didn't follow through with the recipes. Our requests finally convinced some of the "chefs" to share their culinary secrets, and Don Boyd, Venturer coordinator for the Greater Toronto Region, sent along these gourmet ideas.

DUCK WITH HONEY SOYA GLAZE

2 fresh ducks
apples
salt, pepper
peppercorns
basil
soya sauce
parsley
2 celery stalks
poultry seasoning
bay leaves
onions
honey
butter or margarine
grapes

Wash ducks and place them in a pot big enough to hold both. Add chopped celery stalks, including leaves, 3 onions (quartered) and 3 apples (quartered). Cover ducks with water and add 1 tbsp. poultry seasoning, salt and pepper to taste, 1/4 tbsp basil, a few peppercorns and bay leaves. Boil covered for 1 hour or until gamey taste is gone. Drain. Dry ducks with paper towel and place in roasting pan. Toss quartered onions and apples with poultry seasoning, salt and pepper and 1/2 lb. butter or margarine, and stuff ducks with the mixture. Cover and cook on top of stove until brown (30-45 minutes). Serve with glaze made of 4 parts honey to 1 part soya sauce. Garnish with parsley and grapes.

TROUT SURPRISE BARBEQUE

2 trout
1 tin small peas
1 small lemon
sprig of parsley
2 potatoes
1/2 c. butter
foil

Clean trout, leaving on heads and tails. Place 1/8 c. butter inside each fish, wrap in foil and place on barbeque. Open lid of peas and place on barbeque. Prepare potatoes, wrap with foil and place on barbeque.

RECIPES

When potatoes are done, decorate them with a serrated edge. Do likewise with lemon.

Arrange trout, potatoes and lemon on plate. Smooth remaining butter on top of fish and lay parsley for decoration. Place peas between fish and potatoes. Serves two.
— *Chefs Eric Gutteridge and Kevin Stinson, 3/5th Venturers.*

PINEAPPLE UPSIDE DOWN CAKE
Melt butter in cake pan. Sprinkle 1/2 cup brown sugar in bottom of pan and add 3 spoons of pineapple juice. Cover bottom of pan with pineapple slices and place a cherry in the centre. Prepare a single white cake mix and pour over sliced pineapple. Place in dutch oven (put a few stones in the bottom of oven to prevent cake from burning) and bake 25-40 minutes. Turn out on large plate. Serves 6.

CAMPER'S NO-COOK FUDGE
This recipe from Sarnia's *The Pacemaker* may not be "gourmet", but it's a great bedtime snack at camp. Melt 110 mL butter or margarine in 55 mL boiling water, add 110 mL cocoa, 110 mL dry milk, 1 mL salt, 1 mL vanilla and 1/2 kg powdered sugar. Mix well and spread in buttered pan. Top with nuts if desired, cool in ice chest for half an hour, cut and serve.

THANKSGIVING FARE

For the Meeting Hall
Here's an idea to help your section make the comparison between the richness of our way of living and the realities of life in less fortunate lands. With your section, make and eat *chapatis*, the basic diet of children in many countries of South East Asia and Africa. A child of Cub age in these lands might have one or two *chapatis* for breakfast, one or two *chapatis* with a few vegetables at mid-day, and a repeat performance, perhaps with some lentils, for supper. Try each of these "meals", and then talk.

Recipes

Chapatis
250 mL wholemeal flour
125 mL water
pinch salt

Mix flour and salt in a bowl and slowly add water, stirring to make a soft dough. Divide the dough into 10 pieces and flatten each into a circle. Cover with a cloth and leave for half an hour, then roll out very thin. To cook, place *chapatis* in a lightly greased pan over low heat. Turn often. They are done when crisp and brown.

For the Outdoors

Heavenly Biscuits
250 mL flour
10 mL baking powder
5 mL salt
30 mL butter
30 mL milk powder
15 mL whole egg powder
15 mL wheat germ
125 mL grated cheese
160 mL water

Mix dry ingredients, cut in butter and seal in plastic bag. At camp, all you need to do is add water. Shape biscuits in your hands and place them on a lightly greased foil pie plate. Place a second greased foil plate on top of the first, clamp together with paper clips, and place plate on moderately hot coals. Cook 10 minutes each side.

Fish 'n Trimmings in Foil
2 or 3 filets fish
2 strips bacon
small tin peas
potato
1 tbsp. butter

RECIPES

On foil, lay a strip of bacon, the filets and the second strip of bacon. Add tinned peas, very thin slices of potato, and butter. Wrap and cook on the grill 10 to 15 minutes.

Individual Foil Stew

Roll cubes of beef in seasoned flour and place on foil. Add diced vegetables, 1 teaspoon brown sugar and 2 tablespoons water. Wrap, leaving airspace around the ingredients. Cook slowly on the grill for an hour.

Sausage-Filled Spud

Scoop out the centre of a large potato and fill with chunks of sausage. Wrap in foil and cook 25-30 minutes on the grill, or 15-20 minutes directly on the coals.
— *We thank the **Petawawa District Scouters' News** (Jan. '83) for the three foil-meal recipes.*

Super-Quick S'Mores

What could be easier, or more fun. Each one places a square of milk chocolate on a graham cracker. Then he toasts a marshmallow over the fire or coals and pops it on top of the chocolate as soon as it's done to his taste. The heat of the marshmallow melts the chocolate. Have lots of graham crackers, chocolate and marshmallows on hand.

Lemon Drink

Make the lemon syrup at home and carry in a plastic bottle. At camp, add cold or hot water to make a delicious drink. Squeeze juice from fresh lemons into a saucepan. Stir in as many cups of sugar as you have lemon juice. Place on moderate heat and stir until sugar dissolves. Simmer at the same heat until the syrup is thick.

RECIPES

QUICK METRIC CONVERSIONS

MEASURES
250 mL – 1 cup
175 mL – 3/4 cup
125 mL – 1/2 cup
 60 mL – 1/4 cup

15 mL – 1 tbsp
 5 mL – 1 tsp
 2 mL – 1/2 tsp
 1 mL – 1/4 tsp

COOKING TEMPERATURES
 70°C – 150°F
100°C – 200°F
120°C – 250°F
140°C – 275°F
150°C – 300°F
160°C – 325°F

180°C – 350°F
190°C – 375°F
200°C – 400°F
220°C – 425F
230°C – 450°F
240°C – 475°F

PAN SIZE EQUIVALENTS
33 cm – 13 in.
25 cm – 10 in.
20 cm – 8 in.
10 cm – 4 in.
 5 cm – 2 in.

30 cm – 12 in.
22/23 cm – 9 in.
12 cm – 5 in.
 7 cm – 3 in.

NO-RECIPE COOKING PROPORTIONS
- 5 mL salt per 500 g (1 lb.) meat
- 15 mL baking powder per 500 mL flour
- 2 mL salt per 250 mL flour
- 30 mL flour per 250 mL liquid to make sauces or thicken juices

FOIL COOKING TIMES
Beef
- roast: 20 min. per 500 g at steady heat
- cubes: 45 minutes
- ground (patties): 15 minutes

RECIPES

Chicken
- whole: 1-1-1/2 hours
- pieces: 30-35 minutes

Fish
- whole: 20-30 minutes
- fillets, steaks: 10-15 minutes

Lamb
- chops: 40-45 minutes
- cubes: 45 minutes
- shank: 1 1/2 hours

Carrots
- whole: 45-60 minutes
- sliced: 20 minutes

Potatoes
- whole: 40-60 minutes
- sliced: 10-15 minutes

Corn: 20-30 minutes

Wieners: 5-8 minutes

Porkchops: 30-45 minutes

MEAL IN FOIL

For each serving, put 1/4 chicken on foil with an onion slice, a small sliced carrot and a small sliced potato. Season. Add 15 mL water and a pat of butter. Seal, leaving room for expansion. Cook on coals, turning several times, for about 30 minutes.

RECIPES

HOT SOUP FOR A WET DAY
750 mL water
3 chicken bouillon cubes
45 mL butter
250 mL instant potato flakes
500 mL milk
2 slices bacon, crisp cooked and crumbled
Heat water, bouillon cubes and butter. Add potato flakes and milk and heat thoroughly. Before serving, sprinkle with bacon. Serves 6.

FESTIVE FOOD FUN

Snack Swords: For a different snack one meeting night, provide banana slices, cheese slices and pretzel sticks. Invite boys to spear a slice of cheese, then a slice of banana on a pretzel, and try some "sword swallowing".

Stained Glass Cookies
You're planning a special Christmas celebration but don't have a kitchen at your meeting place. Perhaps you'll hold a regular meeting at someone's home so that the boys can prepare a few goodies for your party. Beavers and Cubs will enjoy making these festive cookies. The idea comes from *Making Your Own Traditions — Christmas*.

You need chilled ice-box cookie dough (perhaps prepared ahead by a leader), bright coloured lifesavers and foil-covered baking sheets.

The boys pinch off small pieces of dough and roll into 6 mm (1/4") thick strips which they use to outline shapes on the foil-lined sheet. Easiest are circles, squares, triangles, hearts and Christmas bells, but some boys may want to do more elaborate "drawings". Pinch the ends of the dough together firmly to hold.

RECIPES

Put the candies into a plastic bag and crush with a rolling pin. Boys then fill the openings in their shapes with the crushed candy. Bake for 8 to 10 minutes at 190°C, cool completely and peel off foil.

These cookies also make nice tree danglers. Keep the dough a little thicker at the top and poke in a hole for hanging before you bake them.

SNOWMAN COOKIES

This idea, from Manitoba Council's *Beaver Tales*, is another winner at a home meeting. For each four snowmen, combine 1/2 cup icing sugar, 1/2 cup butter or margarine and 1 teaspoon vanilla. Stir together 1/2 cup rolled oats, 1 cup sifted flour and 1/4 teaspoon salt. Combine with sugar/butter and mix well.

To make his snowman, each boy rolls one 4 cm dough ball for the base, one 3 cm ball for the middle, one 2.5 cm ball for the head and two 1.5 cm balls for arms. Put arms on a separate cookie sheet. Bake cookies at 325°F — 15 minutes for arms, 20 minutes for the rest.

When the snowmen pans are still warm from the oven, the boys roll them in icing sugar (place about a cup in a shallow dish).

To make the frosting with which they can glue their men together, mix a cup of icing sugar with a tablespoon of milk.

RECIPES

CAMP GRAVY MIX

Stir together 2/3 cup corn starch, 1/2 cup dry instant beef or chicken bouillon, 2 tablespoons dried parsley flakes. Store in air-tight container.

To make gravy at camp, melt 1 tablespoon butter in saucepan, stir in 2 tablespoons mix and 1 cup water. Bring to boil, stirring constantly and boil about a minute. Makes one cup.

You can use the same mix for a raisin sauce to serve with ham. Follow basic recipe but decrease water to 3/4 cup and mix in 1/2 cup applesauce and 1/2 cup raisins.

FUN FOOD

*We thank **The Beaver's Bark** from the Northern B.C. Region for the first two fun recipes, and Scouter Brenda Porteous, Prince George, for sharing the resource.*

Three Blind Mice

For each boy, you need a piece of melba toast, three pitted olives, a slice of cheese and three chow mein noodles.

The boys put their toast on a baking sheet, line up three olives on top of it and cover them with a slice of cheese. Place under the broiler until the cheese melts. Before they eat, let each boy insert a chow mein noodle tail under the cheese for each mouse. Looks funny — tastes yummy!

Apple Smiles

You need red apples cored and sliced, peanut butter and miniature marshmallows.

Each boy spreads one side of an apple slice with peanut butter, puts three or four marshmallows on top of the peanut butter, and makes a sandwich by placing another slice of apple on top. Show off the apple smiles to each other, then eat.

Scouter Sandra Hards, North Bay, Ont., sent us the 1st North Bay's resource book. Here are some of her colony's favourites.

Salad Dessert
Mix and toss together one cup of each ingredient: walnuts or pecans; drained pineapple chunks; mandarin oranges; coconut; sour cream; marshmallows; bananas. Enjoy.

Mini Pizzas
For eight pizzas you need:
1 can Bisque of Tomato soup
garlic to taste
1 teaspoon crushed oregano leaves
4 English muffins or burger buns, split
1 cup shredded Mozzarella cheese
Combine soup, garlic and oregano in saucepan and heat. Spread mixture on muffin or bun halves, top with shredded cheese. Broil until cheese melts. Boys can also make happy faces (In their pizzas with slices of pepperoni, green pepper, etc.

Peanut Butter Play Dough
250 mL peanut butter
250 mL corn syrup
60 mL powdered sugar
60 mL powdered milk
Mix ingredients well. After they've washed and dried their hands, give Beavers chunks of dough to knead, roll, cut, and create with. They can lick their fingers with impunity and, when they've finished creating and sharing their creations, they can eat them.

RECIPES

Goo Mix-Ups

Make *Chocolate Goo* from: 3 cups sugar, 1/3 cup cocoa, and 3/4 cup milk. Boil eight minutes, stirring constantly, then stir in a stick of margarine and a teaspoon of vanilla.

Make *Marshmallow Goo* from: 5 cups marshmallows and 1/2 stick butter or margarine. Stir over medium heat until marshmallows melt.

When a Goo cools to the sticky stage, mix in any goodies that catch your fancy. Try your favourite dry breakfast cereals, raisins, peanuts, coconut, marshmallows, peanut butter, fruit... Then, on a sheet of waxed paper, form balls or lollipop shapes to put on sticks, or roll flat, or create a creature or... Chocolate goo mix-ups in a hand decorated package make a good Easter gift for a boy to give to someone special.

NO-BAKE GOODIES

The October *Sharing* column featured our first response to a request for no-bake recipe ideas for Beavers (Letters, J/J'86). Soon after, we received another batch of favourites from Scouter E. Lutes of Salisbury, N. B. They're perfect if you're planning a Christmas baking night to make treats for your annual party or gift packages for seniors or shut-ins you intend to visit during the holiday season.

Butterscotch Peanut Squares
1/2 cup peanut butter (smooth or crunchy)
2 small packages butterscotch chips*
1 cup butter or margarine
coloured miniature marshmallows
* (You can substitute chocolate or peanut butter chips or use a combination.)

Recipes

Melt together peanut butter, butter and chips. Remove from heat, cool slightly, and stir in marshmallows to taste. Spread in a lightly greased 20 cm square pan and cool before cutting.

Haystacks
Melt a 12 oz. package butterscotch or chocolate chips in the top of a double boiler. Remove from heat and stir in one large tin dry chow mein noodles (broken into smaller pieces) and one cup Spanish peanuts. Drop by teaspoonful onto waxed paper and let set. O'Henry fans love 'em.

Munch Bars
1/4 cup butter; 4 cups miniature marshmallows; 1 cup each rolled oats, unsweetened coconut and chopped nuts; 1/2 tsp salt: 1 1/2 cups crispy rice cereal

In a large saucepan, melt butter. Add marshmallows and cook over low heat, stirring constantly until marshmallows melt and mixture is well blended. Remove from heat and stir in remaining ingredients. Press into a greased pan 23 cm x 33 cm. Chill and cut into bars. Store covered in the refrigerator.

Marshmallow Squares
1 cup white sugar; 1 cup margarine; 2 eggs; 1 tsp vanilla; 4 tbsp coconut; box graham crackers crushed; 24 large marshmallows; cup cherries; nuts. Mix sugar, margarine and well beaten eggs. Boil 20 minutes. When cool, add other ingredients and mix well. Spread in 20 cm square pan and refrigerate.

Christmas Feast Traditions
While we think of turkey and trimmings on Christmas Day, in many parts of the world, the traditional feast centres around different foods and is served Christmas Eve. The French *Reveillon* after midnight mass offers oysters and sausages and, in Brittany, the special treat is buckwheat cakes with sour cream. In Norway, Christmas dinner means fish (*lutfisk*) and children tie sheaves of wheat onto high poles

RECIPES

to feed the birds. Lithuanian and Ukrainian feasts include 12 courses, one for each of the 12 disciples, and the tablecloth is spread over a bed of straw to remember the stable where Christ was born. In the Ukraine, cattle often get the first taste of the supper because animals were the first to see Christ. Polish families scatter hay on the floor, leave an empty chair at the table for the Christ child, and serve a fixed number of seven, nine, or 11 dishes. German and Romanian feasts include long thin cakes that symbolize Jesus wrapped in swaddling clothes. And, in Sicily, families decorate the tree with apples and oranges instead of tinsel as a reminder that, when Christ was born, all the trees bore fruit. May the happiness of Christmas be with you as you enjoy your special traditions this year.

Camp Gourmet

Try these recipes at camp this spring and summer.

Corn Fritters: Add a beaten egg to a tin of creamed corn. Crumble and stir in enough soda crackers to thicken. Add salt and pepper to taste. Cook in a greased fry pan like pancakes. Good for breakfast. (*The Fruitbelt Grapevine*)

Sweetcorn Rissoles (Zimbabwe): 1 tin corn, a splash milk, chopped parsley, 1 egg, 1 chopped onion, 1 tsp flour, salt, fat or oil for cooking. Drain and pour corn into bowl. Stir in flour to thicken. Beat egg, add onion, parsley, a pinch of salt and a little milk. Stir into corn. Drop by spoonful into hot deep fat in a pan. Fry each side until light brown. Serve with bacon for breakfast.

RECIPES

Campfire Rice: Mix 1 1/2 cups water, 1 1/2 cups instant rice, 1/2 tsp dry mustard, 1 tbsp butter, salt and pepper, 1 tbsp barbecue sauce, 1 medium onion chopped. Line a deep dish with heavy foil. Put mixture in foil, fold top to close tightly, remove liner from dish and put foil package on grill over coals. Cook for about 20 minutes. Serves 4. (*The Fruitbelt Grapevine*)

BBQ Burgers in Foil: Mix 500 g hamburger with 1/2 cup cracker crumbs, 1 beaten egg, and 1 1/2 tsp seasoned salt. Shape four patties. Top each with a large onion slice and 1 tbsp barbecue sauce. Wrap in heavy foil. Cook over coals 15 minutes, turning twice. Serves 4. (*Manitoba's Beaver Tales*)

Peanut Butter French Toast: Make a peanut butter sandwich. Dip sandwich into beaten egg and milk mixture. Fry in greased pan. (Girl Guides of Canada, Nova Scotia Council's spring newsletter)

No Cook Fudge: Melt 1/2 cup butter or margarine in 1/4 cup boiling water. Add 1/8 tsp salt, 1/2 cup cocoa, 1/2 cup milk powder, 1/8 tsp vanilla, and 500 g powdered sugar. Mix well. Spread in buttered pan and top with nuts if desired. Cool in ice chest for half an hour. Cut and serve. (*Beaver Tales*)

Instant Cheese Cake: Stir strawberry pineapple or peach jam into soft cream cheese. Mix in chopped nuts if desired. Spread between graham crackers. Chill until serving. (*Beaver Tales*)

Fruit Pudding for Four: Mash two bananas. Stir in 1 tbsp peanut butter, 2 tbsp honey and 1/2 cup applesauce. Mix until smooth, put into four small dishes, and sprinkle cinnamon on top.

SPOOKY STUFF FOR FALL PARTIES
Fake Worms: Cook spaghetti, rinse in cold water, spread on cookie sheet to dry. When noodles are still sticky, roll them in cocoa. Serve worms into eager hands with tongs. (*United Church Observer*)

RECIPES

Monster Milk: Each person needs a glass of milk, a banana, almonds, raisins and a candied cherry. Peel the banana and cut a slit at one end to make a monster mouth. Decorate the monster with a candied cherry nose, almond spikes or scales, and raisin or currant eyes and spots. Put tail end into milk glass, admire, then eat. (*Scouting, U.K.*)

Cheese Mints: small packet cream cheese, 1 1/2 boxes powdered sugar, different colours food colouring, 1/4 tsp oil of peppermint. Combine all ingredients in large bowl and mix until creamy. Roll dough into small balls. Flatten with fork. Eat. Yum! Takes away that monster aftertaste!

EATING AROUND THE WORLD

You don't have to go far from home to eat international. We've collected these recipes for camping from a variety of sources, among them England's *Scouting* magazine, *BSA's Boys' Life*, and South Africa's *Veld Lore*.

England: Hot Cross Buns (Serves 8)
Mix together 250 g self-rising flour, 60 g brown sugar, 60 g dried fruit or chopped apple, and a pinch of mixed spice. Add two beaten eggs, 1 c milk, and 60 g melted butter or margarine, and mix into a smooth batter. Shape eight small dishes from double foil and grease well. Fill each about a thirdfull with batter. Cut thin slivers of apple with skin on to make across on top of each bun. Bake in a camp oven for about 20 minutes.

France: Les Bananes Flambées (Serves 6)
Make a thick batter from 3 beaten eggs, 3 heaping tbsp flour, and water. Add 1 spoon oil and set aside. Peel and slice 8 bananas in half lengthwise. Dip each piece into batter and fry quickly in hot oil. Sprinkle with sugar. Serve hot.

RECIPES

Greece: Kotopoulo Lemonato (Serves 4)
Quarter a 1 1/2 kg chicken and brown pieces in 1/2 c butter. Put into a casserole and pour over the juice of 1 1/2 lemons and 1/2 c hot water. Sprinkle with 1 tsp salt and 1/4 tsp pepper. Bake covered for 1 hour, basting every 20 minutes. Remove chicken to platter, lap with sauce, serve with rice.

India: Keema Curry (Serves 10)
Heat 1 c oil. Finely chop and fry until golden, 1 onion and 4 garlic cloves. Add 3 large sliced tomatoes and mix thoroughly. Add 2 spoons curry powder, 3 cinnamon sticks, 1 spoon turmeric, 3 whole cloves, and salt to taste. Stir in 2 kg ground beef and cook slowly until done. Serve with rice and Sambals, banana slices, coconut, and chutney on the side. To make vegetable Sambals, finely chop onions, tomatoes, and green chilies, mix together, season to taste with salt, marinate in vinegar, and garnish with lettuce.

Ireland: Potato Pie (Serves 4-6)
Boil 1 to 2 kg potatoes, mash and mix in salt, pepper, a little ground nutmeg, 5 tbsp butter, and 1 egg yolk. Place half the mixture in the bottom of a buttered pie dish, top with 4 hard boiled sliced eggs, 50 g cheddar cheese cut into strips and 60 g salami cut into strips. Cover with remaining potato mixture, criss-cross with a fork, dot with butter, and bake in a hot oven for 15 minutes.

South Africa: Oatcakes (Serves 6-8)
Mix together 2 c oatmeal, 1/4 tsp salt, and a pinch of baking soda. Add 1 tbsp melted butter or dripping and a little hot water to bind. Knead dough into a round shape, roll out thinly, rub surface with oatmeal, and cut into 6 or 8 pieces. Place each piece on a hot greased griddle (or doubled sheet of aluminum foil) until edges begin to curl. Brown the other side in front of the fire.

RECIPES

USA.: Peanut Butter Granola (6 cups)
Preheat oven to 120°C Measure 2c rolled oats, 1 c wheat germ,
1/2 c sesame seeds and 1/2 c coconut into baking pan and stir to mix.
Beat together 2/3 c peanut butter, 1/4 c honey, 2 tbsp vegetable oil
and 1 tsp vanilla, pour over the dry mixture and stir until well coated.
Bake 45 minutes, remove from oven, and break up mixture by lifting
with a spatula and letting it drop back into the pan. Let cool.

STAMP POT
from Greybeard

My friend and former assistant, John Tabak, gave us this recipe for a simple one-pot patrol meal after a visit to his native Nederlands. In Dutch, the name sounds like "stumpit", and it translates literally as "mashed pot".

John used garlic sausage in his Stamp Pot but says any kind of meat will work. In Norway, they use fish. It may be necessary to fry the meat a bit in the pot first, then pour off the grease. Experiment.

You need potatoes cut in 3 cm cubes; chopped onion; diced carrots, turnip or other vegetable; diced sausage, wieners or other meat: salt, pepper and seasonings to taste; butter or margarine; milk (optional).

Put potatoes, onion, and vegetables into a large pot, cover with water, add meat, and boil until done. Remove meat and drain off most of the water. Add milk (if desired), butter, and seasonings. Mash the vegetables and potatoes together. Return meat to pot and reheat if necessary.

CHEESY SPUD HASH
Each person needs a potato, a slice of cheese, and a small pat of butter. Grate or shave potato and cheese and mix together with butter. Pile the mixture on a double thickness of foil, wrap up and put into hot coals for about 20 minutes. Remove from fire, allow foil to cool, unwrap and enjoy.

RECIPES

CRISPY BANNOCK & VARIATIONS

In the outdoors, bannock is a quick and satisfying replacement for bread. This crispy bannock recipe serves nine people.

750 mL flour
750 mL cornmeal
750 mL oatmeal
160 mL powdered milk
140 mL sugar
5 mL baking powder

Mix ingredients with enough water to make a dough, then fry the dough, bake it in a reflector oven, baking pans, or foil wrap, or wrap it around a green stick and toast it over the fine.

For delicious variations, try adding such ingredients as:
- crushed tinned peaches, cherries or fruit cocktail
- crushed fresh raspberries or blueberries
- raisins and cinnamon
- shaved cheese and fried bacon bits
- dehydrated apple chips and cinnamon

POPCORN IDEAS

Popcorn is often a favourite camping snack. Although it's great warm with butter and a bit of salt, you can also dress it up.

Sugar & Spice Popcorn
8 cups popped corn
3 tablespoons sugar
1/2 teaspoon cinnamon
1/3 cup butter or margarine

Melt butter over low heat. Add sugar and cinnamon and stir until sugar dissolves. Drip over popcorn and toss until well coated.

RECIPES

Apple Corn
16 cups popped popcorn
1/2 cup butter or margarine
1 cup chopped, dried apples
1/2 cup brown sugar
1 teaspoon apple pie spice
Keep popcorn warm while you melt butter and add apples, sugar and spice. Cook mixture over low heat for about 5 minutes. Pour over popcorn and toss well to coat.

HIGH ENERGY GORP

On a winter outing, you need plenty of high energy snacks to keep you going. To make an individual portion for two days, mix up a handful of each ingredient. For a patrol-size portion for a weekend winter camp, mix together
1 kg Wheat Chex
1 box Honey Nut Cheerios
250 g dried banana chips
750 g shelled sunflower seeds
1.5 kg walnuts
1.5 kg pecans
1.5 kg cashews
1.5 kg peanuts
2 kg Reeses Pieces
2 kg M&Ms
1.5 kg raisins
And, remember, GORP spelled backwards means: no Picking Raisins Out, Guys!

RECIPES

SNACKING LOGS
Here's another nutritious high energy idea for winter outings. Mix together one cup each of peanut butter, honey or corn syrup, skim milk powder, raisins, and graham water crumbs. Stir in 1/4 cup sunflower seeds. Shape into logs or balls and chill.

CHEESE & BACON ROLLS
For a quick lunch on a winter outing, roll bacon slices around chunks of cheese and fry.

ZIP-LOCK BAG OMELETS
On winter camps, it's wise to keep cooking simple. At home, prepare and freeze this one-portion boil-in-a-bag breakfast we found in *Canadian Guider* magazine. You need 2 eggs; 2 tbsp milk or water; 2 tbsp shredded cheddar cheese; salt and pepper.

Beat together eggs and liquid with seasonings. Add cheese. Pour into a small ziploc bag, close securely, and freeze. To cook, place bag in a pot of boiling water (keeping it away from the sides of the pot) for a little less than five minutes. As it cooks, squeeze gently with tongs once or twice to distribute the egg evenly.

ASSEMBLY LINE CAKE
Here's a great indoor activity idea for a winter Cub camp. Make it to celebrate a birthday or just a super weekend together. Organize the Cubs in three groups, give each group a large mixing bowl, a list of ingredients, directions, measuring utensils and mixing spoon, and set them to work.

When all bowls are ready, they pour the contents into a large greased and wax paper lined pan for baking. Provide ready-made icing for frosting and lots of sprinkles and goodies they can use to decorate the cake. If it's for a birthday, don't forget the candles.

RECIPES

For each mixing bowl you need:
2 cups flour
1 cup sugar
1/4 tsp salt
125 g butter or margarine (buy packages with individually wrapped quarter portions)
3 tsp baking powder
Mix together with fingers until crumbly and add: 3 eggs; 1 tsp vanilla; 1 cup milk. Beat until smooth.

QUICK PEANUT FUDGE
Beavers can have fun making this no-cook treat for themselves or as their contribution to a group banquet or bake sale. In a large bowl, mix together 1/3 cup butter or margarine, 1/2 cup corn syrup, 3/4 cup chunky peanut butter, 1 tsp vanilla, 1/2 tsp salt. Gradually stir in 3 3/4 cups sifted icing sugar. Press into an 8x8 pan, cut into serving pieces.

HINTS

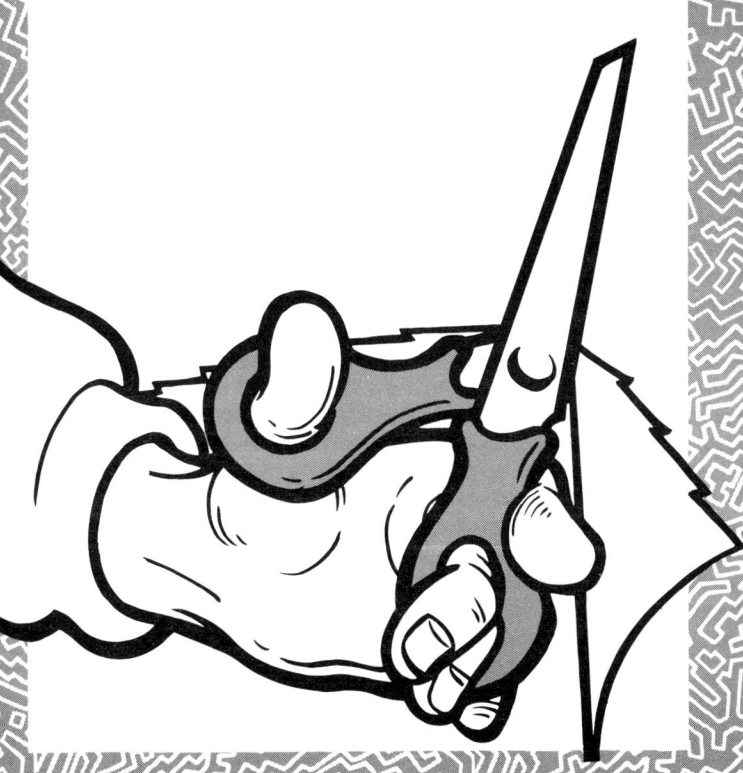

Hints

- Save inner cardboard tubes from kitchen and toilet rolls, stuff with waste paper and use as firelighters.
- Cut a rubber glove, when discarded, into thin strips to create varied rubber bands.
- Did you know that the egg white left in empty egg shells makes good glue? Use it for scrapbooks, etc.
- Stick interesting coloured pictures from magazines onto cards and cut up into jigsaw puzzles. Store in a plastic bag.
- If you spill anything onto clothing it is always best to try and remove the stain with *cold water first*. Hint from a dry-cleaning expert who says too many people rush to rub chemicals or hot water into spot and thus "fix" it forever.
- If you are painting and have some paint left over, put lid on *firmly* and store upside down. Then, if a skin forms on remaining paint it will be at the bottom when you reopen the tin.
- The next time you wonder what to do with your boys, why not try some of the local amenities — the kind of things tourists to your area do? Have you ever been on a local boat trip or to the top of your highest building?
- When using a bucket for a messy job, line it with a plastic bag which can be thrown away afterwards.
- The best way to clean windows is to use wet newspaper, followed by dry newspaper.
- A large sheet of plastic, carried on long trips, is useful in many ways — from ground sheeting to an impromptu tent. Similarly, always carry a folded plastic bag for taking home interesting finds, for carrying water in emergencies, etc.
- Do the handles get hot on those old cooking pots you take camping? Buy plastic coated fuse wire and make a neat job of winding it all along the handle, tucking the ends in.
- Enjoy scrambled eggs but don't get stuck with a hard-to-clean pan. Rinse it out with cold water first and leave a very thin layer of water in the bottom before adding egg. Hey presto! Easy to clean.
- To separate egg yolks from the whites, crack egg into a saucer. Turn an eggcup upside-down over the yolk. Tip off white into a basin.

Hints

- Take the backache out of washing messy pans by always filling used pans with cold water straight away.
- When popping corn, you'll get the best results if you place corn in the freezer for a day, or as long as you can, beforehand.
- Save your used eggshells in a jug of water. In a few days it will be ready to use on your indoor plants, as the resultant liquid makes a good plant food.
- The Hand Thermometer enables you to try on your campfire, recipes which specify a cooking temperature. Of course, the secret of any campfire cooking is to try and maintain steadily glowing coals, but once you have your fire in this state, you can gauge its approximate temperature by using your hand.

Hold your bare hand over the coals and count off seconds ("1 and 2 and 3..."). Your temperature guide is the number of seconds you can stand to hold your hand over the fire.

— If you have to remove your hand between four and five seconds, you have low heat (about 150 degrees C.).
— If you remove your hand between three and four seconds, you have medium heat (about 175 degrees C.).
— If you must remove your hand before you can count to three seconds, you have high heat (200 degrees C.).

To find the temperature you want, raise or lower your hand and you will know where to set your cooking utensil. No matter what you are cooking, the results will be more consistent if you maintain an even or near-even heat. And, by using your hand thermometer, you will assure that your meal cooks at the rate which will produce the tastiest results every time.

(Thanks to *Scouting in New South Wales* for this hint.)

HINTS

- Waxed-paper milk cartons have several lives left in them after the milk is gone.
— make a drinking cup by cutting off the carton about three inches from the bottom
— make a water scoop by cutting off the top
— cut a container into slivers, wrap them in plastic and put them in your pocket for emergency kindling on a camping or hiking trip.
— make a leak-proof mini-garbage can by opening up the top of the container, and putting in your scraps.
- It's much easier to wash soot off the pans you use over your campfire, if you coat the outside of the pans with a thick layer of dishwashing liquid before you cook.

- A discarded roll-on deodorant bottle makes an excellent insect repellent applicator because it enables you to keep 'bug dope' off your hands and out of your eyes. Snap off the pastic top or snap out the ball, rinse out the bottle and refill with your favourite liquid repellent.

- Give your boys a headstart on spring. Cut off large plastic bleach or detergent bottles, fill the base with soil and use it as a starter tray for seedlings.

- Small seedling trays or pots also can be fashioned from aluminum foil. (*Thanks to Reynolds Aluminum*).

Christmas Shadow Play

If your colony, pack or troop hasn't time to stage a full-scale Christmas production this year, try a shadow play using the story from an appropriate Christmas carol. *Good King Wenceslas* or *The Little Drummer Boy* are two that come to mind. All you need are cardboard props, a white sheet strung up in front of the audience, and a strong light about six feet behind the sheet. As the music plays, the actors mime the story behind the sheet. If you dampen the sheet before you present the play, the shadows of the players will be stronger and sharper.

Hints

Cake Auction

So your pack wants to raise money for a special good turn they'd like to do this Christmas? Try this idea, adapted from *Scouting* magazine, B.S.A. Hold a parent and son cake auction. Each Cub and his parent are to make a cake together and bring it to a special meeting where it will be judged under such categories as yummiest; flattest; most colourful; most interesting; gooiest; etc. After the judging give everyone a taste of each cake and auction off the remains. Fun and profitable!

Foil Hints

• Make Christmas cookies shaped like stars and bells, wrap them in aluminum foil and hang them on the tree. They'll stay fresh for eating and make a nice treat for unexpected guests both young and old.

• Coin collectors can keep their coins from tarnishing by wrapping them in aluminum foil.

— *thanks to Reynolds Aluminum*

Envelope Activities

On occasions when the older boys seem bored, provide "envelope activities" for Beavers who can work independently or in pairs without supervision. Cut out some of the good animal puzzles and mazes you'll find in magazines like **OWL**, cover them with clear Mac Tac and slip them into envelopes along with a felt-tip marker. After a Beaver has traced the maze or finished a puzzle, his work in felt-pen can be easily erased and the maze returned to the envelope for another boy to try another time.

— *thanks to WOODPILE, Kootenay Boundary Region.*

Hints

Box of Sticks

Scouting (U.K.), May 1981 issue, suggested a practical and economical addition to a pack or troop equipment box: a large collection of round sticks.

To make them, cut dowelling into approximately 20 cm lengths and smooth the ends with sandpaper. As long as you have lots of sticks, their uses are virtually unlimited for games, contests and indoor obstacle courses.

For example:

• Substitute sticks for hands in a game involving a ball. Any handling of the ball must be done with two sticks, either chopstick style or in any other manner you can devise.

• Try relays in which sixes or patrols vie with each other to build the tallest tower in the shortest time or, after the tower is constructed, to take it down, one stick at a time, in the shortest time without having the whole structure collapse.

• Have teams compete to see how many sticks they can balance on a matchbox.

• Use sticks for model pioneering projects.

• With sticks as rollers under a flat piece of wood, hold contests to see which six or patrol is first to ferry successfully one of its members across the room on a "rollerboard".

Outdoors

• Make your Cubs keen to learn the knots they'll find useful at camp by teaching them to tie knots in licorice. An American Cubmaster reports in *Scouting (BSA)* that he uses red and black licorice whips rather than rope to teach new knots. When a Cub shows the correctly tied knot, he's allowed to eat the licorice. He then collects another couple of pieces with which to try another knot. The Cubmaster says knot-tying sessions have become very popular and "nearly 100 percent effective".

HINTS

• If your canoe leaves a snake-wiggle wake on the water, you've loaded it too heavily in the bow. Keep the weight slightly to the stern for easy steering.

• Make handy fire-starters by filling egg carton cups with lint from the clothes dryer and pouring melted paraffin wax over the lint. Break off a cup to start each fire.

• Keep water boiled over a wood fire free of that smokey taste by throwing a clean sliver of wood into the water while you're boiling it.

• You say that some of the eggs you carried along acquired a few cracks en route? You can still boil them successfully if you first wrap them in tissue. Use string to tie the tissue closed like a purse around the egg.

Dian Thomas, author of the Roughing it Easy *books, offers good tips on outdoor griddle cooking.*

• You need even heat for griddle cooking, so use the griddle only over coals or on a stove. It won't work successfully over a campfire.

• Use a squeezy bottle filled with cooking oil for easy, even griddle greasing.

• To test the griddle temperature before cooking, let a drop of water fall onto the surface. If the water simply lies there and bubbles, the griddle is too cool. If the drop pops and jumps, it's time to cook. If it spatters and disappears, the griddle is too hot and should be raised a bit from the heat source.

• The day is hot and breezy and you want to keep your drinking water cold. Wrap the water container in a wet cloth and hang it in the open from the branch of a tree. It's as good as putting it in a regular fridge.

• On that same hot day you can keep your dinner meat cold by wrapping it in foil and burying it in the ground.

• When you've finished cooking, set your cooking pot off to one side. Perhaps if you give them their own plate, the bees, wasps, flies and other pests will stay away from yours.

• Speaking of pests, remember that mosquitoes and biting flies seem to like dark coloured clothing and the perfumed scents of many

Hints

grooming products (soaps, shampoos, colognes. etc.). Dress so that you won't attract the biters, and try using unscented grooming aids.

• Certain fibres can be damaged by insect repellents. Don't apply repellents to spandex (from which many bathing suits are made), rayon, or Dynel fibres. Tent fabrics, plastic and painted surfaces also can be damaged by insect repellents.

• An insect repellent will not keep bees, wasps or hornets from stinging you. Your wisest move is one away from stinging pests.

Try using 35 mm film canisters when collecting insect specimens. A drop of alcohol makes the canister a fine killing jar. Label the canister with tape and keep the specimen in it.

HINTS FOR PAINT

Powdered tempera is the most economical form of poster paint. Mix 3 parts paint to 2 parts water.

Make your own acrylic paint by adding white glue to prepared tempera.

When you're painting large surfaces, mix the paint with liquid starch instead of water. It will be less runny.

To simulate oil paint, mix powdered tempera with buttermilk instead of water, and stir to mayonnaise consistency.

Mix tempera with liquid detergent to make a paint that will stick well to glass, metal, aluminum foil, plastic, milk cartons and balloons.

Paint eggs with a water and white glue mixture tinted with powdered acrylic or food colouring. They'll be stronger and easier to handle. Before painting, clean eggs by soaking them 48 hours in bleach so that all membrane dissolves.

White glue diluted with water makes a good undercoat for a surface you want to paint.

HINTS

For flesh tones, mix poster paint in this order: 2 tbsp white; 4 drops brown; 1 drop red; 2 drops yellow.

Make your own finger paint. Dissolve 1 cup starch in cold water. Slowly add 4 to 5 cups boiling water, stirring constantly over low heat until mixture is thick, smooth and clear. Remove from heat and quickly stir in 1 cup soap flakes. Colour with powdered tempera.

Keep acrylic paints tightly capped. If they dry out, add boiling water a little at a time and stir. When cool, the paint should be as good as new.

Mix food colouring with water or liquid starch for painting onto fabric.

Place jars of paint in muffin tins to avoid spills.

Remove top of an empty roll-on deodorant bottle, fill with paint and replace top. Painting becomes a neater activity when you roll it on.

Use a clean, empty window-spray bottle for a spray gun when spray painting. Place the object you are painting into a large box so that the paint spatters are confined to the inside of the box.

An old piece of oilcloth makes an excellent surface for finger painting practice.

For a finger painting you want to keep, paint on glossy white shelving paper.

GLUE HINTS

Clear silicone glue, available at hardware stores, is the best glue for plastics and milk cartons.

Contact cement is the best glue for rubber and wood.

To make a heavy duty glue, mix cornstarch with regular white glue until you have the thickness you want.

Tacky white glue is especially good for gluing foam and styrofoam. A little goes a long way, and it works well for gluing things onto plastic bottles.

HINTS

To make your own plaster glaze, mix equal parts white glue and water. Paint onto plaster to prevent it from deteriorating.

PLASTIC TIPS

It's easier to cut a plastic container if you soak it in very hot water immediately before cutting.

Lightly sand plastic before decorating with felt tip markers. Make sure markings stay by spraying the finished product with acrylic fixative.

Aluminum Foil & Camping

Most outdoors people are quite aware of the value of aluminum foil for camp cookery. Reynolds Aluminum also offers a few other outdoors ideas you might want to consider.

• Wrap fishing gear in aluminum foil to keep line from tangling and hooks from rusting. By lining the compartments of a tackle box with foil, you can prevent rust damage to plugs and other equipment.

• Wrap a wet washcloth in a foil package and put it into your pack. You'll have a handy "wet-wipe" for cleaning hands and face after a satisfying camp meal.

• Aluminum foil provides good packaging material for a camper's personal toilet articles.

• When it comes time to pack up at the end of a camp, a wet toothbrush, face cloth and bar of soap wrapped in foil won't dampen the other things in your kit.

Predictions & Estimations

• Mist in a valley or over water at sunrise is a sign the day will be fine. Heavy evening dew also means a fine day will follow.

• Unsure of where you're heading? To find direction, place a short stick upright in the ground and mark the point on the ground where

Hints

the tip of the stick's shadow falls. After about 10 minutes, put another mark on the place on the ground where the tip's shadow falls. A straight line drawn through the two marks will point east and west. The first mark you made will point west.

• Try this method of metric height estimation. You need a stave or long broomhandle, a metric rule, and a friend. Walk nine paces from the tree, pole or tower on which you want a height estimation and stick your stave upright into the ground at that point. Walk one pace further and lie down so that you're doing your eye-balling from ground level.

Sight through the stave up to the top of the object you're measuring, and have your friend slide his finger down the stave until it is in line with your sighting. To find the height of the object you're estimating in centimetres, measure in centimetres the height of your friend's finger from the ground and multiply by 10. If you want to know the object's height in metres, divide the height of your friend's finger from the ground by 10. In other words, if the distance between the ground and friend's finger is 60 cm, the height of the object you're measuring is 600 cm or 6 metres.

— *thanks to* **Scouting in New South Wales**

Safety

• To prevent night accidents in camp, use phosphorescent paint to mark the edges of latrines, the tops of the corner pegs of tents, etc.
• Learn to paddle a canoe in a kneeling position with buttocks resting on the edge of the seat or thwart. This position keeps you in the canoe on rough water and allows you to reach out to grab that eddy with reasonable assurance that the canoe will follow. Use big sponges for knee pads. They also double as water sponges.

Hints

Checkerboard Cake

When you need a big cake for a special occasion, the work and expense is usually foisted onto one good-hearted mother. This idea enables you to divvy up the baking. Have each mom (or boy) bake a single 8x8 layer cake. Direct half of the bakers to ice in one colour and the other half to ice in another colour. When the cakes arrive, arrange them in a checkerboard pattern to make one beautiful giant cake. Even after everyone has had a piece or two, you'll likely find some individual cakes are left intact. Auction them off to give the evening a lively end and earn a few dollars for replenishing the kitty or donating to a favourite cause.

— *thanks to Al Webster, 3rd Bells Corners, Ontario*

Sewing Hints

Before starting to sew a tough material like denim or canvas, stick the needle into a bar of soap. The coating will help the needle slide more easily through the fabric.

To make sure you don't sew a pocket together while sewing a badge on the front, slip a jar lid, preferably plastic, into the pocket, then fearlessly sew away.

Starting Line Control

If your group tends to jump the gun during relays, slow them down by making them start from a prone position. A runner lies on his back and stays in that position until the previous runner stoops to tag him off with a tap on the toe of his shoe.

Recycled Rubber Gloves

Collect discarded rubber gloves and cut them into rubber bands of different shapes and sizes for a multitude of uses.

Burr-free Boots

To help them shed burrs easily, rub the laces of your hiking boots with paraffin before hitting the trail.

HINTS

Indoor Campfire

A flickering candle-log gives a nice atmosphere to an indoor sing-song. Bore candle holes into an old log, stick in plain white candles, fire them up and douse the electric light.

Packing Hints

Keep a dry bar of soap in your sleeping bag to combat musty odours which develop during damp-season camping.

If you carry along eggs, avoid cracks (and worse) by packing them in your flour or sugar.

Put a few grains of rice into the salt shaker to prevent salt from sticking.

Keep your toilet roll dry by packing it in a coffee tin with a snap-on lid.

Fires & Cooking

Waxed milk cartons are an excellent source of emergency kindling. Cut cartons into slivers, wrap a bundle of them in plastic and carry them along in your pack.

Stuff cardboard toilet or paper towel tubes with waste paper and use as fire-lighters.

Make a shallow pot deeper by fashioning for it a liner of doubled foil which stands higher than the pot rim.

Camp Hints

- Avoid "burnt offerings" from a camp oven by placing the baking pan on a shelf about 4 to 5 cm above the bottom of the oven.
- If a Cub at your camp has to take medicine, give him a break by letting him suck on an ice cube to numb his tongue before swallowing the vile stuff.

Hints

- Ice cubes are also handy when you have to remove a splinter from a hand or foot. Use the ice to numb the area around the splinter before "operating".
- Make your own insect-repelling candle from an ordinary thick candle. Drill a 25 mm (1") deep hole near the wick, fill the hole with citronella, and cover it with melted wax. Let Cubs try it at camp.
- When Cubs handle evergreens or cones, they can remove the sticky sap from their hands easily if they use baking soda instead of soap to wash.
- Flashlight batteries dead? To recharge them, place them in a freezer for about two days. This trick will work several times on the same tired batteries.
- If you're having a problem cleaning a pan, rub the area with salt. It works.
- You're getting ready for camp, and decide to bring along that bag of marshmallows you've had around for awhile. So what if they've gone a little dry and hard. You can soften and freshen them up in a jiffy. Put them in a brown paper bag and place in a warm oven for a few minutes.
- Did you know you could waterproof matches by dipping the tips in nail polish? To light them, strike on a small square of sandpaper.
- The little plastic tags from bread and bun packages are great for pinning up wet bathing suits and towels at camp, and they take up a whole lot less packing space than clothespins.

Nature Craft Hints

- Make necklaces from dried beans or barley by soaking the beans or barley overnight to soften for stringing. If you want to add colour, put food colouring in the soaking water.
- The petals from large pine cones, when painted white and strung, make authentic-looking claw or teeth necklaces. To soften them so that you can easily string them with a needle, soak them in hot water for half an hour. You can also string cantelope or watermelon seeds tomake an Indian-style necklace.

HINTS

- Wash and dry feathers collected at camp. If you have lots, you can put them into a pillow case and do the job in an automatic washer and dryer. To dye the feathers, boil water, vinegar and food colouring together and dip them into the mixture.
- Preserve leaves by placing the stems in a solution of two parts water to one part glycerin and leave them until the leaves have absorbed the glycerin.
- They will turn from a greenish brown to a rich dark brown in about two weeks. If you want them to remain green, add green food colouring to the mixture.
- To dry flowers, bury the heads in a half and half mixture of cornmeal and dry boric acid.

Crafty Hints

- Glue plastic coffee can lids to the bottoms of small bottles of paint or glue. They make it impossible for kids to tip the bottles, and they catch the drips.
- To prevent screw tops from sticking to paint or glue jars, smear the thread with vaseline before recapping the jars.
- Shoe polish bottles with daubers are easier than paint brushes for small children to work with. Rinse well, then fill with water colours.
- An idea for a Cub craft centre: make a holder for art paint brushes by glueing a row of empty thread spools to a strip of wood. Paint and decorate.
- Empty plastic toothbrush containers are ideal for storing art brushes as well.
- To make a good textile paint for decorating T-shirts and the like, dissolve crayon shavings in turpentine; one part crayons to two parts turpentine.

Hints

- New crayons won break as easily if you wrap them with cello tape. Try it on the next supply of crayons you buy for the colony craft box.
- Gather up the crayon stubs in your craft box, place on a foil-lined cookie sheet, and put into a warm oven. When they're soft, roll them into a multi-coloured crayon ball. Your Beavers will love it.
- Spray chalk or charcoal drawings with hair spray to prevent them from smudging.
- If you first heat the knife in boiling water, you'll have an easier time cutting polystyrene tiles.
- When scissors are dull, sharpen them quickly by snipping through a sheet of fine sandpaper four or five times.
- Making decorations for a traditional celebration like Christmas, Easter or Valentine's Day? Use cookie cutters to press out shapes from plastic foam trays. If you want to cut out your own shape, use a nail file. You'll find it cuts better and easier than scissors.
- When you want to add sparkle to a decoration, place glitter in a salt shaker. Even small hands will be able to apply it neatly.
- When Beavers are going to string beads or other items, make it easier by applying two coats of clear nail polish to the ends of each string. You can get the same effect by dipping the ends of the string in white glue.
- When your crafty kids get rubber cement stuck to their hands, give them a little dab of vinegar in each hand and tell them to rub. The vinegar will dissolve the cement.
- Prepared wallpaper paste will keep well if you store it in jam jars with good tight lids.
- If you want a really quick-drying glue for a project, pour a little white glue into a disposable lid and add some flour. Mix well. The result is a tacky glue that will dry fast.
- If you're planning projects with blown eggs at Easter, paint the blown shells with clear-drying glue. It strengthens the shells and makes them easier to handle.

Hints

• Before screwing it into a piece of wood, poke the screw into a bar of soap. It will go into the wood much easier.

• To give a project a good shellac finish, apply two coats, the first coat thinned three parts shellac to one part shellac thinner.

Here's an Idea!

If Hallowe'en trick 'n treating is still the custom in your neighbourhood, you have a great opportunity to do some recruiting. Along with the candies in the treat bags you hand out, include a *Join Scouting* invitation card. High light some of the great activities Scouting offers and sign off with the address of the nearest meeting place and the names and telephone numbers of the colony, pack and troop Scouters and the Venturer advisor.

Going Hiking? Toughen your feet for a major hiking trip by applying rubbing alcohol to the soles twice a day for about 10 days. And get both yourself and your boots into condition by taking several smaller hikes before the big trek.

To protect your feet from blisters, smear soap on the inside of your inner sock at the heel and underneath the toes. Carry along a bar of soap and, when you feel your feet become tender, give it a try.

Recycle your rubbish and give the environment a break.

Discarded rubber gloves make effective handgrips when you have to loosen a tight-fitting screw lid, flashlight top, etc. (*Hazel Tagg, Peace River, Alta.*)

Polythene wine bags are ideal camp water containers, small and virtually weightless when empty. The tap is easy to remove and self-seals when re-installed. You can also use wine sacks as inflatable pillows, swimming floats and slightly lop-sided balls for wacky outdoor games.

Hints

How about broken *aluminum tent poles*? Cut them to size. screw them onto a suitable wooden mount and use them as flag holders.

Cut irreparably *torn groundsheets* into 50 cm strips to make banners advertising coming events. etc. If you use paint to make your signs, add a bit of liquid detergent to help it stick to the plastic.

Make miniature rafts from discarded *soft-drink tins*. Equip the rafts with candle lights and launch them ceremoniously (in the camp lake at night.

Convert *dry felt-tip markers* into paintbrushes with their own caps. Simply clean the tip thoroughly with soap and water and let dry a few days.

Instead of tossing it, use an old *shower curtain* as a groundsheet for camping.

Clean *plastic milk bags* make super strong water proof packs for dry mixes of camp biscuits, pancakes, cereal, etc. Fill the bag and seal it by putting a piece of paper over the open end and pressing with a warm iron. Label and add cooking instructions. (*Outdoor Canada. May'84*)

• Save *metal bottle caps* to make fire starters. Place two 5 to 6 cm candle wicks or pieces of waxdipped absorbent string at right angles to each other in a cap (tie together in the middle to avoid having them fall over if you use all the wax), leaving about 1 cm extending on each side of the cap. Pour in melted candle or paraffin wax. When cool, fold over the wicks. Carry these small fire starters in a 35 mm film can, along with some wooden matches. Keep them level while burning to avoid spilling wax so that you can use them several times. The closer together you adjust the wicks, the hotter and more concentrated the flame. (*Outdoors Canada: Charlie Teets, Calgary Alta.*)

HintS

Hints for Camp

To keep mosquitoes away rub the inside skin of an orange peel on face, arms and legs.

If a young boy sprains a hand or foot and you want him to soak it in ice water for awhile, put some sort of toy (boat, duck, etc.) into the pan of water to keep him from becoming bored.

Bake biscuits at camp without a reflector oven. Prepare the biscuit dough and put it into a small baking pan. Place three or four pebbles into the bottom of a cooking pot large enough for the baking pan to fit inside. Set the biscuit pan on the pebbles in the cooking pot, put on the lid and cook on the stove or over a fire for about five minutes. The pebbles hold the pan off the bottom of the pot so your biscuits won't burn. (*Outdoor Canada,* May '84)

How do you tell if your coals are hot enough to cook the food you want to cook? Try this hand method to test temperature. Hold your hand above the coals at the height you intend to cook the food and count: "One Mississipi, Two Mississipi. etc." If you have to pull away the hand at "Three Mississipi", it's time to put on the steak, burgers or kabobs. If you get to "Four Mississipi", the coals are ready for toasting bread or marshmallows. If you reach anywhere between five and seven Mississipi, you have a slightly slower cooking temperature good for pork chops or spare ribs.

If you can't reach "Three Mississipi", the coals are too hot for anything. (*Canadian Guider*, Mar/ Apr '85)

Use a teepee fire which concentrates heat where you need it for quick heating, and replenish often with small sticks.

Carry matches, salt, or dry soup mix in water proof 35 mm film canisters. These handy little packages are also great for holding clues you want to hide in the undergrowth for night treasure hunts or camp wide games. (*Scouting* magazine, U.K.)

Carry "chips in a can" on a hike. When everything else is wet, this snack-pack makes a great fire-starter because of the oil. If you don't need them for fire-making, you can eat them.

HINTS

If you take a pillow case camping, you can make a pillow for sleeping each night by filling it with clothing.

To prevent batteries from wearing down if a flashlight is accidently nudged on while you're travelling, put the flashlight batteries in backwards.

Plastic net bags from oranges or onions make excellent soap holders at camp. You can hang them over the washbowl with soap inside, and use the soap without taking it out of the bag.

Kitchen foil can add extra warmth to your boots. Trace each foot on a piece of foil and add a 5 cm border. Place the foil inside your boots, shiny side up so you can benefit from radiant heat.

If you burn the inside of a cooking pot, shake cream of tarter into the pot, fill with water and bring to a boil. Boil for a few minutes, pour out water, and wipe clean.

Give fried fish extra flavour by adding onion soup mix to the flour or cornmeal you use for a coating.

If your vehicle bogs down in snow, mud or sand on the way to camp, you can use a hubcap as an emergency shovel.

Craft Tips

We thank Beaver leader Jo-Anne Wood of Grandora, Sask., for these useful craft suggestions and hints.

- Does your section seem to go through a lot of glue in a very big hurry? If you're simply glueing paper, you can thin down white glue with a bit of water to stretch it.
- When spreading glue over a large area, use a paintbrush.

If you tear rather than cut tissue paper for collage work, you get a much more subtle blending of colours.

- Beavers find threading the eye of a needle and sewing much easier if they work with embroidery needles and heavy thread.

HINTS

- When small children are making mobiles, use wool or heavy string to put them together. Fine thread is a source of frustration because it tangles so easily.
- Save all your scraps of tissue or crêpe paper for dyeing dried corn and peas. Prepare dye by pouring boiling water over the paper. Let sit until the water is the colour you want, strain out the paper add dried corn or peas to the water and bring to a boil again. Strain vegies out of water and place on newspaper to dry. The colours are beautiful.
- Don't discard those small bits of paint, either. Instead, mix them together to make new colours — a good learning process for the boys.
- To give a velvet finish to a paint job on a styrofoam project, add a few drops of liquid detergent to tempera paint.
- Be careful when choosing paint to use on styrofoam because some types dissolve the foam. Avoid gold paint in a jar.
- For finger painting, pour some liquid starch on finger painting paper and spread, then add dry tempera and let children do their thing.
- To remove dried scum or hard bits from old paint, strain through a nylon stocking. Fasten the stocking to a jar or can with clothes pins and let the paint drip through.
- Nylon net is great for cleaning paint brushes and for taking paint off the hands without scratching. Use the net in combination with any liquid soap or detergent.
- To cut styrofoam easily, use a coping saw or bread knife with a see-saw motion.
- Foil or plastic cups make very good molds for plaster of paris. To keep the mess to a minimum when you're working with plaster of paris, you need one adult to manage each four or five children. Use lots of newspaper and plastic to cover the work area and floor around it.
- If you use flour and water paste to make papier mâché, remember to add salt to the mixture. It makes it easier to mix smoothly and helps prevent the growth of mould as the project dries.
- To make little legs for a project, you can glue on wooden beads. If you don't have beads, make your own. Roll up small wads of tissue

HINTS

paper, saturate with glue, and attach to the bottom of the project. Paint when glue is dry.

• Picking up sequins is easier if you use toothpicks. When glueing on sequins, put a bit of glue on the toothpick to hold the sequin until you attach it to the craft project.

• To put shingles on your craft house roof, glue on small squares of newspaper or construction paper in overlapping rows. When glue is dry, paint.

Foil Hints

• When you need extra plates, cups, or bowls for baking or serving, make temporary dishes from foil. An easy way to do it is to shape the foil over the bottom of suitable containers.

• Cover the ice in a picnic cooler with foil to help it last longer. Keep the water in your canteen cooler by wrapping the canteen in foil.

• Use foil ring dividers for frying eggs. Put rings in the greased pan and drop an egg into each ring.

• Toast sandwiches by wrapping them in a foil envelope and placing them on the embers or a hot plate for a few seconds.

• Because foil-wrapped foods tend to scorch where they are in direct contact with coals, use a double wrapping of heavy duty foil and turn food frequently during cooking.

• Melt chocolate without leaving a potful of mess by wrapping the chocolate in a square of foil and floating it on very hot water.

• To make a sprinkler top for a vinegar or oil bottle, shape a piece of foil over the bottle opening, secure with a rubber band, and punch small holes in the foil.

• Save clean-up time by lining casserole, baking and frying pans with heavy duty foil before cooking in them.

Hints

- When cooking over coals or a small fire, line the fire box with heavy duty foil and build the fire on the foil. It reflects the heat and distributes it more evenly for more efficient cooking. Clean-up is easy, too. Simply bundle up the ashes and drippings when you're done.
- When it comes time for washing up, a crumpled ball of foil makes an excellent scouring pad for pots and pans.

*— Thanks to Manitoba's **Beaver Tales***

More Outdoors Tips

- Put safety first on a night hike by highlighting clothing with reflector tape and tying a white cloth around the arm.
- Feet sore after that hike? Give them a massage by rubbing your arches over a tennis ball.
- You love roasted marshmallows but always burn the outside? You'll always have the perfection of a melted middle inside a golden crust if you dip the marshmallow in water before holding it over the flame.
- Make waterproof firestarters by tightly rolling a newspaper to a diameter of about 38 mm. Tie string around it every 50 mm, then soak it in melted paraffin. When the wax is hard, cut the fire stick into 50 mm lengths. Package in plastic bags to carry in your pack.
- Large #10 cans, usually available free from restaurants, are great for boiling water and cooking food. Their light weight makes them ideal for backpackers, and you can stuff them with other things (stove, food, and clothing) to save space.
- Distribute the weight in your pack according to the kind of ground you are covering. For walking trails and gentle terrain, pack heavy items high and close to your back so you won't have to lean too far forward to align your load over hips and legs. For climbing, skiing, and rough terrain, place heavy items in the centre of the pack close to your back. In either case, remember to pack narrow enough that your load doesn't block the natural swing of your arms.

Hints

Good Conduct Candle

If you're looking for something other than a point system to give your pack an incentive to behave well, here's an interesting idea from Boy Scouts of America's *Scouting* magazine.

The Good Conduct Candle is lit at the start of every meeting and burns until the end. If, however, someone misbehaves, a leader blows out the candle, and it remains out until it's relit at the next meeting. When the candle has completely burned down, treat the pack to a special outing or pizza feast. The more steadily the candle burns, the sooner it burns down and the sooner the Cubs get their treat. You can bet that no one will want to be the guy who causes a "blow out".

The Inspection Train

Scouting (UK) magazine suggests giving inspection a zap of fun. Line up the Cubs one behind the other, each with his hands around the waist of the boy in front, to make a train. Start the train chugging around the room, then blow a whistle to signal a stop, call the name of a station suggesting an inspection item (e.g. Wigtown for hair), and carry out the inspection for that item. Those who don't meet the standard break from the train to make a bridge. The train chugs on to other stations where other items are inspected.

The magazine's other station names are Denton (teeth), Shoeburyness (shoes), Neeston (knees), Nailsea (nails), and Handforth (hands), but you can probably have some fun coming up with your own. Not a bad idea to use one night when your pack is working on a transportation theme. Do you have other ideas suitable to other occasions? Send them in!

Emergency Tinder

A tip from Roger Brunt in *Outdoor Canada* points out that branches at the base of a pine or spruce tree are dead and make excellent tinder for an emergency fire. After snapping them off, crumple their tips and twigs into a tight ball to ensure the flame will

HintS

spread before you run out of fuel, wedge the ball between two rocks, then crisscross larger sticks broken from the branches on top. Put the match right under the ball to light the fire. Small crowded evergreens have more dead lower branches, he advises.

Bits & Pieces

• Find it hard to sew on badges and crests straight? Tape them in place first with two-sided tape. When you are half-way done the sewing, remove the tape.

• To sew buttons on uniforms, use dental floss or elastic thread rather than ordinary thread. Dental floss lasts longer and elastic thread allows some "give". Thanks to Hazel Tagg, Red Deer, Alta.

• Save a handbook that's getting battered looking by putting on a transparent contact paper cover.

• To avoid losing the small parts of something you're assembling, secure a long piece of sticky tape to your work area and stick the parts onto the tape to keep them from rolling away.

• A little chalk rubbed on the blade of a screwdriver will help prevent it from slipping and damaging the screw.

• Make simple bootscraper doormats for the stoops of camp cabins or the main door of your meeting hall by nailing bottle caps, serrated edges up, to pieces of plywood.

• Hands covered in stains after a craft or work project? Try rubbing them with a raw potato. It gets even the stubborn ones.

Fixing Fire Damage

Look around any spot that has been used as a campsite and you will usually find half a dozen fireplaces. Man seems to have a nesting instinct that requires him to make his own personal hearth before he is at home in a place.

A recent study conducted by the Sierra Club Outing Committee shows that, each time a camper uses an open fire, 1.2 square metres

HINTS

(4 square ft.) of ground is destroyed and 5 kg (11 lbs.) of wood consumed. We can not continue to use open fires indiscriminately.

Help fix fire damage. If you come across a site with several big or little fireplaces, you can obliterate many of them. Where fires were built on grassy spots, clear away the ashes, litter and rocks, then place a thick layer of fallen evergreen needles over the burned-over spot. Your efforts will go a long way to help restore a damaged area.

— *Thanks to Mike Marlow and* The Grapevine, *Fruitbelt District, Ont.*

One Minute Boil

Save fuel, time, and the possibility of boil-over damage to your camp stove by practising the One Minute Boil. Bring food to a boil, reduce heat and boil gently for one minute, then cover the pot tightly and remove from the heat source for 10 minutes or so. The food continues to cook by its own heat and both you and your stove are free to prepare another course.

— *from Daymar Adventure Centre, Ont.*

Save the Popcorn Pot

To avoid burning the pot when you're popping popcorn, line the bottom with foil, shiny side up.

(Daymar)

Coffee & Eggs

Save having to use another pot in the morning. After the coffee has finished brewing, put an egg in the coffee pot for five minutes. Result? A soft boiled egg, ready to eat. Good coffee, too.

— *Hazel Tagg, Red Deer, Alta.*

Cocoa Powder Tire Trick

A puncture in your bicycle tire? When you are repairing it, pour in about a teaspoon of cocoa powder through the valve hole. The next

Hints

time the tire gets a puncture while you're out riding, the air rushing out will draw the powder with it and quickly choke the hole, giving you only a slow leak. As a consequence, rather than having to push the bike home for repairs, you will be able to replace the air lost in the initial rush and ride back.

—*Thanks to **Scouting in New South Wales**, Australia.*

Get the Ketchup Flowing

When you open a fresh bottle of ketchup and can't get it going, insert a drinking straw and push to the bottom. It admits enough air to start an even flow. *(Hazel Tagg)*

Camp Repairs

• To banish paint odour when repainting the cookhouse, add two tablespoons vanilla extract to each quart of paint. A large cut onion placed in a big pan of cold water will also absorb paint odour. *(Hazel Tagg)*

• Use a matchstick to fill out a hole where a screw needs tightening. *(Scouting U.K.)*

• Rub candle stubs along the edge of a saw to help it glide better. Sticky drawers also respond to this treatment. *(Scouting U.K.)*